Internationalizing
the Medium-sized Firm

Internationalizing the Medium-sized Firm

Per V. Jenster
J. Carlos Jarillo

HANDELSHØJSKOLENS FORLAG
Distribution: Munksgaard International Publishers Ltd
Copenhagen

© Handelshøjskolens Forlag 1994
Set in Plantin by Grafisk Værk A/S, Denmark
Printed in Denmark by Reproset, Copenhagen 1994
Cover designed by Kontrapunkt
Book designed by Jørn Ekstrøm

ISBN 87-16-13232-7

Series A
COPENHAGEN STUDIES IN ECONOMICS AND MANAGEMENT, NO. 3

Preface

Most well-known business schools have for a long time prescribed an action-oriented philosophy of management education. This philosophy argues that students of business must do in order to achieve proficiency, and that managers succeed or fail not so much because of what they know, but as a result of what they do.

It is with this philosophy in mind and the experience of 20 years of management education that this book on internationalizing the medium-sized enterprise has been developed. The cases are all based on in-depth field research and close collaboration with the managers and companies described. We believe that the user will find this collection of 12 cases to be pedagogically sound, appealing to the class participants, stimulating to teach, and focused on the essential problems of managing firms going international.

In addition, all the cases have been thoroughly tested and refined by experienced professors of leading business schools in teaching situations with students and executives of many different nationalities.

This book can be used successfully in several different formats.

Firstly, it can be used as a comprehensive case supplement to any of the texts focusing on international business and management available on the market. Secondly, it can be used in conjunction with a set of readings and articles on international strategy issues. Thirdly, it can be used as a stand-alone book to support the instructor's own cases and lectures, as a supplement to a management decision simulation game, or as a corollary to student group projects. Finally, the book may serve as the guiding document for the development of managers and owners of enterprises which are pursuing opportunities abroad.

Per V. Jenster and J. Carlos Jarillo

Contents

1. Introduction

1.1 Going International: A Tough Issue for Medium-sized Firms[1]

Not long ago, a participant in an IMD program came with a specific question. His company, a large Spanish engineering firm, had decided to start a process of internationalization, and they had to decide whether to set up the first international office in Mexico or in Paris. There were good reasons for both. Mexico had the same language, a booming economy, and there were some contacts with Mexican engineers and Government officials that could be put to use. Paris, on the other hand, offered next-door ease of operation, similarity in economic and social environment, the chance to pick up some superior technology, etc. All those reasons sounded convincing, but since the company had only the resources to open one office... which one should it be?

These kinds of questions are re-occurring all the time as companies, both large and small, go international. They must decide:

a) Where to go – Geographically, customer segments, etc.

b) How to go – Nature and sequence of internationalization process: Export or set up a foreign plant? Do it alone or in a joint venture? Buy a foreign firm, or start a subsidiary? Send company managers or hire locals? Adapt the company's products or services to foreign tastes or maintain consistency?

c) What – Understanding the implications and necessary changes to current management process and how to go about implementing appropriate change.

Success in the internationalization process will depend on the answer given those questions, but all too often internationalizing the company

[1] The authors have based this chapter on an article by Carlos Jarillo, *Going International: Better Know Why You're Doing It* which appeared in IMD's *Perspectives for Managers, #1*, 1992, and a note by Per Jenster, *Managing Internationalization*, April 1992, funded by the Industrial Development Authority of Ireland.

fails to achieve its aims, or takes much longer than it should. The reason is that these questions cannot be answered without a clear vision of why the company wants to go international in the first place. This "international vision" is absolutely essential for success, yet very often missing: by definition, the companies that need it most are those with the least international experience.

1.2 Growth Alone is Not Enough

Many companies want to go international simply because they have run out of growth opportunities in their market. Often inspired by the encouragement made by government agencies promoting export, they see internationalization as the next source of sales growth. But if there is nothing more to the international vision, the pursuit of growth may turn out to be the road to failure. Simply adding incremental sales will most likely result in a decrease in profits.

Going international is an enormously expensive exercise, both in terms of money and, especially, top management time and attention. Due to the high costs, for internationalization to make sense it must bring added value to the company beyond extra sales. In other words, the company needs to gain a competitive advantage by going international; and going international will not by itself provide advantages. On the contrary, the firm may be worse off than before, even in its home market. In this way, going international has been the beginning of the end for many a company. So, unless the company gets better (not bigger) by going international, it should probably stay home.

1.3 Developing the Vision Competitive Advantage through Internationalization

Four sources of competitive advantage may provide the right reasons for a company to consider going international. Without one or more of them, internationalization is probably not a good idea.

The first reason to go international is to follow customers. As many industries internationalize, they demand international service from their suppliers. Audit and consulting firms experienced this phenomenon many years ago, but it is now underway in industries as diverse as packaging and advertising. International companies are integrating their operations, which creates new demands on suppliers. For example, an auto components supplier who previously sold to a Ford plant in

France is now asked to deliver Europe-wide, and the selling point moves from France to Germany, where Ford's central purchasing function is located. For a local French supplier, this is a big move.

If customers in fact prefer international suppliers – for economies of scale, logistical simplicity, product consistency, etc. – suppliers who can coordinate their activities across national markets will have an edge over purely local competitors. But this is a big if. If customers don't really care, local suppliers will probably be more competitive, because they don't incur the high costs of operating internationally.

The second reason to go international is to gain efficiency – through economies of scale, or by taking advantage of country-specific conditions.

Size is important in many industries. Investments in R&D, manufacturing, or marketing are more easily recouped if they can be amortized over a large unit volume. Every industry has a "minimum efficient scale" below which it is difficult to operate, because fixed costs become prohibitively high. If this "critical size" is too big for a national market to bear, a national industry player must become an international one, absent subsidies or other trade barriers.

This idea is at the root of "market niches". A "market niche" is a market in which the minimum efficient scale is high compared to the total global market. Such a market will sustain only a few competitors. Moreover, all must be international, even if the size of the total market is small. Mountain bike shift gears provide one example: three relatively small companies dominate the world industry, for only a few companies can justify the necessary R&D spending given the market's limited size. Market niches explain why a combination of high R&D investment and vigorous internationalization gives so many small or medium-sized Swiss or German companies a seemingly impregnable position in world markets. In these cases, high technology and internationalization simply require each other.

Companies can also gain efficiency by moving some operations to countries where they can be carried out most efficiently – countries which provide "comparative advantage". Migrating plants in pursuit of lower labor costs are well-known, but companies can also gain by tapping pools of know-how concentrated in specific countries. Logitech, a Swiss-based world leader in the design, production and commercialization of "computer mice" and other peripherals, has its headquarters in Switzerland, manufacturing in East Asia, and product design and marketing in California. It thus leverages geography for maximum efficiency in the different operations needed to carry out its business successfully.

Other companies may deliberately enter those foreign markets which are the most competitive in the world. The company learns from trying to satisfy demanding clients in the presence of strong competitors. The company may certainly not be able to make much money in such an environment, but it makes sure that its competitiveness at home, and in other markets, will be world class. Many British high-tech companies, leveraging a common language, enter the US as soon as they can.

Doing so provides them access to the most sophisticated clients in their industry and, at the same time, builds their credibility back home, as "multinational companies" being able to serve demanding customers an ocean away. Internationalization brings in more than just additional sales, justifying the cost and effort to set up an office 4000 km from home.

The third way a company may gain by internationalizing is through exploiting abroad superior technology or business know-how. In some cases, a company finds a better way to deliver a product or a service, and develops a whole management technology around it, which is clearly superior to anything being done in other countries. It then makes sense for the company to move abroad and try to replicate its success, in the absence of strong local competition. Many American companies, based in what was incontestably the world's leading market, came to Europe in the 50s and 60s with this approach. The extra profits thus generated can be reinvested in R&D, strengthening the company's position through efficiencies; moreover, an international presence may be a plus in following customers. IBM's success in Europe and Japan during the last 30 years followed this pattern.

The fourth, most subtle reason to go international is to spread the company's operations over different countries to defend against competitors. Not long ago, we had the chance to discuss international strategy with a company in the steel distribution business. The company wanted to go beyond its domestic market and start operating in two or three more countries, quickly. When we asked the standard question, "Why do you want to go international in the first place?", the answer was: "We are fed up with foreign competitors dumping on our market, and we cannot do anything about it. If we were selling in their market, we could very easily retaliate". This reason, which doesn't by itself entail gains in efficiency, or better service to customers, and does put a strain on the company's resources, may be vital in markets which are highly concentrated, have high fixed costs, and in which the ability to withstand attack in one country can be assisted by the possibility of counterattacking the aggressor on its home turf.

1.4 Defining the Internationalization Process

Only when a company is clear on the advantages to be gained by going international can it start answering pressing questions about "where" and "how". For instance, the issue of which countries to enter will depend on whether the company wants to increase volume or tap local advantages. The company can rank markets in terms of "country attractiveness": barriers to entry, market potential, resources to be gained, etc. From what we have already discussed, however, it is obvious that the very concept of attractiveness is dependent on the strategy the company wants to follow. Without it, a superficial analysis ("large market", "unsophisticated competitors", "common culture") will prevail.

A similar analysis can be performed on the issue of the mode of entry to new markets. If the company is trying to leverage plant investment, it will probably go to an export strategy, If the key issue is to amortize R&D expenditures, however, licensing might make sense. Similarly, the joint venture will be preferred when both local manufacture and local expertise is needed.

The nature of the competitive advantages being sought will also determine the kind of organization the company wants to set up with its new international subsidiaries. For some companies, one reason to have different plants in different countries is to open the possibility of shifting some of the work from one country to another following currency movements. But to achieve this kind of flexibility, the company must have wholly-owned subsidiaries, not joint ventures, where the local partner will resist sending work (and profits) to a foreign subsidiary in which it does not have a financial stake: one source of competitive advantage (efficiency) calls for a centralized operation, while another (local knowledge) calls for autonomous operations. If these dilemmas are not foreseen, the company will find itself in untenable positions.

1.5 Facing Up to Change: Understanding the Management Implications

Our observations from a number of clinical studies suggest that the implications of the internationalization process are often not fully understood. One small Irish company with sales less than ECU 4 million was selling in 15 countries, ranging from Iceland to China. The implications of this approach led to blotting administrative and sales costs which significantly hampered the firm's cost position in its domestic market.

In another firm, the internationalization process lowered the company's original emphasis on deepening of customer relationships. Customers interviewed were often positive on the products but surprised at the lack of follow-up. Although sales increased, the firm's retention rate of clients suffered over time.

The internationalization may also come in conflict with international pricing policies. For example, some firms have been confronted with its lack of clear pricing policy. Even for high perceived value products, some companies are going international by aggressive pricing to get orders at any cost. Lack of knowledge of their real selling support costs. Contribution from particular orders are often not known.

This also show how the lack of clear vision and strategy has implications for the rest of organizational activities, because they lead to poorly articulated resource allocation decisions which leave sales staff and distributors undirected and often uncontrolled. This often goes hand in hand with little marketing research/intelligence gathering, and leaves the firm with few insights into present or future needs and requirements.

Problems develop not only when an order is lost but also if the firm is successful. One electronics company obtained an order in Japan equal to 40% of sales. However, the management time involved in overseeing the contract led to unhappiness among existing customers.

All these illustrations obviously lead one to raise questions related to the management skill base. According to our studies, the management of medium-sized firms often have a technical background and only limited formal commercial training. Because of this skills shortage, these firms often tend to downplay the financial controls, whilst spending much efforts on chasing new sales and handling crises. As the internationalization process evolve, the lack of controls further highlight the underlying systemic problems. With little understanding of working capital requirements and cash flow management, the foreign ventures become larger leading to poor profitability due to higher than expected start-up costs of the international effort. In short, lack of a strategic approach to new market development creates a management stretch which detracts from the problems in the domestic business.

It is therefore not a surprise that our research has shown that a few successful companies were able to create a solid basis for international development. The companies with successful approaches embraced a long term perspective with a clear vision. Growth was not seen incrementally, but in terms of specific strategic milestones. To accomplish this growth, specific structures and controls were put in place as early as possible. Financial controls, reporting systems and management team building were identified as the building blocks necessary to create the basis for long term sustainable growth.

Setting objectives to focus market and product development efforts was a formal step taken early in the internationalization process. Tightly defined business definitions emphasized pricing for profit rather than for sales growth. Emphasis was also placed on appointing experienced business people to the company boards, thereby assuring a dispassionate person to help identify and probe into assumptions and plans.

The successful companies also elected to contain growth within the financial resources comfortably available. While too little financing limited growth, too much external financing put the company at the mercy of the financiers looking at short term dividends rather than long term growth potential.

1.6 Conclusion

Going international should not be seen as just an "extra" activity of marginal importance. In today's globalizing markets, there is no room for marginal competitors. The international dimension of a company, in the long run, will wither, disappear or be an essential dynamic component of its overall competitive strength.

The centrality requires consensus in the company. Very often, the international push is driven by some particular senior manager's interest. Other executives may fear the unknown and feel (rightly in the short term) that profits are to be made in the home market, with current clients. This type of situation increases the risk of going international, as international operations are seen by many within the organization as marginal. Developing a clear vision of why going international is going to strengthen the whole company is the first step in gaining everybody's commitment. The internationalization process can then be implemented with more planning and less trial and error, addressing the host of necessary decisions on location, mode of entry, organization style, etc., in the context of explicit strategic goals. Without this analysis and the whole company's commitment, chances for success are slim, and those managers who were uncomfortable with the necessary adjustments to a more sophisticated company will be proven right – to the detriment of the future competitive position of the company.

Finally, the company must expect managerial strains, as its systems, probably well adapted to a hands-on management style, prove inadequate to an international operation, where critical trade-offs between overall consistency and local diversity have to be made. These strains are showing right now not only in companies trying to go international, but in multi-international companies which have exhausted their first or second learning cycle, and must upgrade to a new level. For them, the kind of analysis we have described is a valid, and necessary, as it is for the first-time internationalizer.

By the way, the Spanish engineering company mentioned earlier has recently opened its first international office in Lisbon, where one of its clients is building a large plant, and has asked them to direct the job.

2. Organization of the Cases

The 12 cases are organized to reflect, if not the progression, then the changing nature of internationalization issues faced by the organizations as they evolve through the various stages of international perspective and reach. However, let us warn that the cases often span a number of different topics, just as real life management issues are rarely placed into clean and easy separable categories for discrete decision making. The complexity of managing internationalization is exactly rooted in the interactions between distinct problem sets, conflicting functional responsibilities, variations in international priorities, friction between vendors and buyers, political and economic paradoxes and role needs of various decision makers in the organizations.

 1. Panda Furniture – Belgium/U.S.A.
 2. Toro: Industrial Flavors – Norway
 3. Delissa in Japan
 4. Glamoxgruppen – Norway
 5. Iskra Power Tools – Slovenia
 6. The Cochlear Bionic Ear – Australia
 7. Jac Jacobsen Industrier A/S – Norway
 8. Jordan A/S – Norway
 9. Cochrane S.A. – Chile
10. Fundación Chile – Chile
11. Mentec Ltd. – Ireland
12. Benetton S.p.A. – Italy

3. Learning from a Case

The analysis of a case used to examine a business situation is very different from skimming through a news paper article or reading a book. In general, we recommend that a four step process is followed in the preparation process.

1. *The overview.* Read quickly through the case. Try to highlight or note down the names of key decision makers, locations, dates and sticking numbers.

2. *Deepen your understanding.* With the overview behind you, read the case thoroughly. Make sure you have a full comprehension of all the aspects of the case. Try to identify contradictions and paradoxes.

3. *The analysis.* Now you are ready to undertake the analysis of the case. You must attempt to get the fullest understanding of following three aspects:
   a. Industry trends, customers and competitive dynamics
   b. Company analysis, including financial issues
   c. Strategic issues and options.

4. *Decisions and actions.* After the analysis you should now be ready to consider the various alternatives. Place yourself in the role of the decision maker (s) and decide what you would do in this situation. What decision would you lean towards and what advantages and disadvantages are the consequences of your choice(s). Finally, consider how the implementation of your decision would have to proceed and what the reactions would be.

If the case is used in a teaching situation, the professor may have assigned specific study questions which will help you focus in on specific issues. You certainly will have prepared answers to these questions, but do not consider those answers sufficient for what would constitute a proper preparation of the case.

The case method is a *student-centered* approach to learning and involves a classroom situation where students do most of the talking. The role of your professor is mainly to ask question, thus encouraging student interactions on ideas, analysis and recommendations. The professor will also ask you to justify your comments, clarify the logic of your recommendations, set priorities and go beyond the case and draw on your own experience or other cases and articles you may have read. As the discussion in class unfolds, do not hesitate to take a stand on an issue or even present a contrary perspective. High points will also be given to the student who is able to place case facts and issues in theoretical frameworks, in order for the class to develop more generally applicable heuristics on resolving the key issues of internationalization.

The student participation is such a fundamental part of the educational process that if a class participant is not fully prepared, he or she is unlikely to benefit from the class session. The discussion in class is a unique opportunity to learn more about yourself, your colleagues and their experience or views and the decision making in organizations. However, your gain will very much depend on the effort you and your colleagues put forth. So be prepared!

4. Cases

1. Panda Furniture

This case was prepared by Professor Peter Killing, as a basis for class discussion rather than to illustrate either effective or ineffective handling of an administrative situation.

In the spring of 1982, Mr. Jan Winkler, the Chairman of Panda Furniture, was searching for a president to manage Panda's newly formed U.S. subsidiary. After six months of examining résumés and interviewing potential candidates, Winkler, in conjunction with an American consultant, had narrowed the list to two candidates. Both were American and both appeared eager to take on the challenge of building a new company from scratch.

Winkler's plan was to build a 50,000 square foot plant in North Carolina to produce foam-filled casual furniture similar to that manufactured and sold by Panda in Europe. It was anticipated that the U.S. operation would reach an annual sales level of $3 million within two years and pass the break-even point within 12 months of start up. The American market for casual foam furniture was estimated to be approximately $50 million per year and growing at a rate of 25% per annum.

Company Background

Panda was formed in Holland in the early 1900s. Originally a producer of metal springs for mattresses and furniture, in 1960 the company became a manufacturer of finished mattresses and a limited range of furniture. Jan Winkler, the grandson of Panda's founder, joined the firm in the mid-1960s after graduating from Amsterdam University in economics and working for Philips in Holland and Shell in Paris. He entered the firm with some reluctance, promising his father, who was running the company at the time, only that he would carry out some market research which might lead the firm into new markets.

Jan's size up of the company and its markets led him to conclude that the firm faced a number of serious issues. Primary among these were the fact that; (i) many of the firm's customers were backward integrating to produce their own metal springs, (ii) the company faced an acute shortage of production workers, (iii) a joint venture which Panda had entered with a British firm (to produce furniture in Holland, manufactured to the British firm's designs) was on the verge of bankruptcy, and (iv) polyether foam, a product based on a new technology of which Panda knew nothing, was starting to make significant inroads into the company's markets.

These factors, combined with his father's failing health, led Jan to make a full time commitment to Panda, and by 1971 the company had bought out its British joint venture partners, had entered a new joint venture with a polyether producer to supply polyether foam to Panda, and had moved to a new plant location in Belgium which offered an adequate supply of labor.

From this point forward the company concentrated on three product areas, as described below.

Table 1: Product Lines

Product Line	Description	Sales*	
		1975	1981
Mattresses	Polyether foam, spring interior, and latex mattresses, box springs and upholstered beds	78	142
Bedding	Quilts, pillows, quilt covers comforters (duvets), mattress pads and sleeping bags	120	225
Furniture	Upholstered suites and sofa beds	30	75

* Exchange rate was approximately 45 francs to the U.S. dollar in 1981.

Many of Panda's products were sold in the low and medium priced segments of their markets. In Belgium, for instance, Panda sold three lines of mattresses to department stores and had a dominant share of department store mattress sales. However, only about 20% of all mattress sales in Belgium were made through department stores, and traditional furniture stores were somewhat reluctant to carry Panda's lines because they feared that they would be undercut by the aggressive pricing practices of the department stores. Traditional furniture retailers were also reluctant to carry Panda's furniture line which, with its bright colors, absence of wood, youthful appeal, and low prices, was a sharp contrast to their traditional lines. As a result Panda concentrated its efforts on selling furniture through non-traditional retailers that focused on younger consumers. Overall, Panda's sales were 45% direct to department stores, 20% to mail order firms, 15% direct to large retailers, 10% to institutional customers such as hotels and hospitals, and 10% through wholesalers to smaller retailers. *(Several items from the company's furniture line are illustrated in Exhibit 1.)*

Growth in Europe

In 1975 Jan Winkler's father retired from the firm and Jan took over fully as Managing Director. He commented:

> "My father was a typical entrepreneur. He was extremely interested in starting things, but once they were up and going he lost interest. He also liked to work alone and did not spend much time developing the people who worked for him. I intend to put more emphasis on developing our managers and following through with projects past the start-up phase."

Reporting to Jan was Hans van Linden, a 51 year old general manager who had proven quite capable of managing the firm's operations on a day to day basis when he ran the company under the direction of Jan's father. Although very authoritarian in style, he appeared to be effective and his particular strength was in sales. In addition to carrying primary responsibility for marketing and sales, Mr van Linden was responsible for all personnel matters, and for coordinating Panda's marketing and production operations. Jan Winkler was responsible for strategic planning, finance, pricing, organization development and product development. *(An organization chart is provided in Exhibit 2.)*

Since Jan had taken control of the firm in 1975, sales had risen from 228 million Belgian francs to 442 million in 1981, while at the same time profits had increased from 6 or 7 million francs per year to 15-20 million, making Panda one of the most profitable firms in its industry, on a percentage basis. *(For financial statements see Exhibit 3.)* Jan chose to reinvest much of the firm's profit in new equipment. In 1977, for example, he hired a young chemical engineering graduate, Daniel Courage, to assist the firm in developing the equipment and technology needed to produce its own foam blocks from which it could make furniture. After 18 months of experimentation and frustration, the equipment was finally perfected and in 1981 required the attention of only two unskilled operators. Daniel subsequently became Panda's production manager.

In spite of Panda's good track record, Jan Winkler was firmly of the opinion that "past performance is no guarantee of future results". He was particularly concerned that the firm would find it difficult to achieve further significant increases in sales. He explained:

> "The European market is very fragmented, certainly in comparison to the United States. Our home market, the Benelux, has a population of only 25 million and we are now at the point of diminishing returns with respect to what it would cost us to gain further share in this market. We have several major and a number of regional domestic competitors and they are not going to disappear. France and Germany are interesting to us, but because of their nationalism and strong local suppliers, market success would only come if we built local plants – and there is overcapacity in each of these countries already. Local plants would also be necessary because in France and Germany, suppliers from Belgium are viewed as being unreliable, offering poor quality and late delivery!"

As a result of these observations, Jan considered various other areas of the world where expansion by Panda might be feasible. He decided rather quickly that the United States was one of the most interesting alternatives, as it offered a large, affluent, and a relatively homogeneous market. It was also a country which he had visited frequently and was one where he felt comfortable.

> "Personally, I enjoy the United States. I have travelled there a great deal and feel at ease with Americans. Europe, I feel, is becoming more and more socialistic, whereas the United States remains a market economy. I am concerned that Europe may not be a very pleasant place for my children to live 10 or 20 years from now and I want to give them the choice of living in the United States or Europe. My aim is not to get rich overnight, but to gradually build up a solid, sustainable business in the United States."

Entering the United States Market

Winkler's first moves in the United States were to visit a number of furniture manufacturers, to collect Dun and Bradstreet data on firms in the industry, to talk to investment bankers about the business and to read whatever industry reports he could obtain. In early 1981 he took his vacation in the U.S. and attended an American Management Association course for presidents in California "to see if U.S. executives were any sharper or more intelligent than their counterparts in Europe". He also visited a variety of key people in the industry.

These early investigations convinced Jan that neither the mattress nor the bedding business in the United States was very attractive. The dominant firms seemed to be very well established, and it appeared that major advertising expenditures would be necessary to establish a brand name. The bedding business was particularly unattractive as it consisted primarily of very large textile firms that had integrated forward. Many of these firms offered coordinated packages of drapes, sheets and bedspreads which Panda would not be able to match.

In contrast, the casual foam filled furniture business seemed to offer attractive prospects. Winkler noted that this segment of the furniture business seemed to be growing quickly, that firms in the business were small and undercapitalized and many appeared to be managed in a very "ad hoc" fashion. The large traditional furniture manufacturers seemed to be ignoring the foam-filled segment, treating it as a fad not worthy of serious consideration.

These observations lead Jan Winkler to inform several large American public accounting firms that he might be interested in purchasing a small foam based furniture company and to commission a detailed market research study on the casual furniture segment of the U.S. market. The list of manufacturers identified in this study is presented in Exhibit Four. Contact with these manufacturers revealed, however, that few of them were for sale and those that were appeared to be greatly overpriced. Although somewhat disappointed, Jan concluded that the reluctance of these firms to sell confirmed his assessment that the U.S. market was attractive.

The question of whether or not the apparent growth of the casual furniture market in the United States was the result of a "passing fad" or the beginning of a long-term trend was one to which Jan Winkler devoted a great deal of time and attention. The market research study indicated that foam-filled furniture, which was relatively low in price, appealed to the following consumers:

- 18- to 30-year-olds furnishing their first home, apartment or condominium. For these people the furniture played a primary role, in living rooms and bedrooms.

- a 25- to ≥40-year-olds, furnishing secondary rooms in their homes, such as playrooms and dens.
- ≥30-year-olds, buying their second home and looking for a fresh look, perhaps representing a change in lifestyle.

The report also argued that as homes continued to increase in cost they would decrease in size, resulting in a high demand for dual purpose furniture, such as the foam filled chairs and sofas which Panda (and its potential U.S. competitors) manufactured, which could be converted into lounging chairs and beds. Unfortunately, because of their concern with service and delivery times, the major retailers interviewed in the market research study made it clear that they would not even consider carrying Panda's line unless it were manufactured in the United States. Thus it would not be possible for Panda to test market its products by importing them from Europe. The research also suggested that some minor product design changes might be necessary and U.S. fabrics should be used for upholstered surfaces.

A further finding of the market research done for Panda was that a very low proportion of foam-filled furniture, about 10%, was sold through traditional furniture retail stores. Department stores were selling 15-30% of the foam-filled furniture sold in the U.S., discounters approximately 10%, and specialty "lifestyle" stores set up to appeal to young homeowners and apartment dwellers were selling 40-50%. To achieve distribution from its U.S. facility, the report recommended that Panda offer retailers geographical exclusivity on certain products for a period of time, free floor samples and an advertising campaign funded by Panda. Initially the emphasis should be on the dual purpose furniture in Panda's range, with later introduction of upholstered beds and single purpose living room furniture.

Combining the results of the market research study with his own observations, Winkler concluded that the growth of the casual furniture segment (estimated at 25% per annum in the report) was most likely part of a longer term trend and not just a passing fad. Accordingly, he decided that the next step should be a detailed business plan for entering the U.S.

The Business Plan

Working with a firm of consultants that specialized in assisting foreign firms establishing themselves in the United States, Jan prepared a business plan which reflected his belief that Panda's initial entry should create a solid foundation on which the company could grow. He wanted, for example, to buy enough land for current needs, but also take an option for more. He also wanted to build an appropriate plant of decent size. *(Highlights of the business plan are given in Exhibits 5 and 6, and below.)*

- A 50,000 square foot plant would be built to Panda's specifications in North Carolina. North Carolina was chosen in preference to several other areas because it was an established center of the U.S. furniture industry, offering close proximity to several major furniture shows, suppliers and of a local supply of skilled labor.
- The activities to be undertaken in the plant would include the manufacture and cutting to shape of foam (3 employees), the quilting and cutting of textiles (4 employees), sewing fabrics to fit the various shapes and forms of foam (2 employees) and the assembly of these components into finished products (4 employees). Total plant employment in 1982 would be 15 people at an average wage of approximately $200 per week and in 1983 this would probably increase to 20 people.
- A marketing plan would be created with the assistance of an advertising agency. A strong emphasis would be placed on the establishment of creative and innovative marketing techniques, although the traditional tools of trade shows, direct sales to large retailers and manufacturers representatives would also be used.
- Jan Winkler would be involved with the management of the U.S. operation on a part time basis. A full time American president would be hired, together with a production manager, a marketing manager and a financial manager. As necessary, these managers would spend time in Belgium studying Panda's European operations.

The proposed plant included 6000 square feet of space to permit the installation of foam-making equipment similar to that used by Panda in Belgium. The equipment (some of which would be second hand) would cost approximately $60,000 and would provide Panda U.S. an estimated saving of $7.50 per unit of furniture produced. Jan calculated that the investment (plus the salaries of the two employees required to the equipment) would be justified when the plan reached 10,000 units of furniture per year and at higher volumes would provide a handsome return.

Hiring a President

During early 1982, the legal structure for Panda's U.S. subsidiary was finalized, negotiations for the construction of the plant were concluded and Jan Winkler intensified his search for an American president for the new company. As the job description in Exhibit 7 indicates, Jan intended to give the U.S. president a free hand to run the company as he saw fit, with the provision that fixed asset and loan transactions would require Jan's prior approval.

Working with the consulting firm that had assisted him in the preparation of the U.S. business plan and the North Carolina office of a large international accounting firm, Jan identified ten to twenty presidential candidates. After preliminary interviews, however, he decided that only two of these men, John Garfield and David Thomas, were likely to be capable of doing the job. Several more in-depth interviews with each man led Jan to conclude that he felt more comfortable with Mr. Garfield. He explained that Mr. Garfield was more "his kind of person" and a man in whom he felt he could immediately place a high degree of trust.

John Garfield

Until 1981 John Garfield was a senior manager in a major American textile firm. As his résumé indicated (see Exhibit Eight), he had held many positions in this firm over the years, including general management, manufacturing, marketing and administrative jobs. In 1981 Mr. Garfield was asked to transfer to the firm's head office in New York City. After discussing the matter at length with his wife and family, he refused the transfer, preferring to stay in North Carolina where he had been raised, educated and spent much of his early career.

Following his subsequent departure from the firm, Mr. Garfield had unsuccessfully attempted to arrange a leveraged buyout of a local firm. At the time of his interviews with Jan Winkler, he was unemployed.

John Garfield was very enthusiastic about the entrepreneurial aspects of the position which Jan described to him. "It would be a breath of fresh air to work in such a small organization", he said, "and extremely exciting to build a firm from the ground up". He was, however, concerned about the market outlook for Panda's line of casual furniture and, on his own initiative, Garfield visited retailers in a number of major U.S. cities to form an assessment of the new company's chances. His visits left him convinced that Jan's business plan was feasible and that he could do the job.

When checking Garfield's references, Jan found that his former employers described him as "extremely hard working, competent, and honest". The three consultants who interviewed John Garfield at Jan's request were also confident of his ability to do the job and indicated to Jan that he was extremely lucky to have found not only a capable executive but also a prominent member of the Charlotte business community.

David Thomas

David Thomas was equally enthusiastic about the presidential position which Jan outlined to him and, like John Garfield, was confident of his ability to perform it successfully. In fact, Thomas had already done a similar job, in that he had started a U.S. subsidiary in North Carolina for a French furniture company in 1976. As explained in his résumé in Exhibit Nine, Mr. Thomas had built this company to a level of $8 million in sales and 50 employees in a five year period. Because Thomas was still president of this company, it was not possible for Jan to check directly with the parent firm concerning his performance. He did, however, tour Thomas' manufacturing plant and speak with some of his employees while posing as a potential customer. He concluded from the visit that Thomas was indeed a very good marketing and sales executive but that his plant was, at least by European standards, "something of a shambles".

After listening to Jan describe his plans for Panda Furniture in the United States, Thomas volunteered to prepare a marketing plan for the new company, the table of contents of which is presented in Exhibit Ten. Jan was positively impressed with this plan, which reinforced his view that David Thomas had a good feel for the U.S. furniture market. He was concerned, however, that Thomas' extremely sales oriented attitude might not stand him in good stead as a general manager. It was important, Jan believed, that his American general manager, who would be operating alone much of the time, would make decisions on "rational grounds, not on the more emotional basis that one usually finds in sales and marketing managers."

A Time for Decision

In April 1982, Jan had only one item left on his agenda concerning the two men and that was to send John Garfield to Belgium to be interviewed by Panda's managers. He was virtually certain, however, that Garfield would receive a clean bill of health, just as David Thomas had on a visit the previous week. The final decision would then be his to make.

Exhibit 1: Organization Chart – 1981

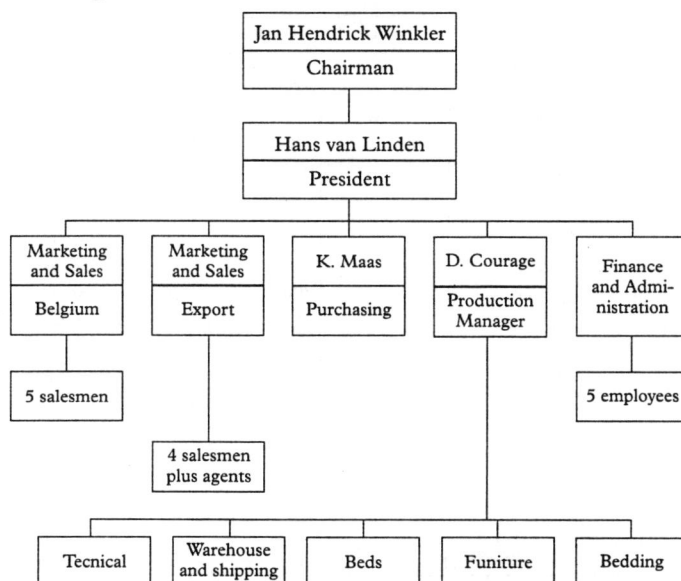

Exhibit 2: Income Statements 1975-1981 (in Millions of Belgian Francs)

	1975	1976	1977	1978	1979	1980	1981
Sales*	229	254	280	318	375	416	442
Gross Profit	75	98	122	163	165	175	184
Personnel Costs	37	46	54	60	67	73	78
General and Administration Costs	6	7	10	12	17	23	25
Selling Expenses	9	11	16	16	19	21	25
Depreciation	14	16	26	51	18	20	20
Interest	5	3	1	1	3	3	(4)
Miscellaneous Expenses	(5)	3	(1)	(3)	(2)	(4)	(4)
Profit before Tax	9	12	16	26	43	40	44
Income Tax	2	5	8	15	23	21	16
Profit After Tax	7	6	8	11	20	19	28

* Price increases during this period averaged approximately 3% per year.

1981 Balance Sheet (Millions of Belgian Francs)

Assets		Liabilities	
Cash......................	34	Accounts Payable	109
Accounts Receivable...........	124	Long Term Debt...............	36
Inventory	36	Capital	14
Total Current Assets	194	Retained Earnings.............	109
Fixed Assets	74		
Total.......................	268	Total.......................	268

Exhibit 3: Competitor Data Collected in Market Research Study

Panda Competition	Plants	Sales $MM 1981^e/1982^e	Employees	Reps	Showrooms
M.L.I.	Tennessee California	12/15	180	40	N. Carolina
Bornemann	Indiana	3/7	60	20	Indiana New York Ohio Florida (2) Illinois Minnesota
Shadow Interiors	Indiana (2)	7/12	250	30	Indiana
Klote Int. Corp	Tennessee	2.5/	50	23	N. Carolina
Aura	Massachusetts	0.6/	16		
DMF	Illinois	5.4/	100	40	N. Carolina
Estia	Ohio			23	N. Carolina
Alternatives	Ohio			33	N. Carolina
Spherical	N. Carolina	1.6/	23	6	N. Carolina (W. Coast)
Thayer Coggin	N. Carolina				N. Carolina
GSF	Massachusetts		11		
Naturest	Colorado	0.25/1	11	15-20	Colorado

^{e} Estimate

Exhibit 4: Proposed North Carolina Plant Investment Schedule ($ 000's)

Uses		Sources	
Machinery	375	Equity from Panda Europe	100
Land and building.	870	Initial loan from Panda Europe[1]	400
Initial working capital	244	Industrial Revenue Bond[2]	1,200
Provision for 1982 loss	289	Subsequent loan from Panda Europe to cover 1983 losses, working capital needs[1]	268
Provision for 1983 working capital	115		
Contingency	75		
	$ 1,968		**$ 1,968**

[1] Interest rate of 11%. No principal repayment for 5 years.

[2] Interest rate of approximately 12%, moves with prime interest rate. Principal repayment begins in 1983. Fifteen year term. It was not certain that Panda would receive this loan, which would be provided by the state of North Carolina, but it seemed likely.

Exhibit 5: Proposed North Carolina Plant Financial Projections ($ 000's)

	5 months 1982	1983	1984	1985
Sales	500	2250	3630	5400
Cost of Sales including	335	1275	1945	2820
labor	66	224	276	369
material	250	1012	1633	2430
Gross Margin	165	975	1685	2580
Selling Expenses	165	450	725	1080
General and admin.	145	380	525	675
Interest	145	120	120	120
Depreciation	80	115	130	135
	535	1065	1500	2010
Pretax Income	(370)	(90)	185	570
Tax	nil	nil	nil	70
Net Income	(370)	(90)	185	500
Operating Cash Flow	(290)	25	315	535
Loan Repayment	-	80	80	80
Additional Working Capital Required	-	115	155	195

Exhibit 6: Job Description for President

---

1. The Day-to-day

The day-to-day management of the company with direct responsibility for

      a) Production & purchasing
      b) Marketing & sales
      c) Finance & administration
      d) Personnel & public relations

a) Production & Purchasing:

      Achievement of required output
      Planning & control
      Quality control
      Labor relations programs
      Selecting reliable and competitive sources of supply
      Buying materials at competitive prices and available in
         conformity with production planning
      Direct product development
      Selection of production manager

b) Marketing & Sales:

      Achievement of minimum target sales/profitability
      Establishing and implementing marketing strategy as
         directed by the Board of Directors
      Selection of Sales Manager
      Selection of Sales representative team
      Selection of advertising and promotional vehicles
      Marketing and Sales planning – constant creativity in design and product marketing technique, distribution channels etc.
      Training of sales personnel
      Direct sales assistance and follow-up
      Setting up and controlling sales incentive programs

c) Finance & Administration:

      Implementing and making proper use of accounting, inventory and general record keeping systems and controls
      Selection of office manager

d) Personnel & Public Rselations:

> Hiring and firing of personnel (those who report to the president with approval of JHW)
> Instituting personnel benefit programs
> Establishing disciplinary and behavior codes

2. Standards of Performance

1. Achieving target sales of business plan
2. Achieving profitability and cost schedules of business plan

3. Restrictions

1. Cannot purchase or dispose of any fixed assets without approval
2. Cannot enter into loan agreements, overdraft facilities, obtain lines of credit etc. without approval

---

Exhibit 7: Résumé – John Garfield

Objective	General management responsibilities in textile, textile related or other fields
Qualifications	Well rounded record of achievement in varied business and other activities including direct marketing, manufacturing, administrative/ finance/ control, technology, and corporate staff responsibilities.
Work experience	Employed by Engel Corporation* since 1960. Information on scope of work and accomplishments can be discussed.
1975-1981	*Group Vice President – Manufacturing Services Charlotte, N.C.* Directed corporate activities for -

Purchasing	Headquarters Administration
Engineering	Energy Planning and conservation
Research & Development	Engel Chemical Company
Industrial Engineering	Engel Printing Company
Licensing	Engel Maintenance Company

Functional missions for these groups covered policy direction and operating support for domestic and international businesses (1980 sales $3.5 billion, 50,000 employees, 85 locations, 1975-80 fixed asset outlays $1.1 billion).

Member of Corporate: Manufacturing Review Committee, Management Development Review Board, "High Potential Employee" Task Force, President's Grievance Committee.

Chairman of Corporate Boards: Environmental Control, Energy Policy, Patents

1974   *President, Engel Fabrics Co. New York, N.Y.*

Consolidated business through merger of two previously separate fabric divisions. Maintained broad Group Vice President duties.

1973   *Vice President – Merchandising New York, N.Y.*

Added responsibilities for Deutsche Engel, Engel Socks, and Engel Wool Company. Continued direct management of Engel Worsteds and Engel Fabrics. Named to Corporate Management Committee and chaired Corporate Wool Committee.

1972   *Group Manager, Engel Worsteds and Fabrics*
New York, N.Y.

Profit center responsibilities for Fabrics, plus continuing duties in Worsteds.

1971   *Executive Vice President, Engel Worsteds*
New York, N.Y.

Managed key company profit center involving developing, styling, marketing, manufacturing, etc. woven and knit worsted blend, and synthetic fabrics for men's and uniform trades.

1970   *Vice President – Administration, Engel Worsteds/Fabrics*
Abbotville, Va.

Directed control, financial, administrative, costing, information processing, etc. activities.

1969	*Vice President – Manufacturing and Division Manager, Engel Fabrics, Nashville, Tenn*
	Managed integrated facilities – raw material procurement through finished goods delivery/service. Products included blankets, women's coating/sportswear, and uniform fabrics.
1967	Controller, Engel Fabrics Division Nashville, Tenn
1965	Controller, Engel Texturizing Division Blue Hill, Ma.
1965	Operations Analyst, Engel Fabric and Raleigh, N.C. Engel Industrial divisions
1963	Planning/Systems Manager, Raleigh, N.C. Charlotte Finishing Plant
1961	Administrative Assistant, Winston-Salem Weaving Plant, Winston-Salem, N.C.
1960	Management Trainee, Raleigh Weaving Plant Raleigh, N.C.
Education	University of North Carolina – Chapel Hill B.S. Business Administration – 1960 Distinguished Scholar
Personal	Age, 43, 6'0", 175 pounds. Married 21 years, son – college sophomore, daughter – twelfth grade.
Other interests	Recent activities: First United Church – Chairman of Budget/Finance Committee, Chairman of St. George's College "Investment for Excellence" Charlotte Chamber of Commerce – President (1979), Vice President, Director Charlotte Day School – Trustee Charlotte Merchants Association – Director Charlotte Rotary Club Charlotte College – Board of Visitors, Executive Committee

Leadership Charlotte – Steering Committee
United Arts Council – Budget/Finance Committee
United Way – Division Chairman, Director
University of North Carolina – Selection Committee

American Textile Manufacturers Institute – Energy
Policy Committee, Wool Committee
North Carolina Textile Manufacturers Association –
Energy and Utilities Committee

Golfing, gardening, backpacking

References	Can be furnished.

* *Disguised name*

Exhibit 8: Résumé – David Thomas

Personal	Year of Birth: 1940 Married, Three Children Height: 5'10" Weight: 180 lbs Military Status: Honorable Discharge
Education	B.A. degree, Michigan State University, 1965. Major: Business Administration. Minor: Economics. M.B.A. degree, Western Michigan University, 1966. Major: Marketing. Minor: Management.
Experience	*September 1976 to Present*

President of a well known furniture manufacturing
company located in Charlotte, North Carolina.

Started a new company as a subsidiary of a major
French furniture conglomerate. My responsibilities
prior to beginning operations included:
...Working with attorneys to create a North Carolina
corporation in December 1976.

...Negotiated to acquire 25 acres of land within the Charlotte city limits

...Worked with an architect and builder to construct a 43,000 square foot building that included production, office and showroom areas.

...Worked with French engineering department to lay out and install all production equipment.

...Set up brokers and opened initial relationships with U.S. Customs Department.

...Sought out and hired a controller, production manager, and production workers prior to start up September 1, 1977.

...Put a sales force of 34 independent agents into the field two months before beginning operations.

...Worked with photographers, printers, and advertising agency to produce catalogs, price lists, publicity releases, market invitations, letterheads, etc.

...Sought out and set up initial resources for packaging glass, staples, glue, machine parts, electrical parts, etc.

After operations began September 1, 1977 built the company to its present volume of $8 million with approximately 50 employees.

Because I am presently employed by this company I would prefer to keep its identity confidential until a personal interview.

September 1973 to September 1976

Director of Marketing for Regent Furniture of Raleigh, North Carolina.

I initiated a new, more dynamic marketing program for a company that had not achieved satisfactory growth or profit in recent years.

Directly responsible for six departments within the company:

1. Sales Management
2. Customer Service

3. Design and Product Development
4. Advertising and Public Relations
5. Fabric Program
6. Showroom Presentation

March 1971 to August 1973

Director of Marketing for Highland Manufacturing Company of Maine, a high quality manufacturer of grandfather clocks since 1899.

Was primarily responsible for introducing a new marketing program which included:
1. Clarification of company's goals and policies
2. Evaluation of company's course of action to obtain these goals
3. Restructuring the line to the "narrow and deep" philosophy
4. Development of a "professional" sales force
5. Realignment of distribution patterns

Net result of this program was an increase in sales from $1.8 million in 1971, to $3.2 million in 1972, to $4.3 million in 1973, to $6.3 million in 1974.

June 1968 to March 1971

Sales representative for Logan's Fine Arts, Inc. covering the states of Ohio, Michigan, Indiana, Kentucky and West Virginia.

Was presented with "Salesman of the Year" award for 1969 and 1970 which included a substantial bonus of U.S. Savings Bonds. This award was based on:
1. Percentage of sales increases
2. Number of new *major* accounts opened
3. The use of professional selling techniques

Was primarily responsible for developing a "programmed approach to major account sales" throughout the company which resulted in significant volume increases. In my territory we realized a 54% increase in two years and this became the top volume territory for the company.

September 1966 to June 1968

Executive trainee for George Coles and Son, Ohio.

Advanced through head-of-stock, branch store department manager and assistant buyer in a department store whose volume exceeded $175 million. Learned all aspects of buying, merchandise presentation, advertising, store operations and the procedures and problems of retailers.

Exhibit 9: David Thomas' Marketing Plan

Table Of Contents	Page
General Management	1
Engineering and Production	1
Finance and Administration	1
Sales and Marketing	2
1. Product	2
2. Distribution	2
3. Promotion	5
A. Total Package Program	5
B. Representation	5
C. Advertising and Public Relations	6
D. Showrooms	6
E. Collateral Material	6
4. Price	6
Exhibits	
A. Survey of Buying Power	
B. Top 100 Department Stores	
C. Top 100 Furniture Stores	
D. The Furniture Market	

2. Toro: Industrial Flavors

This case was prepared by Professor Per V. Jenster and Research Assistant Bethann Kassman as a basis for class discussion rather than to illustrate either effective or ineffective handling of a business situation. This case was developed as part of an Institutional Project on the Management of Internationalization, and conducted in collaboration with the Industrial Development Authority of Ireland.

On a crisp fall morning in October 1990, Jan Emil Johannessen, strategic planner for the Toro division of Rieber & Son, sat in his Bergen office looking out at the fjord as he contemplated the analysis work on his desk. The firm's decision to formally enter into the industrial sales of flavor products had been a challenge to its traditional capabilities in consumer culinary products. In August 1987, management had decided to follow up a 1985 entrepreneurial effort to pursue international opportunities in the industrial flavors business more rigorously *(refer to Exhibits 1 and 2)*. By early 1990, however, they realized that the firm's organizational resources and competencies were already being stretched to the limit. As Jan Emil Johannessen stood reflecting on the European industrial flavor market, he had to acknowledge that some tough decisions needed to be made regarding Rieber & Son's future strategy in culinary products and the international industrial strategy in particular.

Company Background
Rieber & Son A/S

The history of Rieber & Son A/S began in 1817 when the Rieber family from the Kingdom of Wurtemberg set off from Amsterdam aboard the sailing vessel "De Zee Ploeg". Their destination was Philadelphia, but fate led them to Norway instead. During a terrible storm, their ship was wrecked off the Norwegian coast, but they were towed to safety into the harbor of the small town of Bergen.

In 1839, one of the sons of the Rieber Family, Paul Gottlieb, founded the company Rieber & Son A/S, which engaged in various activities, particularly in the building materials sector.

Building materials became the mainstay of the company for the following 100 years. By 1990, Rieber & Son A/S was a professionally managed Norwegian Group with a turnover of approximately NOK 3,200 million and 2,850 employees. The key business areas were Food, Packaging Materials, Road Surfacing Materials and Building Materials. *(Financial data are presented in Exhibit 3)*. The companies' activities ranged from industrial production to purely commercial operations. Each division had its own business concept and, likewise, separate strategies for reaching its objectives.

Over and above the ordinary advantages of group structure, such as management, availability of resources and systems common to all members of the group, there initially seemed to be few points of contact between the individual divisions within the company. Yet, the firm stressed that there was, in fact, commonality in financial management and, to a certain degree, corporate philosophy. Nevertheless, day-to-day synergies among the divisions were limited due to the highly diversified nature of the overall Group.

Strategy and Future Outlook

Rieber & Son's attention had been directed towards the domestic markets with 80% of the company's sales taking place in Norway. Overseas sales were made within defined niches and were mainly linked to the packaging sector and natural stone products. Rieber & Son had concentrated its efforts on growth within sectors often considered "established areas".

The company's strategy was twofold. On the one hand, it was working for a logical further development of all 10 divisions both nationally and internationally. This strategy included both the growth of the divisions' own products, the acquisition of companies well suited to fit into existing divisions and the achievement of competitive advantage through strategic alliances. On the other hand, the firm was seeking further development by taking over various companies in areas where it could achieve a sounder strategic position through the takeover.

Toro

In 1948, Rieber and Son laid the foundation for its current food division, Toro Foods, by introducing Bouillon Cubes, rapidly followed by related dehydrated food products. By 1989, sales of Toro Foods had reached NOK 697 million *(refer to Exhibit 3 for the division's financial results)*. Toro Foods was the most profitable of the 10 Rieber divisions.

With production concentrated in Norway, the firm was proud of its expanding plant outside Bergen, equipped with sophisticated technology for the production of dried products. Air and vacuum dehydration processes were used in internal production while raw materials processed by freeze, drum and spray drying techniques were acquired. By early 1990, annual production had exceeded 11,000 tons of dehydrated foods and ingredients for consumers, catering markets and other food producers.

The firm could proudly point to significant domestic success, despite the presence of large multinational producers, such as Nestlé (Maggi), CPC (Knorr), and Unilever (Lipton). The Toro brand brought the Rieber organization impressive market share results in the Norwegian culinary retail sector with the following products:

Soups	87%
Stews	95%
Sauces	86%
Casseroles	99%
Bouillons	75%

In catering, the firm held similarly strong positions with an overall estimated market share of 70%. *(Refer to Exhibit 4 for details of the Toro Organization.)*

Introduction of Dehydrated Fish Soup
Historically, Toro was a major world player in the whale extract market. The tract was dehydrated and used to add flavor to processed food products. When whaling declined during the 1950s and 1960s, Toro used the knowledge gained in the whaling industry and applied it to other food ingredients. Real success came in 1959 when Toro developed and launched dried soups in sachets. Four years later another breakthrough came when Toro produced dehydrated fish soups. Dehydration, the oldest form of conservation, was actually a fairly simple idea. Water, removed at the beginning of the process, was then added at the time of preparation, without losing any of the product's major nutritive value. The problem was to retain the finer flavors of the raw materials. It was this problem that Toro solved and marketed, initially to the Norwegian market, followed shortly by entry into the Scandinavian market.

Catering

The Toro Catering Division was created as a specialized organization responsible for developing the catering product range, and for sales and marketing in the Norwegian catering market. The division achieved total sales of NOK 102 million in 1989. Despite a decline in the total market, Toro's Catering Division enjoyed an increase in volume. The product line was expanded to include products produced in Toro's factory as well as products from several Norwegian and foreign suppliers of dried, canned, chilled and frozen foodstuffs.

Toro's Catering Division's strategy was to combine high quality with labor saving properties for the user and advantageous prices. The products were specially developed for and adapted to use in catering establishments. The end users of these products included all types of catering establishments such as hotels, restaurants, transport companies and the armed forces. Distribution took place through wholesalers and ships' chandlers.

Expanding to Other Markets

Toro was the undisputed retail market leader in Norway with 90% of the market in dehydrated foods comprising a wide range of products – soups, casseroles, stews, sauces, etc. The quality of these dehydrated foods was perceived to be very high. In addition, Toro had adapted its products to Norwegian tastes.

With the successful launch of its dehydrated fish soup in the 1960s, Toro decided early on to expand into the neighboring Scandinavian market. Through an informal process, the other four Nordic countries (Sweden, Finland, Denmark, Iceland) were targeted. Toro embarked on a niche strategy using distributors and local people to test the market, then tailor the product to the demands of the broader Scandinavian marketplace. Considerable money was spent, especially in Sweden as it was the largest and most attractive market, but the outcome was less successful than had been anticipated.

For 25 years, the market had been dominated by big three players: Unilever, Nestlé, and CPC. These players had the resources to stay in the market long enough to become profitable, had successfully covered the market for many years and had a product line similar to Toro's. Thus, Toro made the decision to retreat from the branded products' market in all the other Scandinavian countries except Iceland.[2] In both

---

[2] In Iceland, a market equivalent in size to the city of Bergen, Toro was able to maintain the dominant position.

Sweden and Denmark, however, Toro's name had become recognized, a fact the firm used to its advantage by producing private label products for two of the largest chains in both countries. Toro sold through the Swedish Cooperative Society in Sweden under the Foodia name and in Denmark under the Irma label. Toro's experience in the Nordic market did not discourage the company from trying to enter the wider European market with export of branded retail lines. The strategy was to develop unique products in Norway and exploit them with niche marketing on the Continent.

In the early 1970s, Toro had developed a range of seafood specialties through a specific process technology for producing tastier fish powder. These products were believed to be superior to those available in Europe. The strategy objective was to introduce the product into as many countries as possible in order to achieve volume through market penetration (in contrast to its first international effort where Toro targeted only the "home market", Scandinavia). However, it soon became apparent that there were many issues which needed to be addressed in order to succeed in the Continental European markets.

First, Toro faced Unilever, Nestlé, and CPC, which together accounted for 80-85% of the market share in dehydrated foods worldwide. These competitors commanded considerable resources and, through sheer volume, were able to bring economies of scale to their product development and market maintenance costs which Toro could not match. In other than fish soups, Toro was at a cost disadvantage because it imported raw ingredients for use in its products and then often exported the finished products to the same countries that the ingredients had come from. In addition to being unable to meet a vast set of packaging requirements, Toro received little support from distributors and agents, who were largely selected using the simplest criteria. This resulted in inconsistent marketing plans which varied from country to country and were insufficient to penetrate the Continental market.

Sales remained flat for 10-15 years while production problems increased due to packaging requirements and small order runs. By 1985 Toro had decided that the Continental niche was too small and required excessive effort for too little profit. It decided to stop selling to the retail market in most European countries, but to keep a presence in those countries where it had the best agents and the highest sales volume. Thus, Toro increased its marketing in Spain, the United Kingdom and the United States, while moving more into private label sales for specific stores in Continental Europe.

By 1986, Toro found at this point in time that the retail market for its products was declining in both absolute and relative terms. Private label sales were largely sold through cooperatives, which were also losing business. Therefore, Toro decided to discontinue its strategy of entering new retail markets in the dried and dehydrated product lines, and to confine its retail food sales primarily to the Norwegian market. Meanwhile, the company discovered an emerging market for expansion – wholesale flavors to the larger European community.

Dabbling in Industrial Ingredients

In the late 1980s, sales remained flat in the finished product sector but continued to rise in the raw materials market. Toro management looked at these results and realized that, over the years, the firm had developed a unique knowledge in the production of seafood and fish powders. Toro also had a strong research and development base in the process and product technology for dry foods, especially relating to taste. Management concluded, therefore, that Toro not only had a role as supplier of finished culinary products to major retailers, but it also had a viable role helping other producers with product formulation and process expertise. To larger firms, Toro offered its special knowledge in fish products, and, to smaller companies, research and development support.

In addition, Norway suffered from a tariff burden on the shelf ready products it exported to the EEC, so it made sense for Toro to sell its knowledge and raw materials to others. During a large strategy meeting in 1988, management decided to limit retail sales to the Nordic market and treat Europe as its industrial market. Having made this decision, Toro withdrew from the finished product sector so as not to compete directly with its potential industrial customers. It was felt that the product segment where Toro had an advantage over its competitors was in the development of natural savory products related to seafood. Consequently, this was the area that Toro targeted for expansion within the European industrial flavors market.

The strategy quickly became a challenge to the various functional disciplines within the organization, partly due to its broad scope. Over the next year and a half, as experience increased, the strategy narrowed down to focus on different distribution methods in various countries and on a more limited product range specifically geared to convenience foods, dried and frozen foods. Using advanced technology and a combination of available first class raw materials, Toro produced a powder with high quality taste. Its R&D unit produced flavor systems which were sold to other culinary companies for use in their products. As demand increased, the majority of powders and granulates of various fish were exported either as semi-manufactured goods, such as stocks and sauces, or as raw material. By the end of 1989, 50% of industrial sales were direct sales to convenience food producers, with the remaining 50% to flavor houses and mixers.

Worldwide Flavor Industry

Because flavors and fragrances used similar materials and technology in production, most producers made both types of products, customarily called the Flavors and Fragrances (F&F) industry. However, the market dynamics (i.e., driving forces for growth) and the bases for competition differed between the flavors and fragrances segments. Fragrances included combinations of natural and/or synthetic raw materials, whereas flavors tended to be less exotic and were usually based on something found in nature.

Growth and profitability of the flavors segment (retail and industrial) had to be viewed in the context of the F&F industry as a whole. Until the late 1970s, the world F&F industry was seen as an extraordinarily high performer. Industry profitability approximated 15% of sales in the mid- to late 1960s and 10% in the 1970s. Since that time, slower growth and increased competitive pressures had reduced profitability to about 6-7% industry-wide. For the past 10 years, real sales growth averaged 5-6% per year, reaching $5.8 billion in 1987. Because of widely fluctuating world currencies, especially the dollar, actual growth was difficult to estimate; however, expected growth was projected to be roughly 5% per year through 1992.

Valued at nearly $2.6 billion in 1987, flavors comprised nearly 45% of the total F&F market, with 15% of the total flavor market from savory flavors. Western Europe and the United States were the largest regional markets, together accounting for 63% of world flavor sales. Japan was the third major market. Consumption in the rest of the world was significantly lower. However, the USSR and the Far East were identified as having the greatest growth potential.

Industry Trends

In the 1960s, artificial flavors accounted for 75% of the market, while natural flavors accounted for 25%. These percentages were reversed by the late 1980s. Although natural flavors were more costly to develop and could not withstand all techniques of food processing, most of the major flavor houses oriented their development programs to meet the growing demand for natural flavors. As the costs of flavor ingredients continued to rise and product development became costly and complex, strategic acquisitions became an important means of company growth. Most of these acquisitions were made for market reasons: to gain a base in a particular regional market, to acquire a market niche, to allow for R&D expansion in an area, or to acquire a talented flavorist or a key food account.

Despite the high level of merger and acquisition activity, the world flavor industry remained highly fragmented. This was not expected to change, although Arthur D. Little, a management consulting firm, predicted that an acquisition slowdown would occur through the early 1990s. Continued success in the industry required an enhanced working relationship with customers in order to understand their changing needs better and thus be able to offer more applications research and technical service.

Companies in the F&F business spent significantly more on R&D than did most participants in their end-use markets. R&D spending varied by company size; the large multinationals spent 7-12% of sales on R&D, while the smaller companies spent 2-5%. Heavy investments in biotechnology focused on developing ways to produce better quality natural flavors at a lower cost. Major research was also conducted to develop more stable natural flavor systems to protect against the effects of processing, packaging, and ingredient interaction. High temperature short-time (HTST) food processing, retorting and microwave cooking, in particular, presented challenges and opportunities to the flavor houses. New techniques to further improve the stability and shelf life of flavors was also being investigated.

In the industrial flavor segment of the market, the growth of processed foods as a percentage of total food consumption was expected to continue through the 1990s, with particularly strong growth in Northern Europe. An increase in sales of savory flavors was anticipated as well. Because of the high cost of research and development, product development would continue to be contracted out to flavor houses, mixers, and raw material suppliers. Overall, ingredients were seen as a profitable area of activity since they did not demand the heavy marketing expenditure required to promote food products to the retail trade. Furthermore, the considerable increase in demand for convenience foods was likely to continue to grow throughout the 1990s, creating new opportunities to expand the market.

Industrial Competitors

The largest producers of seafood products were the Japanese; however, industrial sales from Japanese companies were concentrated almost exclusively in the Far East. In Europe, competition was confined to a limited number of small niche players, primarily located in Norway and France. Of these companies, only one (Isnard Lyraz located in France) produced a high quality product similar to that produced by Toro.

Toro's major competitors in the retail sector (Maggi, CPC, Unilever) were not direct competitors with Toro in the industrial seafood powder area. Although there were areas where some competition existed (HVP and bouillon), by and large, these flavor houses as well as others were Toro customers who purchased and reprocessed Toro's products.

The top 15-20 participants in the F&F industry accounted for the majority of flavor sales; 14 of these companies had sales of $100 million or more *(refer to Exhibit 5)*. The remaining sales were dispersed among some 100 other major producers and nearly 1,000 smaller companies around the world. Thus, in spite of the concentration of sales at the top, fragmentation of the industry was not reduced, primarily because many of the hundreds of small flavor houses were not vulnerable to takeover and because many new companies had entered the business due to the low entry barriers.

Buying Process

Flavor was one of the major differentiating factors among various brands within a food product category. Safety, nutrition, convenience and price were also important, but taste acceptance by the consumer was essential to the creation of brand loyalty. In spite of the importance of flavors to the food industry, food processors exerted considerable pressure on suppliers of food additives. These pressures included demand for natural ingredients, high quality but low cost products, and product diversity to meet the varied tastes of the increasingly sophisticated consumer.

Responding to buyer influence led to tremendous growth in new product introduction (According to Productscan/Marketing Intelligence Service, more than 8,000 new food products were introduced to the European markets in 1987). The trend towards an expanding product market was expected to continue. All of which required a corresponding development in the area of new flavor systems. Product obsolescence – caused by changes in consumer preferences, habits and lifestyles – also occurred at a higher rate in the industry. These factors, combined with the competitive pressures stemming from the food industry, forced flavor suppliers to increase their internal capabilities in product application, basic research and development, technical service, and marketing.

The eruption of more freedom in Eastern Europe and the Soviet Union foreshadowed economic opportunities comparable to the period of international business expansion in the 1950s and 1960s. The internationalization of tastes and increasing health concerns among consumers in all countries presupposed heavy investments in research to keep pace with innovation, or changing the focus to a compounder or blender. As the costs of producing innovative flavors increased, more producers looked to others in the industry for product development, technical expertise and market knowledge.

Many flavor houses predicted that the 1990s would bring a continuation of the flavoring fads of the 1980s – exotic flavorings, natural flavorings and easy to prepare foods. However, the area receiving the greatest interest was in natural flavorings and "healthy" foods. Toro had a fairly large advantage in this area in that all its products were 100% natural, unlike the Japanese whose products were mixed with enhancers and additives. In essence, Toro's processing consisted of taking the frozen blocks of fish filet, crushing and boiling them, drying and milling them. Although this process sounded simple on paper, its technology was quite advanced for the complex production of seafood.

Toro's Initial Efforts in Industrialization

Until 1986, Toro had grown through retail sales and finished products. The decision to enter the European industrial market required a change in sales, distribution and production. Staff that had been working with retail sales and technology was quickly shifted to serve the requirements of an industrial market. It soon became evident that the organization had difficulty with this transition. The staff was not trained to deal with the different requests from industrial customers; specific recipes had to be developed and sold, creating an impact on both R&D and sales; new country-specific regulatory requirements had to be incorporated into the product specifications; and production had to be adjusted to accommodate short runs. There were, however, a number of key strengths which Toro built upon as it entered this new environment. Backward integration (the processing of its own raw materials) continued to be handled by the processing department. The vertical integration allowed Toro to take raw ingredients, process them to specification, and produce a finished product for sale to the marketplace similar to the way it had done in the retail market. Its large, well-staffed research and development department was already familiar with developing a wide range of formulations, and Toro's presence in the retail market lent credibility to its entry into the industrial market.

Sales Department

Focusing on the industrial market required specific sales tasks and behavior which differed from those used in the retail market. Initially, Toro went in with its standard products, but discovered that the customer wanted tailored or specially developed products within short time frames. The salesmen were not prepared to deal with the technical issues raised by industrial clients and were unfamiliar with the amount of effort required to meet these demands, particularly by the research and development department. It was felt that a sales force with technical skills was needed. To meet this new demand, R&D staff were teamed with the sales staff. In addition, one technical sales manager was recruited from the factory and one was hired from the outside. This new staff and technical focus allowed for greater communication between the client and R&D at an earlier stage in the customer relationship, and eliminated basic misunderstandings as to availability of products and the time frames required for production. It raised, however, a different problem – taking research and development staff away from its other tasks. In-house education as well as attendance at seminars helped enhance the skills of both the sales staff and the R&D staff. In fact, one individual from research and development was moved into the sales department to enhance the technical understanding of this unit.

Export sales were split 50/50 – half on finished goods for the consumer and half on semifinished product and raw material. Rieber/Toro's biggest markets for selling fish powders were West Germany (25%), Benelux (20%), the USA (10%) and France (10%). Spain, as a large fish-eating nation, was on the verge of becoming a big market for the company, with sales running at 10% of total industrial turnover. The rest of the sales went to the Far East, Australia and Scandinavia. In Europe, the products were sold through agents; in the Nordic countries the product was sold directly. In 1989, Rieber/Toro decided to apply a model of direct sales representation in the UK added an additional 10% of sales. An English staff of two salespeople and a technical person were obtained when a small distributor was purchased in an effort to gain a better understanding of the English customers' requirements. Small distributors were usually selected in the various countries, because they were more responsive to Toro's needs than were the larger distribution houses, which were perceived to be less loyal. As a common sales strategy, the largest producers and mixers were targeted priorities for both the agents and the sales force.

Large food producers buying directly from Toro accounted for 50% of sales. Selling directly enhanced Toro's ability to offer advice on usage and to provide blended products. Direct sales to flavor houses accounted for 30% of sales. The flavor houses made a living out of extracting taste from raw materials and selling it to the customer at a high markup. Also, the flavor houses had access to an international market which Toro neither knew nor understood. The remaining 20% of sales were to mixers who serviced smaller companies and other industries, such as those in meat-based products *(refer to Exhibit 6)*.

Research and Development

With a budget equivalent to $2.4 million invested each year (representing 2.6% of total turnover), the company was proud of its applied developmental work. The R&D department was responsible for dealing with a customer's technical questions as well as formulating new products and controlling existing ones. With 45 staff members working in its development laboratories and pilot plant, the company was continually testing new methods and ways of handling ingredients.

An industrial market focus, however, strained the R&D department's resources. Used to having one to two years lead time to develop products for the company to sell, the department's position had reversed – it now had to produce products to demand as well as develop new products. As the company focused its emphasis more on the industrial component, staff who had been working in the retail area were moved to the industrial area. Most of these people needed time and education in order to understand the new business focus as well as to deal with the new regulatory requirements demanded by the various countries in which Toro was now selling. Ensuring quality also needed additional resources to comply with the changing requirements of data and documentation. But, perhaps the biggest change was that, as orders came in, products had to be tailor made, reformulated and produced under very tight time lines to meet customer demand. This situation created a lot of internal pressure.

To deal with these new demands, R&D focused on building up its staff to deal professionally with individual customers. Technical staff were assigned to travel with the sales staff and to communicate directly with clients. By being on the scene, the technical staff were able to lay out the product requirements and to identify problem areas early in the process. Within the company itself, increased communication with all departments, but particularly with sales and manufacturing, was emphasized.

Being located so far from the market made it imperative that Toro do everything possible to facilitate communication and product delivery. This strategy required a large investment in new equipment, as well as in personnel training and continually helping the staff to adapt. There were, however, some economies of scale which surfaced. Some recipes were able to be used across borders and, in some cases, industrial projects provided the testing ground for retail products. The research and development department had faced the challenge of being responsive to the developmental needs of the industrial environment well. Nevertheless, continuing the effort to maintain a strong research focus was of some concern to the department manager.

Production

Production problems centered around the difficulties created by small runs as opposed to the larger runs common for products in the retail market. This change affected scheduling and equipment as well as the process used. R&D staff were often needed in the factory to provide hands-on expertise during small trial runs. The short timetables requested by customers exacerbated the issues. To meet these new production requirements, specific small batch, dedicated equipment was purchased. R&D staff continued to be involved in production runs, particularly pilot runs which focused on developing products. The buying department found alternative sources for shellfish in order to have the necessary resources on hand for production to meet client demand. Although communication among the various departments had improved, the increased interaction among the departments involved in production required having constant communication about, and evaluation of, the problem areas.

A New Way of Working

The development of flavorings and natural additives for the international food market forced many changes in the day-to-day operations and the overall aspects of the business. The need for technical and production staff to be located closer to the clients – especially those smaller companies located in Europe – was acknowledged. A strategy was developed which included acquisition of a network of smaller companies already in the industrial market in Continental Europe. Distribution networks were expanded and staff requirements in R&D, Export, and Manufacturing were under constant review. Contacts with flavor houses and agents were expanded. This intense evaluation involving the entire Toro division was geared to speed up and facilitate entry into the industrial market.

With over 40 years of retail marketing and a strong presence in the Norwegian market, Toro had consistently relied on its technical formulation and product expertise. The changing retail environment and the opening of international borders implied that Toro would have to use those strengths to face the many challenges which lay ahead. Jan Emil Johannessen was optimistic that Toro would meet the challenges and succeed in its new industrial environment.

Exhibit 1

Rieber & Søn A/S
Bergen 21.10.85

MEETING NOTES

Action Program – Marine Powders

Objectives:

Primary: To be the world's leading producer of marine powder products.

Secondary: Within marine powder, we will aim to have an assortment of products which cover the main needs of our customers.

We will aim always to be able to deliver products when needed.

We must be competitive with respect to price and quality of our products.

Budget:

	1986	1987	1988	1989
Turnover (NOK mn.*)	7.5	9.5	12.0	15.1
(actual sales)	6.5	9.0	13.5	15.0

Source: Company Records
* CHF 1.00=NOK 4.50

Exhibit 2

Rieber & Søn a/s
26.8.88

Strategy – Industrial Products 1988-1994

Status:
We have a solid point of departure in our own production of dried food products to a discerning market. This has forced us to develop a large degree of proprietary processes and semifinished products of high quality.

With this in mind, we have developed sales of NOK 20 mn., with a satisfactory/good profitability.

The selling process is largely characterized as technical sales to a target group consisting of the technical decision makers in flavor houses and other food producers.

Marine Products
Product/Markets:
- 2 fish powders (one high end, another somewhat lower in costs)
- Crab powder
- Lobster powder
- Crimp powder
- Oyster powder

Strategic Position:
High quality of powders, with some brought forth with own proprietary processes based on natural raw materials. The emphasis is on long shelf life for these products.

Critical Success Factors!
Raw materials and replication of recipes of consistent nature.

Future Possibilities:
As of now, our customers have primarily been flavor houses. This has been a good fit with our pure taste systems, without formulated mix combinations, e.g., hydrolysate spices, starches. However, we assume that the food producers are demanding products with a higher value added dimension.

Thus, we see a need for
* less expensive products, e.g., crimp products
* mixed raw materials (different levels of value added)
* developing other extract products in collaboration with universities
* possibly looking for acquisition candidates producing similar or complementary powder products.

Bouillon (Hydrolysate)
Sales 1987 – NOK 9 mn.
Budget 88- NOK 12 mn.

Product/Markets
Internationally, we sell formulated bouillon, that is, hydrolysate with meat extract, spices, etc. Here, our main clients are in the U.K.

Although we do not have strong competitive advantages in pure hydrolysate, we have developed talent in formulating end products. Thus, we have been functioning as a flavor house, and are offering our products in formulated condition to our customers.

Strategic Perspective
We have strong talent in formulating products *vis-à-vis* end producers, based on our own experience in vacuum-based products.

Future Developments
We believe that further efforts in this area should follow the direction pursued in the U.K. This will be emphasized after the purchase of our British agent. Such opportunities may be pursued elsewhere.

Meats
Status
Our own developments in meat based product, particularly for use in micro ovens, are very encouraging. However, as of yet no international sales have been made, partly due to our cost disadvantage created by import restrictions.

Future Developments
Viewed in light of our effort in bouillon, we see certain possibilities which are being pursued.

Budgets
As per attachment.

Source: Company Records

Exhibit 2b: Forecast in NOK

	Growth	87	88	89	90	91	92	93	94
Existing marine powders	10%	9.2	12	14	16	18	20	22	24
Formulated marine powders			1	3	5	7	8	10	12
Acquired mixes			12	13	14	15	16	17	18
Total marine			25	30	35	40	44	49	54
Dried meats			3	6	9	12	15	18	21
Peas, lentils			1	2	3	4	4	4	4
Flavor blends	7%		200	214	228	245	262	280	300
Bouillon			9	12	17	22	27	32	37
Total			**238**	**264**	**292**	**323**	**352**	**383**	**416**

Exhibit 3: Financial Information on Main Areas

(Figures in NOK mill.)	Food		Packaging materials		Road/asphalt		Building materials		Joint costs/ elimination		The group	
	89	88	89	88	89	88	89	88	89	88	89	88
Income Statement												
Net sales	697	657	691	645	654	551	1102	1032	-2	-15	3142	2870
Of which, exports etc., represent	51	49	331	320	24	29	243	163	-	-	649	561
Contribution from sales and other income	424	399	336	315	306	265	383	376	6	2	1455	1357
Operating costs	-152	-143	-86	-78	-80	-67	-132	-139	-10	3	-460	-424
Wage/social security costs	-135	-133	-166	-147	-154	-132	-170	-159	-35	-36	-660	-607
Depreciations	-22	-27	-31	-29	-30	-28	-21	-18	-4	-4	-108	-106
	115	96	53	61	42	38	60	60	-43	-35	227	220
Balance Sheet												
Net operating capital[1]	38	63	68	57	9	-27	242	209	-142	-120	215	182
Capital assets	180	183	200	196	125	111	178	173	223	161	906	824
Net working capital	218	246	268	253	134	84	420	382	81	41	1121	1006
Key figures												
Yield ratio[2]	46%	37%	20%	25%	31%	33%	16%	19%			22%	24%
Turnover rate[3]	2.8	2.5	2.6	2.6	4.7	4.6	2.8	3.0	-	-	2.7	2.7
Profit margin[4]	17%	15%	8%	10%	7%	7%	6%	6%	-	-	8%	9%
Average number of employees	578	573	735	701	524	517	884	884	79	78	2800	2753

1) **Net operating capital.** Receivable plus stock less interest-free credits.
2) **Yield ratio.** Operating result plus financial revenues in percent of average net working capital.
3) **Turnover rate.** Net sales divided by average net working capital.
4) **Profit margin.** Operating result plus financial revenues in percent of net sales.

The average net working capital used in the calculation of the key figures appears as a weighted average of the consumption of capital throughout the whole year, and is thus not directly comparable with the above net working capital which is obtained from the balance sheet at 31 December.

Exhibit 4: Toro Organization

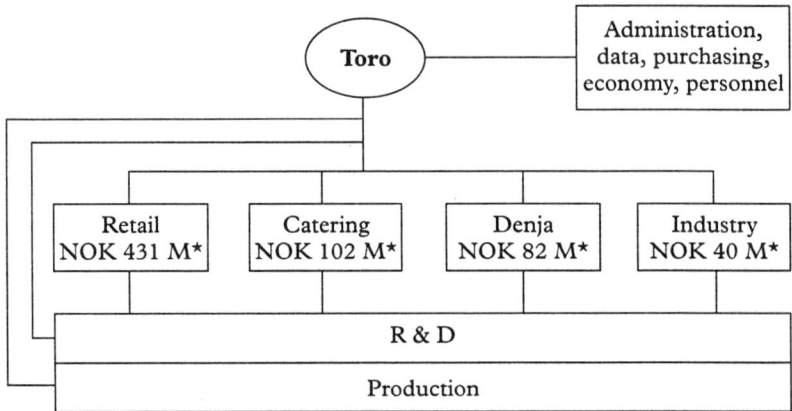

```
                    ┌─────────┐      ┌──────────────────┐
                    │  Toro   │──────│  Administration, │
                    │         │      │ data, purchasing,│
                    └─────────┘      │ economy, personnel│
                                     └──────────────────┘
```

Retail NOK 431 M*	Catering NOK 102 M*	Denja NOK 82 M*	Industry NOK 40 M*

R & D

Production

* *budget for 1989*   570 employees

Exhibit 5: Companies with 1987 Flavor and Fragrance Sales of $100 Million or More

Company/Parent	Headquarters	1987 World Sales (MM$)
International Flavors & Fragrances (IFF)	United States	745
Quest International/Unilever	United Kingdom/Netherlands	635
Givaudan/Hoffmann-La Roche	Switzerland	480
Takasago Perfumery	Japan	440
Haarman & Reimer/Bayer	Germany	350
Firmenich	Switzerland	240
Dragoco Gerberding	Germany	350
Bush Boake Allen (BBA) Union Camp, U.S.	United Kingdom	140
Florasynth-Lautier	France	130
Fritzsche Dodge & Olcott/BASF	Germany	130
PFW Division/Hercules	United States	120
Universal Group/Universal Foods	United States	110
Roure	France	100
Hasagawa	Japan	100
Total		**3,870**

Note: In today's world monetary system of fluctuating currencies, all calculations in current U.S. dollars, or any other currency, are subject to considerable exchange rate distortions. Thus, the dollar sales for each of these companies do not necessarily reflect the company's true size or position relative to the other major players.

Sources: Annual reports and Arthur D. Little, Inc., estimates.

Exhibit 6: Sales to Customers

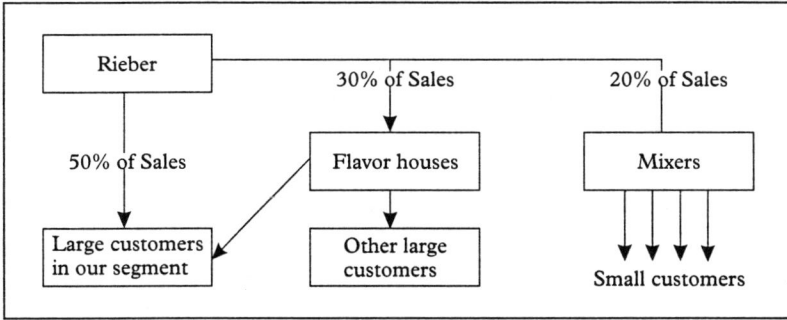

3. Delissa in Japan

This case was prepared by Research Assistant Juliet Burdet-Taylor and Professor Dominique Turpin as a basis for class discussion rather than to illustrate either effective or ineffective handling of an administrative situation. All names and figures have been disguised.

"We can maintain our presence in Japan or we can pull out..."

In the autumn of 1991, Bjorn Robertson, who had recently been named Managing Director of Agria, Sweden's leading dairy products cooperative, met with his team to review the international side of the business. The four men sat around a table piled high with thick reports, Nielsen audits, film storyboards, yogurt cups and a mass of promotional material in Japanese. Agria's "Delissa" line of fresh dairy products was sold all over the world through franchise agreements. Several of these agreements were up for review, but the most urgent one was the agreement with Nikko of Japan.

"In the light of these results, there are several things we can do in Japan. We can maintain our presence and stay with our present franchisee, we can change our franchisee, or we can pull out. But, let's look first at how badly we are really doing in Japan." Bjorn Robertson, looked across the conference table at Peter Borg, Stefan Gustafsson and Lars Karlsson, each of whom had been involved with Agria's Japanese business over the past few years.

Bjorn Robertson read out loud to the others a list of Agria's major foreign ventures featuring the Delissa yogurt brand: *"USA launch date 1977, market share=12.5%; Germany launch 1980, market share=14%; UK launch 1982, market share=13.8%; France launch 1983, market share=95%; Japan launch 1982, market share today=2-3%."* Robertson circled the figure with his marker and turned to look around at his team. "Under 3% after 10 years in the market! What happened?" he asked.

History

Agria was founded in 1967 when a group of Swedish dairy cooperatives decided to create a united organization that would develop and sell a line of fresh dairy products. The principal engineers of the organization were Rolf Anderen and Bo Ekman who had established the group's headquarters in Uppsala, near Stockholm. In 1970, after the individual cooperatives had been persuaded to drop their own trademarks, the Delissa line was launched. This was one of the few "national" lines of dairy products in Sweden. It comprised yogurts, desserts, fresh cheese and fresh cream. In the two decades that followed, Agria's share rose from 3% to 25% of the Swedish fresh milk products market. Rolf Anderen's vision and the concerted efforts of 20,000 dairy farmer members of the cooperative had helped build Agria into a powerful national and international organization.

By 1991, more than 1.1 billion Delissa yogurts and desserts were being consumed per year worldwide. In fiscal year 1990, Delissa had sales of $1.6 billion and employed 4,400 people in and outside Sweden.

Industrial franchising was rare in the 70s, and Swedish dairy products firms did not usually invest money abroad. However, Mr. Ekman's idea of know-how transfer ventures, whereby a local licensee would manufacture yogurt using Swedish technology and then market and distribute the product using its own distribution network, had enabled Delissa to penetrate over 13 foreign markets with considerable success and with a minimal capital outlay. In contrast, Delissa's biggest competitor worldwide, BSN – a French food conglomerate marketing a yogurt line under the "Danone" brand name – had gone into foreign markets, mainly by buying into or creating local companies, or by forming regular joint ventures.

By the time Bjorn Robertson took over as European marketing director in 1985, the Delissa trademark – with the white cow symbol so familiar in Sweden – was known in many different countries worldwide. Delissa was very active in sponsoring sports events, and Bjorn Robertson – himself a keen cross-country skier and sailor – offered his personal support to Delissa's teams around the world. When he reviewed the international business, Robertson had been surprised by the results of Agria's Japanese joint venture which did not compare to those achieved in most foreign markets. Before calling together the international marketing team for a discussion, Robertson requested the files on Japan and spent some time studying the history of the alliance. He read:

"Proposal for entry into the Japanese market
In early 1979, the decision was made to enter the Japanese market. Market feasibility research and a search for a suitable franchisee is underway, with an Agria team currently in Japan.

Objectives

The total yogurt market in Japan for 1980 is estimated at approximately 600 million cups (100 million). The market for yogurt is expected to grow at an average of at least 8% p.a. in volume for the next 5 years. Our launch strategy would be based on an expected growth rate of 10% or 15% for the total market. We have set ourselves the goal of developing a high quality range of yogurts in Japan, of becoming well known with the Japanese consumer. We aim to reach a 5% market share in the first year and 10% share of market within three years of launch. We plan to cover the three main metropolitan areas, Tokyo, Osaka and Nagoya, within a two-year period, and the rest of the country within the next three years."

Robertson circled the 10% with a red pen. He understood that management would have hesitated to set too high a goal for market share compared to other countries since some executives felt that Japan was a difficult market to enter. But, in 1987, six years after the launch, the Japanese operation had not reached its three-year target. In 1991, Delissa's share of the total yogurt market had fallen to 2%, without ever reaching 3%. Bjorn Robertson wrote a note to the Uppsala-based manager responsible for Far Eastern business stating that he felt Agria's record in Japan in no way reflected the type of success it had had elsewhere with Delissa. He began to wonder why Japan was so different.

The report continued with a brief overview of the Japanese yogurt market:

"Consumption

Per capita consumption of yogurt in Japan is low compared to Scandinavian countries. It is estimated at around 5.3 cups per person per year in Japan, versus 110 in Sweden and 120 in Finland. Sales of yogurt in Japan are seasonal, with a peak period from March to July. The highest sales have been recorded in June, so the most ideal launch date would be at the end of February.

Types of yogurt available in Japan – 1980

In Japan, yogurt sales may be loosely broken down into three major categories:

• Plain (39% of the market in volume): Called "plain" in Japan because the color is white, but it is really flavored with vanilla. Generally sold in 500 ml pure pack cups. Sugared or sometimes with a sugar bag attached.

- Flavored (45% of the market in volume): Differentiated from the above category by the presence of coloring and gelifiers. Not a wide range of varieties, mainly: vanilla, strawberry, almond and citrus.

- Fruit (16% of the market in volume): Similar to the typical Swedish fruit yogurt but with more pulp than real fruit. Contains some coloring and flavoring.

Western-type yogurts also compete directly in the same price bracket with local desserts – like puddings and jellies – produced by Japanese competitors.

Competition
Three major Japanese manufacturers account for about half of the total real yogurt market.

Snow Brand Milk Products is the largest manufacturer of dairy products in Japan and produces drinking milk, cheeses, frozen foods, biochemicals and pharmaceuticals. Turnover in 1980 was ¥293,322 million ($1 = ¥254 in 1980).

Meiji Milk Products, Japan's second largest producer of dairy foods, particularly dried milk for babies, ice cream, cheese. Its alliance with the Bulgarian government helped start the yogurt boom in Japan. Turnover in 1980 was ¥410,674 million.

Morinaga Milk Industry, Japan's third largest milk products producer processes drinking milk, ice cream, instant coffee. It has a joint venture with Kraft US for cheeses. Turnover in 1980 was ¥250,783 million.

The share of these three producers has remained stable for years and is approximately: Yukijirushi (Snowbrand) 25%; Meiji 19%; Morinaga 10%.

The Japanese also consume a yogurt drink called "Yakult Honsha" which is often included in statistics on total yogurt consumption as it competes with normal yogurt. On a total market base for yogurts and yogurt drink, Yakult has 31%. Yakult drink is based on milk reconstituted from powder or fresh milk acidified with lactic acid and glucose. Yakult is not sold in shops, but through door-to-door sales and by groups of women who visit offices during the afternoon and sell the product directly to employees."

Along with some notes written in 1979 by Mr. Ole Bobek, Agria's Director of International Operations, Bjorn Robertson found a report on meetings held in Uppsala at which two members of Agria's negotiating team presented their findings to management:

"Selecting a Franchisee
We have just returned from our third visit to Japan where we once again held discussions with the agricultural cooperative, Nikko. Nikko is the country's second largest association of agricultural cooperatives; it is the Japanese equivalent of Agria Nikko is a significant political force in Japan but not as strong as Zennoh, the National Federation of Agricultural Cooperatives which is negotiating with Sodima, one of our French competitors. Nikko is price leader for various food products in Japan (milk, fruit juice, rice) and is active in lobbying on behalf of agricultural producers. Nikko is divided into two parts: manufacturing and distribution. It processes and distributes milk and dairy products, and it also distributes raw rice and vegetables.

We have seen several other candidates, but Nikko is the first one that seems prepared to join us. We believe that Nikko is the most appropriate distributor for Agria in Japan. Nikko is big and its credentials seem perfect for Agria, particularly since its strong supermarket distribution system for milk in the three main metropolitan areas is also ideally suited for yogurt. In Japan, 80% of yogurt is sold through supermarkets. We are, however, frustrated that, after prolonged discussions and several trips to Japan, Nikko has not yet signed an agreement with Agria. We sense that the management does want to go ahead but that they want to be absolutely sure before signing. We are anxious to get this project underway before Danone, Sodima or Chambourcy[3] enter Japan."

The same report also contained some general information on the Japanese consumer, which Bjorn Robertson found of interest:

[3] Chambourcy was a brand name for yogurt produced and distributed by Nestlé in various countries. Nestlé, with sales of $27 billion in 1990, was the world's largest food company; its headquarters were in Vevey (Switzerland).

"Some Background Information on the Japanese Consumer
Traditionally, Japan is not a dairy products consumer, although locally produced brands of yogurt are sold along with other milk-based items such as puddings and coffee cream.

Many aspects of life in Japan are miniaturized due to lack of space: 60% of the total population of about 120 million is concentrated on 3% of the surface of the islands. The rest of the land mass is mountainous. In Japan, 85% of the population live in towns of which over one third have more than half a million people. This urban density naturally affects lifestyle, tastes and habits. Restricted living space and lack of storage areas mean that most Japanese housewives must shop daily and consequently expect fresh milk products in the stores every day as they rarely purchase long-life foods or drinks. The country is fairly homogeneous as far as culture and the distribution of wealth is concerned. Disposable income is high. The Japanese spend over 30% of their total household budget on food, making it by far the greatest single item, with clothing in second place (10%).

The market is not comparable to Scandinavia or to the US as far as the consumption of dairy products is concerned. There are young housewives purchasing yogurt today whose mothers barely knew of its existence and whose grandmothers would not even have kept milk in the house. At one time it was believed that the Japanese do not have the enzymes to digest milk and that, only a generation ago, when children were given milk, it was more likely to be goat's milk than cow's milk. However, with the market evolving rapidly towards "Westernization", there is a general interest in American and European products, including yogurt.

Although consumption of yogurt per capita is still low in Japan at the moment, research shows that there is a high potential for growth. When we launch, correct positioning will be the key to Delissa's success as a new foreign brand. We will need to differentiate it from existing Japanese brands and go beyond the rather standardized "freshness" advertising theme.

Distribution
Traditionally, Japanese distribution methods have been complex; the chain tends to be many layered, making distribution costs high. Distribution of refrigerated products is slightly simpler than the distribution of dry goods because it is more direct.

The Japanese daily-purchase habit means that the delivery system adopted for Delissa must be fast and efficient. Our basic distribution goal would be to secure mass sales retailer distribution. Initially, items would be sold through existing sales outlets that sell Nikko's drinking milk, "Nikkodo". The milk-related products and dessert foods would be sold based on distribution to mass sales retailers. The objective would be to make efficient use of existing channels of distribution with daily delivery schedules and enjoy lower distribution costs for new products.

The Japanese Retail Market
The retail market is extremely fragmented; independent outlets account for 57% of sales (vs 3% in the US). With 1,350 shops for every 100,000 people, Japan has twice as many outlets per capita as most European countries. Tradition, economics, government regulations and service demands affect the retail system in Japan. Housewives shop once a day on average and most select the smaller local stores, which keep longer hours, deliver orders, offer credit and provide a meeting place for shoppers. Opening a Western-style supermarket is expensive and complicated, so most retailing remains in the hands of the small, independent, or family business.

Japan has three major metropolitan areas: Tokyo, Osaka and Nogaya, with a respective population of 11, 3, and 2 million inhabitants. Nikko's Nikkodo, with a 15% share of total, is market leader ahead of the many other suppliers. Nikko feels the distribution chain used for Nikkodo milk would be ideal for yogurt. Each metropolitan area has a separate distribution system, each one with several depots and branches. For instance, Kanto (Greater Tokyo) – the largest area with over 40 million people – has five Nikko depots and five Nikko branches.

Most of the physical distribution (drivers and delivery vans) is carried out by a subsidiary of Nikko with support from the wholesalers. The refrigerated milk vans have to be fairly small (less than 2 tons) so that they can drive down the narrow streets. The same routes are used for milk delivery, puddings and juices. Our initial strategy would be to accept Nikko's current milk distribution system as the basic system and, at the same time, adopt shifting distribution routes. Japan's complicated street identification system, whereby only numbers and no names are shown, makes great demands on the distribution system and the drivers."

The Franchise Contract

Bjorn Robertson opened another report written by Ole Bobek, who had headed up the Japan project right from the start and had been responsible for the early years of the joint venture and who left the company in 1985. This report contained all the details concerning the contract between Agria and Nikko. In November 1979, Nikko and Agria had signed an industrial franchise agreement permitting Nikko to manufacture and distribute Delissa products under license from Agria. The contract was Agria's standard Delissa franchisee agreement covering technology transfer associated with trademark exploitation. Agria was to provide manufacturing and product know-how, as well as marketing, technical, commercial and sales support. Agria would receive a royalty for every pot of yogurt sold. The Nikko cooperative would form a separate company for the distribution, marketing and promotion of Delissa products. During the pre-launch phase, Per Bergman, Senior Area Brand Manager, would train the sales and marketing team, and Agria's technicians would supply know-how to the Japanese.

By 1980, a factory to produce Delissa yogurt, milk and dairy products had been constructed in Mijima, 60 miles northwest of Tokyo. Agria provided Nikko with advice on technology, machinery, tanks, fermentation processes, etc. Equipment from the US, Sweden, Germany and Japan was selected. A European-style Erka filling machine was installed which would fill two, four or six cups at a time, and was considered economical and fast.

Robertson opened another report by Bobek entitled "Delissa Japan – Pre-Launch Data". The report covered the market, positioning, advertising and media plan, minutes of the meetings with Nikko executives and the SRT International Advertising Agency, that would handle the launch, analysis of market research findings and competitive analysis. Robertson closed the file and thought about the Japanese market. During the planning phase before the launch, everything had looked so promising. In its usual methodical fashion, Agria had prepared its traditional launch campaign to ensure that the new Agria/Nikko venture ensured a successful entry into Japan for Delissa... "Why then," wondered Bjorn Robertson, "were sales so low after nine years of business?" Robertson picked up the telephone and called Mr. Rolf Anderen, one of Agria's founders and former chairman of the company. Although retired, Anderen still took an active interest in the business he had created. The next day, Bjorn Robertson and Rolf Anderen had lunch together.

The older man listened to the new managing director talking about his responsibilities, the Swedish headquarters, foreign licensees, new products in the pipeline, etc. Over coffee, Robertson broached the subject of the Japanese joint venture, expressing some surprise that Delissa was so slow in taking off. Rolf Anderen nodded his understanding and lit his pipe:

> "Yes, it has been disappointing. I remember those early meetings before we signed up with Nikko. Our team was very frustrated with the negotiations. Bobek made several trips, and had endless meetings with the Japanese, but things still dragged on. We had so much good foreign business by the time we decided to enter Japan, I guess we thought we could just walk in wherever we wanted. Our Taiwanese franchise business had really taken off, and I think we assumed that Japan would do likewise. Then, despite the fact that we knew the Japanese were different, Wisenborn – our international marketing manager – and Bobek still believed that they were doing something wrong. They had done a very conscientious job, yet they blamed themselves for the delays. I told them to be patient... to remember that Asians have different customs and are likely to need some time before making up their minds. Our guys went to enormous pains to collect data. I remember when they returned from a second or third trip to Japan with a mass of information, media costs, distribution data, socioeconomic breakdowns, a detailed assessment of the competitive situation, positioning statements, etc. ... but no signed contract. [*Rolf Anderen chuckled as he spoke.*] Of course, Nikko finally signed, but we never were sure what they really thought about us... or what they really expected from the deal."

Bjorn Robertson was listening intently, so Rolf Anderen continued:

> "The whole story was interesting. When you enter a market like Japan, you are on your own. If you don't speak the language, you can't find your way around. So you become totally dependent on the locals and your partner. I must say that, in this respect, the Japanese are extremely helpful. But, let's face it, the cultural gap is wide. Another fascinating aspect was the rite of passage. In Japan, as in most Asian countries, you feel you are observing a kind of ritual, their ritual. This can destabilize the solid Viking manager. Of

course, they were probably thinking that we have our rituals, too. On top of that, the Nikko people were particularly reserved and, of course, few of them spoke anything but Japanese.

There was a lot of tension during those first months, partly because France's two major brands of yogurt, "Yoplait" and "Danone" were actually in the process of entering the Japanese market, confirming a fear that had been on Bobek's mind during most of the negotiation period."

Rolf Anderen tapped his pipe on the ashtray and smiled at Robertson.

"If it's any consolation to you, Bjorn, the other two international brands are not doing any better than we are in Japan today."

What About These Other European Competitors?
The discussion with Rolf Anderen had been stimulating and Robertson, anxious to get to the bottom of the story, decided to speak to Peter Borg, a young Danish manager who had replaced Bergman and had been supervising Agria's business in Japan for several years. Robertson asked Borg for his opinion on why "Danone" and "Yoplait" were apparently not doing any better than Delissa in Japan. Borg said:

"I can explain how these two brands were handled in Japan, but I don't know whether this will throw any light on the matter as far as their performance is concerned. First, Sodima, the French dairy firm, whose Yoplait line is sold through franchise agreements all over the world, took a similar approach to ours. In 1981, Yoplait tied up with Zennoh, the National Federation of Agricultural Cooperative Association, the equivalent of Sodima in Japan. Zennoh is huge and politically very powerful. Its total sales are double those of Nikko. Yoplait probably has about 3% of the total Japanese yogurt market, which is of course a lot less than their usual 15-20% share in foreign markets. However, Zennoh had no previous experience in marketing yogurt.

Danone took a different approach. The company signed an agreement with a Japanese partner, Ajinomoto. Their joint venture, Ajinomoto-Danone Co. Ltd, is run by a French expatriate together with several Japanese directors. A prominent French banker based in Tokyo is also on the board. As you know, Ajinomoto is the largest integrated food processor in Japan, with sales of about

$3 billion. About 45% of the company's business is in amino acids, 20% in fats and 15% in oil. Ajinomoto has a very successful joint venture with General Foods for "Maxwell House", the instant coffee. However, Ajinomoto had had no experience at all in dealing with fresh dairy products before entering this joint venture with Danone. So, for both of the Japanese partners-Ajinomoto and Zennoh, this business was completely new and was probably part of a diversification move. I heard that the Danone joint venture had a tough time at the beginning. They had to build their dairy products distribution network from scratch. By the way, I also heard from several sources that it was distribution problems that discouraged Nestlé from pursuing a plan to re-introduce its Chambourcy yogurt line in Japan. Japanese distribution costs are very high compared to those in Western countries. I suspect that the Danone-Ajinomoto joint venture probably only just managed to break even last year."

"Thanks Peter," Robertson said. "It's a fascinating story. By the way, I hear that you just got married... to a Japanese girl. Congratulations, lucky chap!"

After his discussion with Peter Borg, Bjorn Robertson returned to his Delissa-Nikko files. Delissa's early Japanese history intrigued him.

Entry Strategy

The SRT International Advertising Agency helped develop Delissa's entry into what was called the "new milk-related products" market. Agria and Nikko had approved substantial advertising and sales promotion budget. The agency confirmed that, as Nikko was already big in the "drinking milk" market, it was a good idea to move into the processed milk or "eating milk" field, a rapidly growing segment where added value was high.

Bjorn Robertson studied the advertising agency's pre-launch rationale which emphasized the strategy proposed for Delissa. The campaign, which had been translated from Japanese into English, proposed:

"Agria will saturate the market with the Delissa brand and establish it as distinct from competitive products. The concept "natural dairy food is good to taste" is proposed as the basic message for product planning, distribution and advertising. Nikko needs to distinguish its products from those of early-entry dairy producers and other competitors by stressing that its yogurt is "new and natural and quite different from any other yogurts".

The core target group has been defined as families with babies. Housewives have been identified as the principal purchasers. However, the product will be consumed by a wider age bracket from young children to high school students.

The advertising and point-of-sale message will address housewives, particularly younger ones. In Japan, the tendency is for younger housewives to shop in convenience stores (small supermarkets), while the older women prefer traditional supermarkets. Housewives are becoming more and more insistent that all types of food be absolutely fresh, which means that Delissa should be perceived as coming directly from the manufacturer that very day. We feel that the "freshness" concept, which has been the main selling point of the whole Nikko line, will capture the consumers' interest as well as clearly differentiate Delissa from other brands. It is essential that the ads be attractive and stand out strikingly from the others, because Nikko is a newcomer in this competitive market. Delissa should be positioned as a luxurious mass communication product."

The SRT also proposed that, as Japanese housewives were becoming more diet conscious, it might be advisable to mention the dietary value of Delissa in the launch rationale. Agria preferred to stress the idea that Delissa was a Swedish product being made in Japan under license from Agria Co, Uppsala. They felt that this idea would appeal to Japanese housewives, who associated Sweden with healthy food and "sophisticated" taste. The primary messages to be conveyed would, therefore, be: "healthy products direct from the farm" and "sophisticated taste from Sweden". Although, it was agreed that being good for health and beauty could be another argument in Delissa's favor, this approach would not help differentiate Delissa from other brands, all of which project a similar image.

In order to reinforce the image of the product and increase brand awareness, the SRT proposed that specific visual and verbal messages be used throughout the promotional campaign. A Swedish girl in typical folk costume would be shown with a dairy farm in the background. In the words of the agency, "We feel that using this scene as an eye-catcher will successfully create a warm-hearted image of naturalness, simplicity, friendliness and fanciful taste for the product coming from Sweden." This image would be accompanied by the text: "The refreshing nature of Delissa Swedish yogurt; it's so fresh when it's made at the farm."

Also included in the SRT proposal:

"Advertising
To maximize the advertising effort with the budget available, the campaign should be run intensively over a short period of time rather than successively throughout the year. TV ads will be used as they have an immediate impact and make a strong impression through frequent repetition. The TV message will then be reinforced in the press. The budget will be comparable to the one used for launching Delissa in the US.

Pricing
Pricing should follow the top brands, (Yukijirushi, Meiji and Morinaga) so as to reflect a high-class image, yet the price should be affordable to the housewife. The price sensitivity analysis conducted last month showed that the Delissa could be priced at 15% above competitive products."

Launch

In January 1982, Delissa's product line was presented to distributors prior to launch in Tokyo, Osaka and Nagoya. Three different types of yogurt were selected for simultaneous launch:

- plain (packs of 2 and 4)
- plain with sugar (packs of 2 and 4)
- flavored with vanilla, strawberry, and pineapple (packs of 2). (Fruit yogurt, Delissa's most successful offering at home and in other foreign markets, would be launched a year or two afterwards.)

All three types were to be sold in 120 ml cups. A major pre-launch promotional campaign was scheduled for the month before launch with strong TV, newspaper and magazine support, as well as street shows, instore promotions, and test trials in and outside retail stores. On March 1, 1982, Delissa was launched in Tokyo, and on May 1, in Osaka and Nagoya.

1985 – Delissa after Three Years in Japan

Three years after its launch, Delissa – with 2% of the Japanese yogurt market was at a fraction of target. Concerned by the product's slow progress in Japan, Agria formed a special task force to investigate Delissa's situation and to continue monitoring the Japanese market on a regular basis. The results of the team's research now lay on Robertson's desk. The task force from Uppsala included Stefan Gustafsson (responsible for marketing questions), Per Bergman (sales and distribution) and Peter Borg (who was studying the whole operation as well as training the Nikko sales force). The team spent long periods in Tokyo carrying out regular audits of the Delissa-Nikko operations, analyzing and monitoring the Japanese market and generating lengthy reports as they did so, most of which Robertson was in the process of studying.

Borg, eager to excel on his new assignment, sent back his first report to headquarters:

"Distribution/Ordering System
I feel that the distribution of Delissa is not satisfactory and should be improved. The ordering system seems overcomplicated and slow, and may very well be the cause of serious delivery bottlenecks. Whereas stores order milk and juice by telephone, Delissa products are ordered on forms using following procedure:

Day 1 a.m.:   Each salesman sent an order to his depot.
Day 1 p.m.:   Each depot's orders went to the Yokoharna depot.

Day 2 a.m.:   The Yokohama depot transmitted the order to the factory.
Day 2 p.m.:   Yogurt was produced at Nikko Milk Processing.

Day 3:   Delivery to each depot
Day 4:   Delivery to stores.

Gustafsson agrees with me that the delivery procedure is too long for fresh food products, particularly as the date on the yogurt cup is so important to the japanese customer. The way we operate now, the yogurt arrives in the sales outlet two or three days after production. Ideally, this period should be shortened to only one day. We realize that, traditionally, Japanese distribution is much more complex and multi-layered than in the West. In addition, Tokyo and Osaka, which are among the largest cities in the world, have no street names. So, a whole system of primary, secondary and sometimes tertiary wholesalers is used to serve supermarkets and retailers. And, since the smaller outlets have very little storage space, wholesalers often have to visit these outlets more than once a day.

I wonder if Nikko is seriously behind Delissa. At present, there are 80 Nikko salesmen selling Delissa, but they only seem to devote about 5% of their time to the brand, preferring to push other products. Although this is apparently not an uncommon situation in many countries, in Japan it is typical – as the high costs there prohibit having a separate sales force for each line."

Borg's report continued:

"Advertising
Since we launched Delissa in 1982, the advertising has not been successful. I'm wondering how well we pre-tested our launch campaign and follow-up. The agency seems very keen on Delissa as a product, but I wonder if our advertising messages are not too cluttered. Results of recent consumer research surveys showed only 4% unaided awareness and only 16% of interviewees had any recall at all; 55% of respondents did not know what our TV commercials were trying to say.
A survey by the Oka Market Research Bureau on advertising effectiveness indicated that we should stress the fact that Delissa tastes good... delicious. Agria's position maintains that according to the Oka survey, the consumer believes that all brands taste good, which means the message will not differentiate Delissa Research findings pointed out that Delissa has a strong "fashionable" image. Perhaps this advantage could be stressed to differentiate Delissa from other yogurts in the next TV commercial."

Delissa in Japan
– Situation in and Leading Up to 1991

In spite of all the careful pre-launch preparation, ten years after its launch in Japan, Delissa had only 3% of the total yogurt market in 1991. Although Agria executives knew the importance of taking a long-term

view of their business in Japan, Agria's management in Sweden agreed
that these results had been far below expectations.

A serious setback for Agria had been the discovery of Nikko's limited
distribution network outside the major metropolitan areas. When Agria
proposed to start selling Delissa in small cities, towns and rural areas, as
had been agreed in the launch plan, it turned out that Nikko's coverage
was very thin in many of these regions. In the heat of the planning for
the regional launch, had there been a misunderstanding on Nikko's
range?

Robertson continued to leaf through Agria's survey of Japanese business, reading extracts as he turned the pages. A despondent Borg had
written:

> "1988: The Japanese market is very tough and competition very
> strong. Consumers' brand loyalty seems low. But the market is
> large with high potential – particularly amongst the younger popu-
> lation – if only we could reach it. Nikko has the size and manpower
> to meet the challenge and to increase its penetration substantially
> by 1990. However, Nikko's Delissa organization needs strengthen-
> ing quickly. Lack of a real marketing function in Nikko is a great
> handicap in a market as competitive as Japan.
>
> Distribution is one of our most serious problems. Distribution
> costs are extremely high in Japan, and Delissa's are excessive (27%
> of sales in 1988 vs 19% for the competition). Comparing distribu-
> tion costs to production costs and to the average unit selling price
> to distributors of ¥54.86, ($1 = ¥145 in 1988), it is obvious that we
> cannot make money on the whole Delissa range in Japan. Clearly,
> these costs in Japan must be reduced while improving coverage of
> existing stores.
>
> Distribution levels of about 40% are still too low, which is cer-
> tainly one of the major contributing factors for Delissa's poor per-
> formance. Nikko's weak distribution network outside the metro-
> politan areas is causing us serious problems.
>
> 1989: Delissa's strategy in Japan is being redefined (once more).
> The Swedish image will be dropped from the advertising since a
> consumer survey has shown that some consumers believed that
> "fresh from the farm" meant that the yogurt was directly imported
> from Sweden – which certainly put its freshness into question! Ads
> will now show happy blond children eating yogurt.
>
> Over time, the product line has grown significantly and a line of

puddings has recently been added. Nikko asks us for new products every three months and blames their unsatisfactory results on our limited line.

By 1991, plain yogurt should represent almost half of Delissa's Japanese sales and account for about 43% of the total Japanese market. The plain segment has grown by almost 50% in the past three years. However, we feel that our real strength should be in the fruit yogurt segment, which has increased by about 25% since 1988 and should have about 23% of the market by next year. So far, Delissa's results in fruit yogurt have been disappointing. On the other hand, a new segment – yogurt with jelly – has been selling well: 1.2 million cups three months after introduction. Custard and chocolate pudding sales have been disappointing, while plain yogurt drink sales have been very good."

Bjorn Robertson came across a more recent memo written by Stefan Gustafsson:

"Mid-year Results
Sales as of mid-year 1991 are below forecast, and we are unlikely to meet our objective of 55 million 120 ml cups for 1992. At the present rate of sales, we should reach just over 42 million cups by year end

Stores Covered
In 1991, Delissa yogurt was sold mainly in what Nielsen defined as large and super large stores. Delissa products were sold in about 71% of the total stores selling Nikko dairy products. We think that about 7,000 stores are covered in the Greater Tokyo area, but we have found that Nikko has been somewhat unreliable on retailer information.

Product Returns
The number of Delissa products returned to us is very high compared to other countries. The average return rate from April '90 to March '91 was 5.06% vs almost 0% in Scandinavia and the international standard of 2-3%. The average shelf life of yogurt in Japan is 14 days. Does the high level of returns stem from the Japanese consumer's perception of when a product is too old to buy (i.e. 5-6 days)? The level of return varies greatly with the type of product:

"healthy mix" and fruit yogurt have the highest rate, while plain
and yogurt with jelly have the lowest return rate.

Media Planning

Oka's latest results suggest that Delissa's primary target should be
young people between 13 and 24 and its secondary target children.
Budget limitations demand that money be spent on advertising
addressed to actual consumers (children), rather than in trying to
reach the purchasers (mothers) as well.

However, during our recent visit to Japan, we found that Nikko
and the agency were running TV spots-that were intended for
young people and children – *from 11:15 to 12:15 at night.* We
pointed out that far more consumers would be reached by showing the spots earlier in the evening. With our limited budget, careful media planning is essential. Nikko probably was trying to reach
both the consumer and distributor with these late night spots. Why
else would they run spots at midnight when the real target group
is children? Another question is whether TV spots are really what
we need."

Looking at some figures on TV advertising rates in Japan, Bjorn Robertson found that the price of a 15-second spot in the Tokyo area was between ¥750,000 and ¥1,500,000 in 1990 depending on the time it was
run, which seemed expensive compared to European rates *($1 = ¥144
in 1991).*

Robertson continued to peruse the report prepared by Stefan Gustafsson:

"Positioning

I'm seriously wondering whom we are trying to reach in Japan and
with what product. The Nielsen and Oka research findings show
that plain yogurt makes up the largest segment in Japan, with flavored and fruit in second and third positions. It is therefore recommended that regular advertising should concentrate on plain yogurt, with periodic spots for the second two categories. However,
according to Nikko, the company makes only a marginal profit on
plain yogurt, thus they feel it would be preferable to advertise fruit
yogurt.

In light of this particular situation and the results of the Oka
studies, we suggest that plain yogurt be advertised using the exist-

ing "brand image" commercial (building up the cow on the screen) and to develop a new commercial for fruit yogurt based on the "fashion concept". We also believe that, if plain yogurt is clearly differentiated through its advertising, sales will improve, production costs will drop and Nikko will start making money on the product.

Last year, to help us understand where we may have gone wrong with our positioning and promotional activities, which have certainly changed rather often, we requested the Oka agency to conduct a survey using in-home personal interviews with a structured questionnaire; 394 respondents in the Keihin (Tokyo-Yokohama) metropolitan area were interviewed between April 11 and April 27, 1990.

Some of the key findings are as follows:

Brand Awareness
In terms of unaided brand awareness, Meiji Bulgaria yogurt had the highest level with 27% of all respondents recalling Bulgaria first and 47% mentioning the brand without any aid. Morinaga Bifidus was in second place. These two leading brands were followed by Yoplait and Danone with 4% unaided awareness and 14% and 16% recall at any time. For Delissa, the unaided awareness was 3% and 16% for recall. In a photo aided test, Delissa plain yogurt was recognized by 71% of all respondents with a score closer to Bulgaria. In the case of fruit yogurt, 78% recognized Delissa, which had the same level as Bulgaria. Awareness of Delissa was higher than Bifidus and Danone but lower than Yoplait. In the case of yogurt drink. 99% of all respondents were aware of Yakult Joy and 44% recognized Delissa (close to Bulgaria).

Interestingly, the brand image of Meiji Bulgaria was the highest of the plain yogurt brands in terms of all attributes except for "fashionability". At the lower end of the scale (after Bulgaria, Bifidus and Natulait), Delissa was close to Danone and Yoplait in brand image. Delissa was considered less desirable than the top three, especially as far as the following characteristics were concerned: taste, availability in stores for daily shoppers, frequency of price discounting, reliability of manufacturer, good for health. Delissa's image was "fashionablen". [*"Is this good or bad?"* Gustafsson *had scribbled on the report. "Should this be our new platform??? We've tried everything else!"*]

Advertising Awareness

In the advertising awareness test, half of all respondents reported that they had not noticed advertising for any brand of yogurt during the past six months. Of those who had, top ranking went to Bifidus with 43%, Bulgaria 41% and Delissa in third place with 36%. Danone was fifth with 28% and Yoplait sixth with 26%. Respondents noticed ads for Delissa mainly on TV (94%), followed by in-store promotion (6%), newspapers (4%) and magazines (4%); 65% of the people who noticed Delissa ads could recall something about the contents of the current ads, and 9% recalled previous ads. However, when asked to describe the message of the Delissa ads, 55% of the respondents replied that they did not know what the company was trying to say.

Consumption

77% of all respondents had consumed plain yogurt within the past month: 28% Bulgaria, 15% Bifidus, 5% Yoplait, 4% Danone and 3% Delissa. The number of respondents who had at least tried Delissa was low (22%) vs 66% for Bulgaria, the best scoring brand. In the plain category, Delissa was third of the brands mainly consumed by respondents. Bulgaria was number 1 and Bifidus number 2. In the fruit segment (under yogurt consumed within the past month), Delissa was in third place (5%) after Yoplait (10%) and Bulgaria (8%). Danone was in fourth place with 3%. [*"So where do we go from here?" Gustafsson had scrawled across the bottom of the page.*]"

Robertson closed the file on Gustafson's question.

Where Do We Go from Here?

Bjorn Robertson looked around the table at the other members of his team and asked, "What happened? We still haven't reached 3% after ten years in Japan!" Bjorn knew that Borg, Gustafsson and Karlsson all had different opinions as to why Delissa had performed badly, and each manager had his own ideas on what kind of action should be taken.

Stefan Gustafsson had spent months at Nikko, visiting retailers with members of the sales force, instigating new market research surveys and supervising the whole Nikko-Delissa team. Language problems had made this experience a frustrating one for Gustafsson, who had felt cut

off from the rest of the Nikko staff in the office. He had been given a
small desk in a huge room along with over 100 people with whom he
could barely communicate. The Japanese politeness grated on him after
a while and, as no one spoke more than a few words of anything but
Japanese, Gustafsson had felt lonely and isolated. He had come to believe that Nikko was not committed to the development of the Delissa
brand in Japan. He also felt that the joint venture's market share expectations had been absurd and was convinced the franchisee misrep-
resented the situation to Agria. He felt that Nikko was using the Delissa
brand narne as a public relations gimmick to build itself an international image.

When he spoke, Stefan's tone was almost aggressive:

> "I don't know what to think, Bjorn. I know I don't understand our
> Japanese friends and I was never quite sure that I trusted them,
> either. They had a disconcerting way of taking control right from
> the start. It's that extreme politeness... You can't argue with them,
> and then suddenly they're in command. I remember when the
> Nikko managers visited us here in Sweden... a busload of them
> smiling and bowing their way around the plant, and we were bow-
> ing and smiling back. This is how they get their way and this is why
> we had such mediocre results in Japan. Agria never controlled the
> business. Our distribution set-up is a perfect example. We could
> never really know what was going on out there because language
> problems forced us to count on them. The same with our position-
> ing and our advertising... we're selling taste; no, we're selling
> health; no, we're selling fashion... to babies, to grandmas, to
> mothers." We thought we were in we control but we weren't, and
> half the time we were doing the opposite of what we really wanted.
> Bjorn, the Japanese will kill Delissa once they've mastered the
> Swedish technology. Then, they'll develop their own brand. Get
> out of the joint venture agreement with Nikko, Bjorn. I'd say, get
> out of Japan altogether."

Robertson next turned his attention toward Peter Borg, who had a different view of the problem. He felt that the Nikko people, trained to sell
the drinking milk line, lacked specific knowledge about the eating milk
or yogurt business. Borg – who had also taken over sales training in
Japan after replacing Bergman – had made several trips a year to train
the Nikko people both in marketing the Delissa brand, and in improv-

ing distribution and sales. He had also trained a marketing manager. Borg had worked closely with the Japanese at the Tokyo headquarters.

Borg said, "I understand how Stefan feels... frustrated and let down, but have we given these people enough time?"

"Enough time!" said Gustafsson, laughing. "We've been there for over ten years and, if you look at our target, we have failed miserably. My question is 'have they given *us* enough support?'" Turning to Stefan, Borg continued:

> "I know how you feel, Stefan, but is 10 years that long? When the Japanese go into business abroad, they stay there until they get a hold on the market, however long it takes. They persevere. They seem to do things at their own speed and so much more calmly than we do. I agree on the question of autonomy. It's their very lack of Western aggressiveness that enables them to get the upper hand. Their apparent humility is disarming. But, Bjorn, should we really leave the joint venture now? When I first went to Japan and found fault with everything we were doing, I blamed the whole thing on Nikko. After nearly six years of visits, I think I have learned something. We cannot approach these people on our terms or judge them as we would judge ourselves. We cannot understand them... any more than they can understand us. To me, the whole point is not to even try and understand them. We have to accept them and then to trust. If we can't, then perhaps we should leave. But, Bjorn, I don't think we should give up the Japanese market so easily. As Stefan says, they can be excruciatingly polite. In fact, I wonder – beneath that politeness – what they think of us."

Lars Karlsson, the product manager, had been looking after the Japanese market only a short time, having been recruited by Agria from Procter & Gamble 18 months earlier.

> "Bjorn, for me, perhaps the most serious defect in our Japanese operation has been the poor communication between the partners and a mass of conflicting data. I came into the project late and was amazed at the quantity of research and reporting that had taken place over the last ten years by everyone concerned. Many of the reports I saw were contradictory and confusing. As well, the frequent turnover of managers responsible for Japan has interrupted the continuity of the project. And, after all the research we did, has

anyone really used the findings constructively? How much is our fault? And another thing, have we been putting enough resources into Japan?

There are so many paradoxes. The Japanese seem to be so keen on the idea of having things Western, yet the successful yogurts in Japan have been the ones with that distinctive Japanese flavor. Have we disregarded what this means? Agria people believe that we have a superior product and that the type of yogurt made by our Japanese competitors does not really taste so good. How can this be true when we look at the market shares of the top Japanese producers? It obviously tastes good to the Japanese. Can we really change their preferences? Or should we perhaps look at our flavor?

It's interesting. Yoplait/Zennoh and Ajinomoto/Danone's joint ventures could be encountering similar problems to ours. Neither has more than 3% of the Japanese yogurt market and they have the same flavor that we do."

Bjorn Robertson listened to the views and arguments of his team with interest. Soon, he would have to make a decision. Almost ten years after launching Delissa with Nikko, should Agria cancel its contract and find another distributor? Or should the company renew the arrangement with Nikko and continue trying to gain market share? Or should Agria admit defeat and withdraw from Japan completely? Or... was it, in fact, defeat at all? Robertson was glad that he had gathered his team together to discuss Delissa's future... their thoughts had given him new insights on the Japanese venture.

4. Glamoxgruppen

This case was prepared by Research Associate Mark E. Brazas, under the supervision of Professor Per Jenster, as a basis for class discussion rather than to illustrate either effective or ineffective handling of a business situation. This case was developed as an Institutional Project on the Management of Internationalization, and conducted in collaboration with the Industrial Development Authority of Ireland.

In March 1984, Torkell Hatlebakk, Managing Director of Glamox, a commercial and industrial lighting fixture business headquartered in Molde, Norway, smiled as he perused the "coffee cup memo". "This is so like my father," he thought, "to get involved in everything connected with the Glamox image." The memo was a staff member's follow-up to Birger Hatlebakk's decision to standardize the company coffee cup for all of Glamox's domestic and foreign offices – an analysis of the cost/benefit ratios for different cup configurations (shape, colors, materials, logo size, etc.). "What a waste of time," thought Torkell Hatlebakk. "In the end, my father will probably do his own 'research' and settle on a completely different design!"

In any case, he had more serious business to attend to, now that Glamox had been reorganized and its short-term financial crisis resolved. He knew that it was very important to set objectives and priorities for Glamox's medium to long-term strategy. "With our limited financial and managerial resources," he contemplated, "coffee cups are not where we need to focus."

Company Background

Glamox A/S was founded in 1947 in Trondheim, a small city on the west coast of Norway, by Torkell Hatlebakk's father, Mr. Birger Hatlebakk. As a teacher of mechanical engineering at the Trondheim Technical College, Birger Hatlebakk had developed a process for treating aluminum which improved the ability to clean the trays used for milking cows and goats. When he teamed up with a student working on light reflection in 1951, they discovered that "glamoxizing" gave an aluminum surface excellent light reflection properties as well.

Glamox's initial operations were confined to manufacturing industrial light fittings, which were marketed and sold by another Norwegian lighting company, IFA, based in Bergen. This arrangement lasted until 1958. Because the product ranges of Glamox and IFA increasingly overlapped – and competed for sales force attention – Glamox decided to develop its own sales force. In 1956, Glamox had relocated to Molde, a town with some 20,000 inhabitants 300 kilometers southwest of Trondheim, after some disagreements with the Labor government in Trondheim over a fine they had imposed on an "unauthorized" company warehouse.

Mr. Birger Hatlebakk, according to his son, was not a man who focused on technical expertise at the expense of marketing. Rather, he was dedicated to providing the customer with more value for his money and a better way of doing things. To ensure that his company could provide customers with these benefits, he necessarily paid a lot of attention to the technical problems involved in, for instance, tunnel lighting and offshore lighting. (A company brochure proudly claimed that the market had found that "products which are good enough in the North Sea are more than good enough in other places".)

During the 1950s and '60s, both Glamox and IFA made substantial inroads in the Norwegian commercial and industrial lighting market. In 1950, Philips, the large Dutch multinational, had a 90% market share in Norway. Twenty years later, Philips had left Norway, while Glamox and IFA, now full-fledged competitors, built their 1970 market shares to 40% each.

Glamox's International Operations

Glamox first "went international" in 1964, when it initiated a sales agreement with several Swedish wholesalers. Recalling this initial foray into foreign markets 25 years later, Mr. Torkell Hatlebakk described it as a preemptive move to bring Norwegian products to Sweden before Glamox's Swedish competitors entered the Norwegian market. Moreover, the Norwegian market was small, nearly saturated and suffering from a downturn in the construction industry. Getting more market share in Norway would be costly at best. A high degree of competitive, almost personal rivalry had developed with former ally IFA and its CEO, but Birger Hatlebakk decided that Glamox stood a better chance of outdoing IFA abroad than at home.

The arrangement with the Swedish wholesalers lasted ten years. It ended when Glamox's distributors were bought out by other whole-salers. This "trade concentration" temporarily froze Glamox products out of the Swedish market. In response, Glamox developed its own sales force in Sweden.

On the initiative of Birger Hatlebakk, Glamox expanded its sales operations outside Norway. Kjell Bjordal, Glamox's Finance Director, described the expansion. "If you have ambitions for your company, in a country like Norway we instinctively go international because of econ-omies of scale in production and distribution. If we had stayed in Nor-way, we would never get past NOK 180 or 200 million. And if you want to get bigger than that in your domestic market, you must give away some of your profit to do so."

After Sweden, Glamox entered a number of different Western Euro-pean countries, as indicated in *Table 1* below.

Tabel 1: Glamox's Entry into its Major Foreign Markets

Market	Date
Sweden	1964
Denmark	1967
UK	1968
Finland	1972
West Germany	1974
Austria	1976

This sequence for market entry was partly based on the perceived "fam-iliarity" of the market in question. Glamox entered Sweden first be-cause that market resembled Norway. Succeeding countries were targeted because they seemed similar to country markets where Glamox had already gained experience. Glamox followed a consistent pattern in entering each country market. First, extensive studies of the country's lighting market and competitive situation were conducted. Next, an analysis was made of Glamox's internal capabilities *vis-à-vis* that mar-ket. Did the company already have the right products for a given mar-ket? If not, could Glamox develop new products tailored to that market? Could the company finance three years of operations without a profit? Assuming satisfactory answers to these questions, Glamox would estab-lish its own sales force in the new country. Only after profitability had been achieved in a market would Glamox expand into a new country.

In 1978, the company opened a manufacturing plant in Finland to avoid high Finnish import duties, and also to appeal to the Finnish preference for domestically made products. "They basically produce the same goods as we produce here in Molde," said Kjell Bjordal. "But this is a necessary cost of doing business in Finland – we look as if we are a Finnish company. If the Finnish government had not provided such generous subsidies, we probably would not have built this plant." In 1983, the Finnish plant accounted for 19% of Glamox's cost of goods sold.

Under Mr. Birger Hatlebakk's direction, control of Glamox's foreign operations was highly centralized. Although each foreign organization was a separate corporation with its own board of directors, decisions on pricing, positioning and marketing strategy frequently were made by consultation back and forth between the foreign sales office and headquarters – mainly, Birger Hatlebakk himself. Furthermore, each foreign subsidiary was operated as a '"zero-profit entity". The company's accounting system attributed all profits to the headquarters organization in Molde, thus configuring the foreign subsidiaries as cost centers. *(Refer to Exhibit 1.)*

On the positive side, centralization brought the benefits of Birger Hatlebakk's expertise into the day-to-day business of the foreign companies. It also ensured consistency in the overall policy of the company. But Torkell Hatlebakk thought that centralization had its drawbacks. Rapid delivery speed and responsiveness to the customer were important success factors in the business. Both suffered when the local organization had to get clearance from headquarters to, for instance, supply part of an order with competitors' products.

Torkell Hatlebakk also felt that the local organizations were not fully leveraging their knowledge of local market conditions. He expressed himself on this subject as follows:

> "It is very hard for a foreigner to sell in a country. Even though you can learn the language, and even some of the culture, you must fine-tune your mentality. You are very, very dependent on sales forces, and on the local people doing a good job, and on the strength of your local contacts. The local operations are where it happens. You must keep in constant contact with the local markets, talking, because that is where the fight is going on. They (local salespeople) are the ones who have direct dialogue with the customers. Having the contacts in the market is extremely important, and you need to be a little bit aggressive. Success in each country is really entirely dependent on local management."

Distribution

Glamox operated as a supplier to the building construction industry and, for its marine lighting products, the shipbuilding industry. Glamox confined itself to technical, functional lighting, refusing to enter the markets for home lighting or non-fixed lighting. Commercial and industrial lighting sales could be classed in two broad categories: direct sales to electrical installers; and wholesale distribution to electrical supply houses, who in turn sold to electrical installers.

Glamox focused on direct sales to lighting fixture installers through its own sales force. In 1989, 90% of Glamox's sales in Norway were direct sales. Wholesale distribution through electrical supply houses was only significant to Glamox in Finland, where about 25% of sales were to wholesalers, and the UK, where the proportion of Glamox sales to wholesalers was 50%.

Glamox's focus on direct sales was based on several considerations. In the first place, Glamox had little control over the contact between wholesalers and their customers – which negated the competitive advantage Glamox gained by providing well thought out technical solutions to customer needs. Additionally, the direct sale channel was larger, in terms of sales volume, in Norway and in many of the other country markets served by Glamox. Moreover, the average order size for a direct sale tended to be higher than a stock listing with a wholesaler. There were fewer problems with trade terms, such as returns and receivables policies, with the professionals. Finally, wholesalers tended to stock products from the lower end of Glamox's price range, in contrast to direct sales. Consequently, direct sales not only provided generally higher margins, but also supported the quality image that Glamox wished to cultivate.

Moreover, a company sales force was critical to controlling distribution – getting the product in front of the customer in a well-presented but aggressive fashion.

According to Torkell Hatlebakk:

> "Some of our competitors ran into difficulty because they used agents, exclusively, as their foreign sales channels. You can use agents in markets you can afford to lose, but when a large part of your turnover comes from a particular market, you must have control over your distribution. An agent can turn his back on you, but your daughter company must struggle through."

Glamox did not hire away its competitors' sales forces, believing that "mercenaries" would not have enough loyalty or commitment in a struggle. Generally, the company found its salespeople through advertising or word of mouth. "Get hold of some good people and have them refer other people they know and recommend" was Torkell Hatlebakk's summary of the process.

Glamox tried to build a core of experienced salespeople while also achieving some balance in the age distribution of the sales force. Glamox would initially send some of its Norwegian people into the new market "beachhead", but their role was one of training and advising local salespeople and management. As soon as the new salesforce was adequately integrated into Glamox methods, procedures and corporate culture, the "advisers" were withdrawn.

Direct Sales – Electrical Installers

"Installers" included electrical contractors, building consultants, project managers and architects – individuals with final responsibility for the quality and cost of lighting used in their projects. It was difficult to generalize about installers' margins to customers who had contracted for a building, but Torkell Hatlebakk estimated them to be roughly 20-25%.

To sell to electrical installers, it was critical for a lighting products supplier to build a reputation through word of mouth within the building trade. The sales process generally involved personal contact through the supplier's sales force. Customers were interested in discussing different lighting options and in learning more about different lighting possibilities, especially among the "professional" builders – the architects and building consultants. Frequently, Glamox would bring important customers to its headquarters in Molde to demonstrate the advantages of its products and discuss lighting solutions to the customer's problems, en route to closing a sale. In other words, education was part of the Glamox product.

Glamox's success was initially built on a competitive advantage in technology. A glamoxized light reflector produced more light than competitors' offerings, which used painted metal surfaces. Glamox's marketing played up its technical advantage with sophisticated, well-informed sales presentations emphasizing the long-run cost savings, convenience and quality of Glamox products.

Wholesalers – Electrical Supply Houses

Electrical supply houses were the other major distribution channel for commercial and industrial lighting products. A typical supply house was a warehouse type of facility located in an industrial district. Its customers were building contractors for both residential and industrial construction. However, these customers tended to employ fewer people and engage in smaller projects than the installers Glamox reached directly through its sales force. Wholesalers' margins were roughly estimated by Torkell Hatlebakk to be about 30-35%.

An International Product Line

Different countries required different industrial and commercial lighting products, in order to meet idiosyncratic national electrical standards as well as different market demands. A light fitting for Denmark might include the same box, reflector and lamp holder as one sold in Germany. However, the wiring and/or the holes in the fitting would need to be adjusted, or a capacitor included. Recess fittings were influenced by the module design of the ceiling, which varied across national lines. UK wiring boxes were completely different from those used in other European countries.

In order to serve these varying requirements, Glamox widened its product range. By 1984, Glamox's product line included some 850 different products, not including one-off items produced for single orders. Competing against giants like Thom Lighting and Siemens, Glamox won orders for rapid, on-time delivery of small quantity items that the big firms could not be bothered with. Often these were standard Glamox products specially modified for a single order.

The different segments of Glamox's business varied in profitability. In general, project sales to building consultants or architects were more profitable than "routine" sales to installers, particularly when new products were designed for the project. Mr. Hatlebakk felt that the best business was general commercial interior lighting, particularly in sales to small and medium-sized projects. In this segment, marginal contribution (sales minus direct labor and direct material costs) averaged around 50% of sales. Electrical heating, industrial lighting and marine/offshore project work were almost as attractive. Outdoor lighting and interior effect lighting were relatively less attractive segments, but still enjoyed marginal contribution margins above 35%.

The concept of standardizing and "rationalizing" its product portfolio often surfaced at Glamox, but was never adopted. Mr. Ola Slagstad, Glamox's Technical Director, summarized the outcome: "The only time we really reduce the number of variations is when something doesn't sell, in which case we stop making it." Essentially, enlarging the product range to meet the diverse needs of customers was seen as key to Glamox's success.

Production

This large product range created several problems for Glamox. The company's production lines were only in operation about 88% of available production time, since producing multiple products on the same production line required frequent tooling changeovers. These changeovers averaged two hours for a completely new product, and slightly less when a minor adjustment (like changing the number or position of the wiring holes) was required. By generating more idle time in the workforce, the changeovers aggravated Glamox's high labor costs-Norwegian wages for manufacturing workers were among the highest in the world. Production scheduling was complicated and as a result of this and the frequent changeovers, throughput time averaged five days.

In 1983, Glamox had launched a 3-year plan to invest NOK 12.5 million annually in new equipment. The company hoped to improve productivity and reduce labor costs with these investments, and through several training programs for its workforce.

Glamox's cost structure is presented in *Table 2* below.

Table 2: Glamox's Cost Structure

Activity or Input	% of Ex-Factory Price
Product development	5
Raw materials and components	35
Manufacturing labor	13
Depreciation	2
Marketing and sales	20
General and administrative	15
Shipping	5
Manufacturer's margin	5
Total	**100**

Product Development

New product ideas originated inside Glamox's Technical Department or with Mr. Birger Hatlebakk. According to Mr. Slagstad, getting product ideas from the sales force had been tried, but "they only want us to make whatever Philips has".

Glamox had two different processes for new product development. "Custom" products were developed and produced to order by a small group known as the "Project Department". New "custom" products involved either limited modifications to products in the "standard" catalog, or fabrication of completely new designs. Strain on the prototype shop was considerable; they operated under heavy time pressure to produce new drawings and new tooling, and to deliver the customer's order within the time frame agreed to. Moreover, developing and producing the custom products was highly dependent on outside suppliers for timely delivery – particularly of electronic components used in, for example, emergency lighting equipment.

Additions to Glamox's standard product line, on the other hand, were developed manually in a prototype shop run by Glamox's Technical Department with a staff of 20 draftsmen and mechanical engineers. Since these products were produced to stock, rather than to customer orders, time pressure was relatively minimal. Rather, the main production issue revolved around inventory management, and the main problems concerned incorrect demand forecasts or production scheduling.

Diversification and Crisis, 1972-1983

Glamox entered the electrical heating business in 1972, by initiating manufacture of wall and skirting heating systems for commercial and industrial use. This move capitalized on some available synergies in production and distribution. Electric heating panels used the same basic components and production processes as lighting equipment. The distribution channels for industrial lighting and heating products frequently overlapped. In Norway, for instance, about half of heating product sales were made through the same distribution channels Glamox used for its lighting products. In the early 1970s, Glamox did pioneering work on electronic thermostats. The company also won several national and international awards for its heaters – "functional solutions which also meet the requirements for flexible use of space and design criteria". By 1983, heating equipment comprised 18% of total Glamox sales.

Other Glamox efforts at diversification were not as successful. Mr. Birger Hatlebakk's long-time passion for motor vehicles brought him to invest NOK 30 million during 1972-80 to start Moxy, a truck company. Birger Hatlebakk designed the trucks himself, large vehicles whose six-wheel drive feature made them extremely mobile in difficult terrain and positioned them to compete head-on against a similar Volvo product. The elder Mr. Hatlebakk had envisioned Moxy becoming the largest company in the Glamox group, but by 1982 Moxy had been through bankruptcy twice and was acquired at a bargain basement price in 1983 by a group of British truck dealers.

In retrospect, Torkell Hatlebakk attributed Moxy's bankruptcy to undercapitalization of the company and to his father's desire to have complete control, which made it difficult to attract investors. Additionally, the Norwegian government authorities never bought the idea of a native Norwegian motor vehicle. Consequently, state development funds and tax credits did not materialize.

> "After the dealers took over, the company did fine. It is now about the same size as Glamox, so my father was, in a sense, correct in his forecast. If we could have solved these [funding] problems, done some good marketing, and got some good new management into the company, it would have worked for us."

Glamox had also acquired two small local businesses – a printing company (1979) and an iron foundry (1964). Printing was motivated by Birger Hatlebakk's interest in local politics. The iron foundry was able to fabricate some parts for Moxy's manufacturing operations, but was mainly seen as an investment opportunity. Neither business ever turned a profit for Glamoxgruppen.

Torkell Hatlebakk Reorganizes Glamox

Torkell Hatlebakk took over as Glamox's Managing Director in August 1980, in the midst of financial crisis. Poor performance by the non-core businesses, coupled with slippage at Glamox as Birger Hatlebakk's attention was absorbed elsewhere, pushed the group into a net loss for the year. Moreover, using Glamox's cash to fund Moxy and the other non-core businesses had left Glamox operating on a thin shoestring of working capital and deferring needed production line investment.

Torkell Hatlebakk brought several new managers into Glamox and began getting the situation turned around. Glamox's workforce was cut from 850 to 600 (626 to 449 for Norway, 45 to 20 for Sweden) in 1981-82. "Fortunately, general economic conditions in this area were not too bad at this time," he recalled. "We had no demonstrations and not too much unfavorable reaction. Things were very quiet. People seemed to realize that something needed to be done. We cut Germany to a one-man operation but, otherwise, all the cuts were in Norway, pretty much through straight layoffs. Actually, the biggest problem was that our banks stopped our credit."

The printing business was sold in February 1981, the foundry near the beginning of 1982. Moxy went through bankruptcy once in 1981, was restarted by a group of external investors without success, experienced a second bankruptcy in 1982 and was sold in 1983. During 1982, Glamox equity was written down to zero. The company was recapitalized with NOK 15 million of shares sold in 1982 and NOK 10 million in 1983. This financial restructuring reduced the Hatlebakk family ownership of Glamox from 100% in 1981 to 3% in early 1984, including the interest held by a group of investors organized by Torkell Hatlebakk's brother-in-law. Subsequently, Glamox returned to profitability, posting net income of NOK 8 million on NOK 208 million sales in 1983. *(Refer to Exhibits 2-4.)*

Glamox's Position in Early 1984

With Glamox's financial crisis under control, Torkell Hatlebakk at last had time to take stock of the company's position and set some directions for the future. He had prepared a number of short memos based on information he had obtained from his father, various members of his staff and his own experience. These memos are summarized below.

The European Industrial Lighting Industry

In 1984, the industrial lighting industry was highly dependent on new construction and, therefore, the cyclical swings related to it. However, about 20% of sales were for replacement of older lighting fixtures. Replacement periods ranged from 3 years for retail shops to 20 years for industrial and outdoor lighting, but these life cycles were becoming shorter.

Overall, the lighting business was starting to benefit from the increasing importance of services in the European economy. Service businesses were generating demand for higher priced, more frequently replaced lighting products. More people were working indoors, and customers were paying more and more attention to total lighting effect as a source of productivity and workforce comfort. Costs were also increasingly seen from a long-term perspective – not only initial installation but subsequent maintenance, service and durability.

Lighting was increasingly a service business rather than a manufacturing industry driven by technology. However, technical innovation – and the ability to finance it – remained important competitive factors. Small and medium fittings manufacturers were branching out from their traditional national bases to seek foreign distribution and cooperative design agreements (like the Italian designs Glamox used for some of its outdoor lighting products). Survival depended on having a broad range of products and access to distribution channels. Strong local distribution and local identity were necessary even for companies with a full range of products.

The traditional demarcation between lamps [e.g., bulbs or fluorescent tubes] and fittings was breaking down in the face of these market changes. Leading European lamp makers like Philips, Siemens' Osram subsidiary, GTE/Sylvania, and Thom EMI were increasingly offering "total lighting solutions", instead of obliging customers to make product-by-product decisions. The easiest way for a bulb maker to get into the solutions business quickly was to buy independent fittings manufacturers. As a result, Glamox had received a couple of offers.

It was expensive and difficult for small newcomers to establish themselves with special products because distribution networks were relatively static. Also, good new products could be copied easily and quickly.

Markets/Potential Markets

The Nordic countries accounted for over 80% of Glamox sales in 1983. Its market share was also highest in these countries. *(Refer to Exhibit 5.)*

Norway was the company's most important market, providing 45% of sales. This market was relatively stable. There were few Norwegian competitors and they did not seem to represent a major threat to the status quo. Foreign competitors had only a small share of this market and would also have needed to overcome domination of the distribution channels by Glamox and IFA. Additionally, they would have faced difficulties in achieving close contacts with Norwegian officials and customers. Glamox's sales development in 1982 was satisfactory as market share improved despite attacks by foreign, especially Swedish, suppliers.

The company's Swedish sales had declined by 24% since 1980, but then gained slightly in 1983. Large wholesale distributors dominated this market, and Glamox had problems competing on price. Finland was Glamox's second most important market, having shown strong growth in recent years – 64% since 1980 compared to 7% for Glamox overall. Local production, integration and closeness to the customer were important advantages, as protectionist sentiment in Finland was stronger than anywhere else in Scandinavia.

The Danish market had been difficult due to its heavy focus on energy saving. However, Glamox's concentration on energy-economic lighting systems gave good results in 1982. Schools and public buildings were an important part of this market, but they were hurt by budget cuts. On the other hand, private sector investment was expected to increase in the short run. The company's sales in Denmark had increased by 8% during the last four years.

In West Germany, Europe's largest market, no company had even 10% market share in 1983. Instead, there were half a dozen manufacturers at around that level, with several more not far behind. Only Siemens and AEG were quoted publicly. Because the others, like Trilux, Erco, Staff, Hofmeister and RZB, remained determinedly private, it was difficult for predators of any nationality to acquire a local German partner.

The German market was the "quality leader" for lighting – the way France was for perfume. Most of Glamox's production equipment was made in Germany, and a lighting product accepted in Germany was likely to succeed elsewhere. Frequently, Glamox had taken a mature or declining product which had been successful in Germany and given it new life by migrating it to the UK, and then, sometimes, to a "third life" by migrating it to Spain or some other marginal market.

Glamox's real strength in both Germany and the UK was minimal outside the offshore/marine market segment. Offshore/marine offered some possibility for a global segment-based strategy, but it would be difficult to execute. On the upside, product specifications were relatively undifferentiated along national lines-shipping was a relatively international business. The company had good market share positions in Scandinavia and the UK. Its products were well accepted at the high end of the quality scale. Best of all, there were few strong competitors in this market segment.

On the other hand, the shipping market was depressed in 1984, with heavy price competition. Moreover, the bidding process involved in winning marine orders was complicated and protectionism was rampant, especially in Japan and Korea, the world's two leading shipbuilders. Even in Europe, builders frequently purchased from national suppliers. Finally, a global strategy in the marine segment would require significant resources for worldwide service and worldwide dual sales – to shipbuilders and shipowners.

Competitors

Overall, the Western European market for commercial light fittings in 1984 was still much less concentrated than in the US, where the top four suppliers accounted for more than 50% of the market. The top eight European suppliers held only 41% of the market. *(Refer to Exhibit 6.)*

This picture changed, however, if the situation were taken country by country. Except for Germany, the top four suppliers held between 85% of the national market (in Austria) and 69% of the market (in Denmark). In every country, one or more lampmakers was present among the top four makers of fittings.

Conclusion

"Despite our recent brush with bankruptcy," thought Torkell Hatlebakk, "this company has a great deal of resilience. We are barely on our feet again, but we must go forward, not stop. And we must choose our direction wisely. A big company can afford to make mistakes, but we've just about reached our limit in that department. We need courage and optimism, but we also need some success... quickly."

Exhibit 1: Organization Chart, 1983

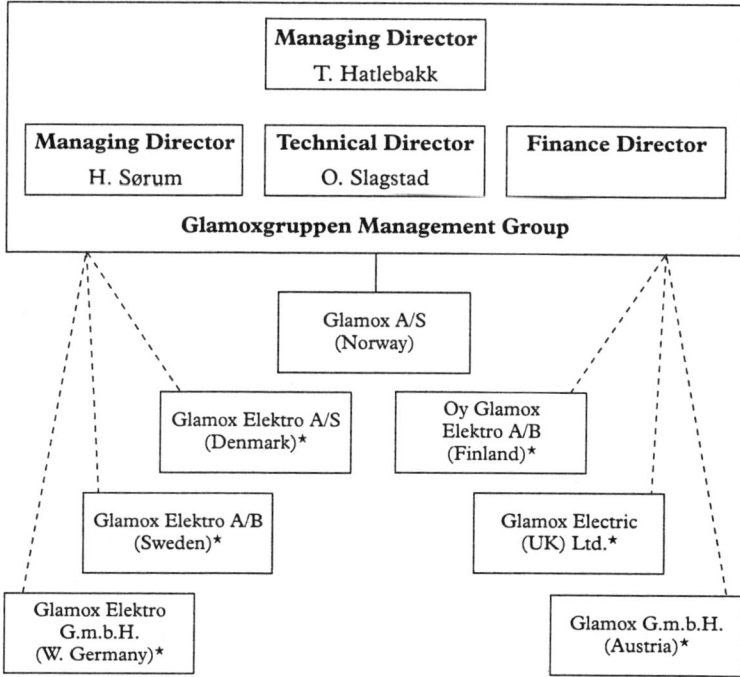

* Foreign subsidiaries report to local board of directors

Exhibit 2: Glamoxgruppen Income Statements (Millions of NOK[1])

	1982	1983
Operating revenues	190	208
Operating costs:		
Raw materials and goods		
intended for resale	62	71
Wages and social security	72	79
Depreciation	5	5
Bad debts	1	2
Changes in stocks of		
work in progress and finished goods	4	1
Other operating costs	32	39
Total operating costs	176	197
Operating profit	14	11
Net financial expenses	6	3
Profit before extraordinary items	8	8
Extraordinary items:		
Profit on sales of fixed assets	13	–
Result of the composition[2]	26	–
Depreciation development costs	(1)	–
Other extraordinary income, net	-	1
Extraordinary items, net	38	1
Profit before taxes	46	9

[1]NOK/$1.00, annual average, per IMF 6.4540   7.2964
[2]Special one-time extraordinary gain for write-down of liability to creditors in connection with financial restructuring.

Glamox's 1983 sales by:

Product line	%	Country	%
Lighting	71.6	Norway	45.3
Heating	18.4	Finland	17.6
Other	10.0	Denmark	12.1
	100.0	Sweden	9.4
		Austria	4.1
		UK	3.2
		W. Germany	0.6
		Other	7.7
			100.0

Exhibit 3: Glamoxgruppen Balance Sheets (Millions of NOK[1])

Assets:	On December 31,	
	1982	1983
Current assets:		
Cash and cash equivalents	10	11
Customer bills receivable	1	3
Accounts receivable	34	34
Other receivables.	2	3
Inventory2.	45	45
Total current assets.	92	96
Long-term investments.	2	12
Fixed assets:		
Machinery, vehicles, fixtures	15	20
Buildings.	7	5
Total fixed assets.	22	25
Total assets.	116	133
Liabilities and Equity Capital:		
Current Liabilities:		
Accounts payable, suppliers.	15	22
Wages, taxes and social security.	9	12
Other current liabilities.	15	14
Total current liabilities	39	48
Long-term liabilities:		
Mortgage loans.	30	25
Other long-term liabilities.	2	3
Total long-term liabilities	32	28
Conditional tax-free allocations.	5	10
Equity capital:		
Share capital (NOK 1,000 per share par value.	15	25
Statutory reserve.	3	3
General reserves.	22	19
Total equity capital	39	47
Total Liabilities and Equity Capital	116	133

[1]NOK/$1.00, year end (IMF).	7.0540	7.7222
[2]Inventory	**1982**	**1983**
Raw materials.	13	13
Work in progress and components.	10	11
Finished goods	23	21

Exhibit 4: Glamoxgruppen Sources and Uses of Funds (Millions of NOK)

	1982	1983
Sources of Funds		
Funds from operations:		
Profit before taxes	46	9
Ordinary depreciation	5	5
Other.	(3)	(2)
Total funds from operations	48	12
Funds from external sources:		
Issuance of new shares	15	10
New long-term liabilities	1	3
Book value of fixed assets sold	13	2
Total funds from external sources	29	15
Total sources of long-term funds	77	27
Uses of Funds:		
Investment in fixed assets	2	15
Investment in long-term receivables and investments	–	10
Reduction of long-term liabilities.	19	7
Total uses of long-term funds	21	32
Net sources (uses) of long-term funds	56	(5)
Funds provided from (used by) changes in non-cash working capital:		
Short-term receivables	6	(4)
Inventory	5	–
Bank overdrafts	(21)	1
Accounts payable, supplier	(14)	8
Other current liabilities	(29)	1
Funds from (for) non-cash working capital, net	(53)	6
Increase in cash	3	1

Exhibit 5: Glamoxgruppen Market Share in Western European Markets, 1983 Commercial/Industrial Lighting Fittings

Country	Total	Sales* Glamoxgruppen	Glamoxgruppen Market Share (%)
Norway	200	64	32.00
Finland	240	24	10.00
Denmark	160	32	20.00
Sweden	317	19	6.00
UK	1,800	6	0.33
Austria	300	4	1.33
West Germany	2,100	1	0.05
Other	N/A	19	N/A

* (millions of NOK)

Exhibit 6: Western European Market Shares, Commercial/Industrial Lighting Fittings, 1983

Company/Nationality	Market Share
Thorn Lighting (UK)	11.0%
Philips (Neth.)	9.0
Siemens (W. Germany)	5.3
Zumtobel (Austria)	4.3
GTE/Sylvania (US)	3.8
Europhane (France)	3.3
Trilux (W. Germany)	2.5
AEG (W. Germany)	1.8
Others	59.0

5. Iskra Power Tools

This case was prepared by Research Associate Robert C. Howard, under the direction of Professors William A. Fischer and Per V. Jenster, as a basis for class discussion rather than to illustrate either effective or ineffective handling of a business situation. This case is part of IMD's institutional research program on Managing Internationalization.

As he walked through his factory one frigid winter morning in January 1991, Miro Krek, General Manager of Iskra Industrija za Elektricna Orodja in Kranj, Yugoslavia, commented to his visitors, "There are certain things we need to do in aligning our marketing and manufacturing. As you walk through here, you can see that our efficiency could easily be improved by 10-15%. For example, we could put in longer lines and plan larger volume runs to get better efficiency. At the same time, we are considering concentrating our manufacturing on certain parts such as motors." Placing his hand on his chest, he said with considerable emotion, "Motors are at the heart of any power tool – we need to manufacture them!"

For Iskra's management, the situation in Yugoslavia was tumultuous. Krek explained, "Over the last three months, Yugoslavia has undergone incredible political change towards adapting a Western style market economy. As this change has touched all aspects of our society, so it has forced us to rethink our entire power tool business. The question for me is, "Should we try to become a major player in the West and East European power tool markets or, should we only focus on a few select markets or customers? Then, too, what would be the consequences for the Iskra organization?"

Soon after the government approved several free enterprise laws in Yugoslavia in January 1989, revolutions occurred in many of the neighboring countries in Eastern Europe. Prior to those events, Iskra had concentrated its sales primarily on Western power tool markets, where the management believed their competitive advantages were low labor costs and, to a lesser extent, a few niche products. In fact, until January 1991, these two dimensions had formed the basis of Krek's plans for leading the Iskra Power Tool Division into the 1990s. Now, however, with Europe's political landscape in upheaval, new markets were emerging, and old advantages were threatened. Consequently, it was necessary to review the interrelated issues of manufacturing and marketing power tools.

As Krek saw it, there were at least three options available for Iskra Power Tools. First, continue to capitalize on Yugoslavia's low labor costs and compete on price in Western markets. Alternatively, Iskra could build on the two major successes that it had enjoyed, and manufacture and market a select few power tools in Western niche markets. Third, the management of Iskra Power Tools could try to build on Yugoslavia's tradition as a commercial link between East and West, and develop the power tool markets of Eastern Europe.

Along with the above, Miro also had the continuing worry of how to preserve Iskra's domestic position at a time when the firm was under direct attack from a Black & Decker assembly operation in Yugoslavia. With less than two weeks to prepare for his final presentation to senior management of the Iskra Group, Krek knew a full review of the options for the 1990s was necessary.

The Iskra Group of Companies

The Iskra Group of Companies was founded in Ljubljana in 1961 through the merger of four major electrical companies in Slovenia, Yugoslavia's northernmost republic. The group based its name on the oldest of these companies – Iskra – which also meant "spark" in Slovenian, and symbolized the electronic nature of the group's products. By 1991, Iskra had become the leading electronic and electrical manufacturer in Yugoslavia, manufacturing and marketing a broad range of products through 14 domestic subsidiaries and 18 foreign offices. Moreover, in Slovenia, Iskra was home to roughly 25,000 employees, making the Iskra Group of Companies the largest Slovenian employer.

Iskra Power Tools

Although the Iskra Group was founded in 1961, the origins of some of its companies could be traced to the end of World War II or earlier. What became Iskra Power Tools, for example, had begun as a textile company in Kranj during the 1930s when Czechoslovakian textile manufacturers moved their operations to Northern Yugoslavia to take advantage of the low-cost labor force. During World War II, the Nazis gained control of Yugoslavia and transformed the textile facility into a military factory for aircraft engine parts; in the process, they transferred substantial metal working and engineering skills into the Iskra factories.

Throughout the post war era, the mechanical expertise brought to Iskra by the Germans grew increasingly intertwined with electronics, supported by the expertise in Iskra's electronics companies. Until the early 1950s, Iskra's employees had channeled that expertise into industrial and consumer products for rebuilding the Yugoslavian infrastructure and meeting the needs of the domestic market, respectively. Included among the group's industrial products were electric power meters, transformers, capacitors, and electric motors. In the consumer area, typical products included automotive electronics such as starters, alternators and voltage regulators, and household appliances such as vacuum cleaners, toasters, and power tools.

In time, the Kranj production facility became too constrained to continue manufacturing the entire Iskra product offering, and several products were transferred to other sites in the area. Power tool production, however, along with kilowatt meters and telecommunications switching equipment remained in Kranj. *(See Exhibit 1 for the Iskra Power Tools organization chart.)*

Iskra Commerce

As was typical in many centrally-planned economies, the production and distribution of Iskra Group's products were partitioned into separate responsibilities. While the factories concentrated on production, a separate sales organization, Iskra Commerce, was founded in 1961 to handle the marketing and distribution responsibilities of the organization. Originally, Iskra Commerce had served as a central commercial organization, conducting all purchasing and selling for the Iskra Group of Companies – both inside and outside Yugoslavia. In the early 1970s, following marked growth in size and responsibility, Iskra's domestic companies began to purchase and sell directly in Yugoslavia. However, Iskra Commerce retained responsibility for foreign commercial intercourse.

In foreign markets, Iskra Commerce continued purchasing and selling for all companies within the Iskra Group until the late 1980s. Thereafter, Iskra's foreign companies, like the ones in Yugoslavia, began to establish direct commercial links with suppliers and buyers. Mitja Taucher, former Senior Adviser of Iskra Commerce, recalled the organization's mission, "When Yugoslavia had strong regulations regarding imports, it made a lot of sense to channel all the group's purchases and sales through one organization; the group was stronger as a whole than as individual companies. Now, however, with the changes in Yugoslavia concerning imports and the strength of our individual companies, it makes sense for Iskra Commerce to serve in a different capacity."

The Power Tool Industry

Generally speaking, power tools included any tool containing a motor that was capable of being guided and supported manually by an operator. Thus, power tools played an intermediary role between traditional hand tools and sophisticated machine tools. Typical products in the power tool family included the household drill, circular saw, jigsaw, router, angle grinder, hedge trimmer, chain saw and less familiar and more specialized products such as nut runners and impact wrenches used in assembly line manufacture. The wide availability of electrical energy and the relatively low cost of electric tools facilitated their use in small workshops, the building and construction industries, and in households.

Analysts and participants classified the industry into two broad segments according to end usage: professional and hobby. In the professional category, users worked in industries such as assembly-line manufacture, foundries, shipbuilding, and woodworking. The building and construction trade, on the other hand, covered both user segments; that is, tools dedicated to the professional builder as well as tools designed for the home enthusiast or do-it-yourself (DIY) market. Worldwide, power tool purchase behavior varied as a function of labor costs and disposable income. Generally, the professional power tool sector was most developed in high labor cost countries; the DIY market tended to be more pronounced in countries with higher personal disposable incomes.

In 1989, the worldwide electric power tool industry was valued at just over DM 10 billion[4], with sales concentrated in three major markets: North America, 28%; Europe, 47%; and the Far East, 18%. Although the industry had grown an average of 3% per annum on a worldwide basis since 1980, market growth rates varied considerably among individual countries (as indicated in Table 1). Within Europe, where the in-

---

[4] In 1989, average exchange rates were 1 ECU = DM 2.02, and US $1 = DM 1.88.

dustrial segment had traditionally dominated, Germany, France, Great Britain and Italy represented 75% of the region's sales (as summarized in Table 2).

Table 1: % Growth of European Power Tool Markets in 1989 & 1990

Country	% Growth 1989	Country	% Growth 1990
Portugal	20	Greece	35
Spain	18	German	18
Italy	15	Portugal	18
Greece	15	Italy	12
Finland	12	Netherlands	10
Austria	12	Sweden	10
Sweden	10	Ireland	8
Great Britain	8	Belgium	6
Germany	8	Spain	6
France	8	Austria	4
Belgium	8	Denmark	3
Switzerland	8	Switzerland	3
Netherlands	5	France	0
Ireland	5	Great Britain	0
Denmark	-5	Norway	0
Norway	-5	Finland	-3

1989 Source: Databank   *1990 Source: Bosch*

Table 2: 1989 Unit Sales in Europe's Four Largest Markets

Country	Thousands of Pieces	%European Sales
Germany	7,000	28
France	5,000	20
Great Britain	4,300	17
Italy	2,500	10
Other Countries	6,200	25
Total	25,000	100

Source: Bosch

Segments and Channels

Professional tools were traditionally bought in hardware stores, from wholesalers, large tool specialists or from a manufacturer's or distributor's direct sales force. Quality products suited to specific tasks, durability, and after-sales service were viewed as important buying criteria. In addition, some manufacturers of high-end tools viewed education and problem-solving as part of the sales effort, with trained sales people needed to meet the technical requirements of the user.

In the hobby segment, customers bought from wholesalers, hardware stores, department stores, home centers, mail order houses, and hypermarkets. In this segment, manufacturers considered image, product quality, and price as important purchase factors. Also in this segment, competition was becoming increasingly like that of other consumer products, namely, brand name and packaging were gaining in importance relative to other product features. At the low end of the market, products were designed to meet an expected lifetime use of 25 hours. At the high end, on the other hand, which tended to enlarge as the market matured, there was more emphasis on durability and ergonomic characteristics, similar to professional products.

In Europe, a shift in purchasing patterns had led to a shift in the distribution of power tools. In the professional sector, direct sales had begun to play a more significant role in the distribution process, particularly in the more mature and structured markets. And, in the consumer segment, the volume of tools sold through mass merchandisers was growing at the expense of conventional tool sellers. In short, increased specialization in power tool usage, combined with a proliferation of applications, was leading manufacturers to establish more direct links to professional users and more visible links to the DIY segment. The volume of power tools sold through any one of these channels varied as a function of country. Generally speaking, the markets in Northern Europe were more mature and more structured than those in the Mediterranean countries. Likewise, mass merchandisers and direct sales played a more significant role in the North than in the South. *(Table 3 contains comparative data on power tools sold through different channels in Germany vs Italy.)*

Table 3: % of Country Sales by Distribution Channel – 1990

Channel	DIY Segment Germany	Italy
Wholesalers	5	25
Hardware Stores	55	45
Department Stores (Mass Merchandisers)	15	11
Home Centers	21	-
Others (Cash & Carry, Mail Order)	4	19
	Professional Segment	
Direct	10	-
Hardware	50	55
Wholesalers	40	25
Large Tool Specialists (Mass Merchandisers)	-	20

Source: Black & Decker, Iskra Company Records

Manufacturing

Power tools embodied a range of technologies including a motor shaft around which copper wire was wound to form an armature, gears, plastic or metal housing, switches and cables. In conjunction with a trend in production specialization in the post war era, power tool manufacturers relied heavily on subcontractors to produce many of these components. Generally speaking, the major competitors only made components that were central to the performance of the final product, such as the motor. *(The following bill of material summarizes the key elements in a typical power tool.)*

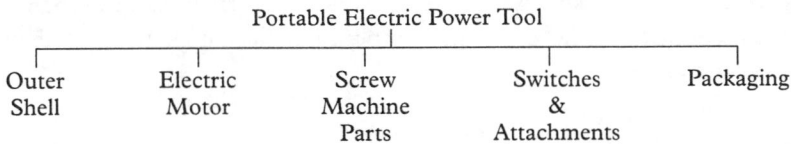

Portable Electric Power Tool

Outer Shell	Electric Motor	Screw Machine Parts	Switches & Attachments	Packaging

Typically, power tools were mass produced, although the extent of mechanization varied with the volume of production, nature of the product, and the efficiency of the individual manufacturer. According to one industry analyst, purchased materials accounted for 50% of a power tool firm's manufacturing costs, machining 15%, diecasting/molding 9%, motor winding and assembly 12%, and final assembly 14%.

Trends

By the late 1980s, a number of trends began to influence the level and nature of competition in the worldwide power tool industry. Among these were a growing preference for battery-powered tools, globalization of the industry, and the opening up of Eastern Europe.

Battery-powered Tools

During the 1980s, battery-powered (also known as cordless) tools benefited significantly from advances in technology. Because of their low energy storage, initial battery-driven products were limited to the smaller jobs of the DIY market. However, the combination of superior power storage and lighter materials that were developed during the 1980s permitted battery-operated tools to be used in more demanding applications, thus facilitating their penetration of the professional market. At the end of the 1980s, cordless tools represented 20% of all power tool production worldwide and, like many products using electronics, the Japanese were particularly adept at developing cordless power tools. During the 1990s, advances in materials science and battery technology were expected to increase both the usage life between recharges and the number of applications cordless tools could handle.

Globalization

Throughout the 1980s, the electric power tool industry became increasingly globalized, enabling larger players to have an operational flexibility unavailable to smaller companies. By decreasing a firm's reliance on a single market, multinational power tool companies were able to leverage their positions worldwide. That is, firms with manufacturing as well as sales in many markets were able to exploit uncertainties in exchange rates, competitive moves, or government policies far better than their smaller rivals.

Eastern Europe and the USSR

During 1989, communist dictatorships across Eastern Europe were replaced by a variety of governments which, in general, expressed their commitment to develop market economies. Analysts believed that these developments would influence the power tool business in two ways. First, these newly-opened markets and their power tool manufacturers were expected to be the targets of firms already established in the West. Secondly, once the legal issues surrounding privatization became clear, the surviving power tool manufacturers in Eastern Europe could begin to restructure their own operations, and market their products at home and abroad.

Competition

In 1989, there were approximately 75 power tool manufacturers worldwide. Generally speaking, these competitors could be grouped into two categories: large multinationals and, primarily, domestic manufacturers. Typically, the large players offered a full range of power tools to both the professional and the DIY segments, as well as a complete line of accessories such as drill bits, saw blades, battery packs and after-sales service. Smaller power tool manufacturers, on the other hand, tended to concentrate production on a limited line of tools, augmented by OEM products to one or a few segments of the market. Although these small firms lacked the product offering of their larger rivals, they were well known and respected for their expertise in their chosen fields.

Black & Decker

Black and Decker was the largest power tool maker in the world. With manufacturing plants in 10 countries and sales in nearly 100, the company reported 1989 power tool sales of $1,077 million. With approximately 25% of the total market, Black & Decker commanded a worldwide share more than twice that of its next biggest rival. Like most of its competitors, the company segmented the industry into professional and DIY sectors; between the two, Black & Decker derived two-thirds of its revenue from consumers and one-third from professional users.

In addition to its sheer size, Black & Decker enjoyed a number of competitive advantages. New product introduction, for example, was a high priority; the company launched 77 products in 1989 alone and, in the same year, new and redesigned products accounted for 25% of revenues. By 1991, the company expected new entries to represent more than half its sales.

In Europe, where Black & Decker pioneered the introduction of products to the DIY segment, its name was virtually synonymous with power tools. In Britain, for example, it was not uncommon for DIY remodelers to "Black & Decker" their homes. And, in France, individuals "plugged in" to the social scene were said to be "trés Black & Decker".

One company spokesman attributed his company's success to proper market segmentation and a restructuring that had begun in the mid-1980s. Thus, when the market for power tools as a whole was growing at a rate of only 5-6%, Black & Decker achieved 11% growth in 1989, twice the rate of the markets served, due in part to its concentrated focus on accessories and cordless products. Although the latter grew 30% in 1989, Black & Decker's successful identification of the trend toward cordless products allowed its sales in this segment to grow by 70%, reaching $100 million in 1989.

From the mid-1980s onward, the management of Black & Decker devoted significant attention to "globalizing" its worldwide operations and, by the beginning of the 1990s, design centers, manufacturing plants, and marketing programs were adept at making and selling products to a worldwide market. As early as 1978, Black & Decker had undertaken the standardization of its motors and armature shafts, and it had, over the years, consistently pursued manufacturing approaches that combined product variety with volume output such as: dedicated lines and facilities for specific items (focused factories and group technology); flexible manufacturing systems (FMS)[5], just-in-time manufacturing (JIT)[6], and significant vertical integration of the fabrication and assembly process. In addition, Black & Decker achieved substantial cost savings through global purchasing programs and saved millions of dollars by restructuring its manufacturing facilities. In one facility, for example, the company standardized production around a limited number of motors. In another case, the company consolidated production of drills from five different plants to two.

To strengthen its presence in Eastern Europe, Black & Decker had recently established an assembly operation via a joint venture in Kranj. Although the company owned only 49%, its proximity to Iskra was seen as a serious challenge to the latter's position in Yugoslavia. And, in May 1989 in Czechoslovakia, Black & Decker entered into a joint venture to produce DIY tools and lawnmowers for the Czechoslovakian and West European markets. Once the joint venture reached full capacity, planned for the start of 1990, Black & Decker intended to cease production at its French and Italian facilities, and rely on its new Eastern European manufacturing platform.

[5] Flexible manufacturing systems consisted of sophisticated computer-driven lines, with relatively independent routing and intelligent machining centers.
[6] JIT referred to the Japanese-inspired approach to manufacturing which had originated with the philosophy of continuous improvement, superior quality, low changeover costs, and greatly reduced work-in-process inventories.

Makita

Based in Japan, the Makita Electric Works had entered the power tool market in the 1950s. In the mid-'70s and the 1980s, Makita established itself in a number of foreign markets by emphasizing its price competitiveness. At one point in the mid-'70s, for example, Makita products were selling at price levels that were 20-30% lower than the industry average. Nonetheless, by the beginning of the 1990s, Makita had established a solid reputation for quality and after-sales service, supported by a 3-day repair policy. And, through engaging a large number of distribution outlets in target markets to promote and service its products, Makita had climbed to number two in the industry by 1991.

In; contrast to Black & Decker, Makita concentrated only on the professional segment of the market, with a broad range of tools for professionals. The company attributed its success in overseas markets to superior after-sales service and a close working relationship with well-informed retailers who kept in touch with consumers regarding the latest in product development. Beginning with two factories in Japan in the mid-'70s, Makita had decided to globalize its operations during the 1980s, establishing factory operations in the US, Canada, and Brazil.

In Europe, Makita's 1989 sales increased by 15% and, in the same year, a company spokesman stated that Makita intended to become the largest power tool supplier in the region. In a step towards fulfilling that vision and meeting the company's expressed goal of supplying 25% of European sales with locally manufactured products, Makita began constructing a new power tool plant in the UK in March 1990. Scheduled to begin operating in early 1991, the plant would initially make cordless and percussion drills, angle grinders and circular saws for the professional sector. Ultimately, however, the plant was to produce only electric motors. As of January 1991, Makita had not begun to compete in any of Iskra's markets.

Robert Bosch

Robert Bosch was the third largest power tool producer in the world and had manufacturing plants in Germany, the USA, Brazil, and Switzerland. Like Black & Decker, Bosch produced a variety of power tools for both the professional and the DIY segments, buying the portable tool division of Stanley Tools in the US in 1979. The company was particularly strong in Europe where it distributed through all channels. In 1990, despite an unfavorable trend in the $/DM exchange rate, Bosch's sales increased 14% to over DM 2.2 billion.

Following the unification of East and West Germany, Bosch management announced plans for a joint venture with VEB Elektrowerkzeuge Sebnitz to assemble power tools in Dresden (formerly East Germany) to be distributed through the latter's network of 1,400 hardware outlets. By the end of 1990, the Sebnitz facility was a fully-owned subsidiary and earmarked for DM 50 million in investment, initially for producing one-handed angle grinders and small drills. In the longer term, the management of Bosch planned to concentrate all export production in Sebnitz.

Skil was a major manufacturer of power tools based in the US, where the company was originally known as a professional tool supplier. More recently, however, Skil had concentrated on developing tools that fulfilled needs somewhere between the professional and consumer levels. In Europe, Skil had positioned itself in the Nordic markets as a professional tool company. It approached the rest of Europe, on the other hand, in the DIY market with a strong price emphasis, and was particularly strong in Germany and France.

Niche Players

Aside from the larger multinational power tool companies, there was a host of successful, albeit smaller, players in Europe which pursued niche strategies. In Germany, for example, Festo and ELU were well known for their fine-crafted woodworking tools, especially circular saws. Likewise, Kango, a British company, was renowned for its percussion drills. Generally speaking, niche players in the European power tool business charged premium prices and earned the majority of their sales in their home markets.

(See Exhibits 2 and 3, respectively, for a summary of Iskra's competition according to category, and a competitor positioning diagram prepared by a team of Iskra management.)

Iskra Power Tools' Competitive Position

Market Development

From its beginning in the early 1950s, the Iskra Power Tool division concentrated its sales in the Yugoslavian market. Ventures into Western Europe did not begin until the 1960s when the management sought to expand its product offering, consisting primarily of electric drills, based on the company's expertise in small electric motors. The cornerstone of this expansion strategy was exchange programs with other power tool manufacturers.

In 1966, Iskra entered into a cooperation agreement with Perles, a small power tool manufacturer in Switzerland. In exchange for Perles' angle grinders sold under the Iskra name in Yugoslavia, Perles received Iskra's drills which it distributed through its own network under the Perles label. In 1971, Iskra management sought to build on the Perles name and distribution network by acquiring the Swiss-based manufacturer. Mitja Taucher commented that, in the early 1970s, Iskra management realized they would have difficulties with an unknown name in Europe and, thus, decided to acquire Perles. "Perles is still in existence mostly for its name, not its manufacturing capacity, which is small," recalled Mitja. He added, "It was a good name across Europe for large angle grinders and some drills."

Bolstered by its first co-marketing arrangement with Perles, in 1972 the management of Iskra entered into an agreement with Skil Europe. In exchange for Iskra's small drills, sold under Skil's name through its European distribution network, Skil supplied Iskra with percussion drills, belt sanders and circular saws, sold in Yugoslavia under the Iskra name.

Eastern European Ventures

Following the first of a series of oil crises that began in 1973, it was difficult for Iskra to continue its expansion plans into Western markets. As an alternative, the management of Iskra Power Tools began to strengthen business ties with its socialist neighbors in Eastern Europe.

Czechoslovakia

Iskra's Eastern European experience began in 1978 with Naradi, a power tool manufacturer, and with Merkuria, a trading company, both based in Czechoslovakia. Due to a lack of convertible currency in Czechoslovakia, Iskra devised a three-way trading agreement: Perles shipped drills from Switzerland to Naradi, which marketed the products under the Naradi name, and to Merkuria, which sold products under the Iskra name. In turn, both Czech firms delivered products to Iskra; the process was completed when Iskra sent its power tools to Perles in Switzerland. Although Iskra achieved nearly a 10% market share through these two agreements in Czechoslovakia, its success was not without problems.

One executive stated that the weak point in the process was the power tools from Czechoslovakia; tools made by Naradi did not measure up to the quality standards demanded by Yugoslavian consumers. Moreover, after a few years, Naradi's products were out-of-date in comparison to competitors' offerings. Finally, because of the difficulties posed by the lack of real distribution channels or a service network in Czechoslovakia, Iskra management terminated the agreement in 1988.

Poland

Iskra had also participated in a cooperative arrangement to exchange power tools with Celma, a Polish power tool manufacturer. Like the agreement with Naradi in Czechoslovakia, Iskra marketed Celma's products under the Iskra name in Yugoslavia. However, Celma's products were of such low quality that Iskra soon found itself inundated with repair requests. Consequently, the management of Iskra devised a new agreement for close cooperation on specialty tools such as shears, steel cutters and die grinders.

USSR

More recently, Iskra Power Tools had tried manufacturing in the USSR. After five years of negotiating with the Institute for Power Tools in Moscow, in 1984, the first 100 power tools were brought to Yugoslavia. Unfortunately, due to the length of the negotiating period, the products were out-of-date on arrival. Like the previous efforts in Czechoslovakia and Poland, Iskra brought its Russian efforts to a halt.

Refocus on Western Europe

Like many firms that manufactured in and exported from Yugoslavia, Iskra earned a certain level of income from the domestic market. Although that income was not guaranteed, limited competition in the Yugoslavian power tool market had almost always provided Iskra with a source of funding to manufacture tools sold outside the country. By the beginning of the 1980s, however, the management of Iskra Power Tools grew concerned about becoming too dependent on the domestic market. Moreover, when it combined the uncertainties of the domestic market with its unsuccessful ventures in Eastern Europe, the management concluded it was time to resume strengthening ties with Western power tool producers.

Iskra as OEM Supplier

ELU

In 1980, Iskra signed a cooperation agreement with ELU, a German manufacturer of woodworking tools. Despite Iskra's successful development and initial manufacture of a small circular saw for sale under the ELU label, the management of ELU cancelled the agreement after two years. According to Branko Suhadolnik, Export Manager for Iskra Power Tools, Iskra was simply unable to supply the quantity of saws specified in the contract because of delays in starting production.

Kango

Iskra also began manufacturing for Kango, a UK company specializing in drills. In exchange for Kango's rotary hammer, sold under the Iskra name in Yugoslavia, Iskra provided Kango with circular saws sold under the Kango name in the IJK.

Iskra as Volume OEM

Skil

In the mid-1980s, Iskra management expanded its cooperation with Skil. In addition to supplying Skil with a small drill, Iskra provided a small angle grinder, a circular saw, and orbital sander. These items were sold under the Skil name in support of Skil's low price strategy. In November 1990, the management of Iskra approached Skil to discuss strengthening their partnership still further. However, as of January 1991, no additional cooperation had been agreed to.

Ryobi

In 1990, Miro Krek and Branko Suhadolnik began negotiating a joint venture agreement with Ryobi from Japan. Suhadolnik explained that Ryobi was considering Yugoslavia as an entry point into the European Economic Community and wanted to capitalize on Yugoslavia's comparative advantage in labor costs. In return for supplying angle grinders to Ryobi, Iskra was to market Ryobi's battery-operated power tools in Yugoslavia. Although the management of Ryobi was impressed with Iskra's products, they said that the manufacturing costs were too high; to meet Ryobi's terms, Iskra had to invest in more equipment. Shortly thereafter, the management of Ryobi decided to postpone further dealings in Eastern Europe until the political environment stabilized.

Bosch

In its most recent effort to supply a foreign manufacturer, Iskra approached Bosch concerning a router that complemented Bosch's offering. This deal, too, nearly succeeded, but was contingent on Iskra's dissolving its independent sales network in Germany and elsewhere. Because Bosch was not willing to purchase what Iskra management believed was the required volume necessary to compensate for the loss of its sales network, Iskra declined the offer.

In summary, the management of Iskra had made several attempts over the years to increase its attractiveness to foreign firms. With Skil, a generalist in the power tool industry, Iskra's competitive advantage was being a low-cost supplier; with ELU, Kango and Bosch, on the other hand, Iskra's success was based on the high perceived value of a niche product. With Ryobi, price competitiveness and market presence in Eastern Europe were important.

Iskra's Products and Channels

At the beginning of 1991, Iskra marketed a range of 200 products; 10 of these were obtained from other manufacturers via exchange agreements, while the balance were designed and produced by Iskra alone. Roughly speaking, accessories accounted for 20% of Iskra Power Tools' turnover, while drills and angle grinders accounted for approximately 50% and 30%, respectively, of tool sales. *(See Exhibit 4 for an overview of Iskra's product offering.)* Outside Yugoslavia, Iskra distributed its own products under the Perles name, almost exclusively through specialist hardware outlets in both the DIY and professional segments. In addition, Iskra Commerce marketed Iskra's power tools through its own offices. Although the influence of the latter was declining, Suhadolnik commented that, until the late 1980s, Iskra Commerce's foreign companies often made policies to survive for the short term, with little attention to the long term. For example, in those markets where the two organizations overlapped, prices sometimes differed between Iskra Power Tools and Iskra Commerce for the same products. More recently, he added, Iskra management had succeeded in changing this policy but, Suhadolnik commented, "To change something with a life of its own is not so easy."

In Yugoslavia, where Iskra had a market share of 50% in 1989, the company sold its power tools through Iskra Commerce with its own network of shops in each republic. However, the company had a significantly larger market share in Serbia than in Slovenia or Croatia. According to Branko, natives of the latter two provinces, because of their proximity to Italy and Austria, were not only better informed as to Western power tool alternatives, but could more easily access these alternative products. Power tools were also sold through the Iskra Power Tools sales organization, and directly from the factory in Kranj.

Design

In 1990, the design group at Iskra consisted of six people, all working primarily with pencil and paper. By contrast, their Western counterparts worked with computer-aided design (CAD) systems. Despite the lack of modem design equipment, the Iskra design team possessed strong artistic talents and lacked the engineering bias of Western designers. In describing the evolution of the relationship between design and manufacturing at Iskra, one manager commented that, until the early 1980s, there was a "We draw, you make" attitude. A few years thereafter, employees in the two functions began taking a more interdisciplinary approach to designing and making Iskra's power tools. Designers, for example, began asking those in manufacturing about the costs associated with individual parts; those in manufacturing, on the other hand, asked designers for new technological solutions. "Yet," recalled one designer, "new solutions were not possible because they required too much investment in new technology."

As of January 1991, there were two ways of concentrating on new product development at Iskra Power Tools. One was via direct cooperation with manufacturing on existing product lines, a process which tended to focus on minor changes and had been practiced for at least 15 years. The second pertained to new products and was primarily concerned with shortening product development time, through interdisciplinary teams, to a level comparable to Iskra's competition.

Not unlike the design-manufacturing relationship, the interaction between design and marketing was based on a philosophy of "We design, you sell". Beginning in the mid-1980s, however, this relationship also began to change as collaboration with Iskra's partners – Skil and Perles – on new designs began to increase, and greater and earlier cooperation between the two functions began to evolve.

Iskra was receptive to ideas from the marketplace, communicated to the design team via Iskra's customers and foreign distributors. In 1988, for example, Iskra formed a multidisciplinary team to determine which products had to be produced in the subsequent five years, at what price and what quantity. In the export market, ideas were solicited from Iskra's agents and distributors via an annual conference. As for feedback from end users, Iskra conducted market research for both its professional and its DIY customers, albeit only in Yugoslavia. (See Table 4 for design information at Iskra Power Tools.)

Table 4: Information on Iskra Power Tools' Design Function

Year	1982	1983	1984	1985	1986	1987	1988	1989	1990
No. designers	5	5	5	5	5	3	6	6	5
Average age	40	41	42	42	43	35	37	40	41
Years of experience (absolute)	38	43	48	49	54	20	26	28	33
Reconstructed products	6				7				3
Modifications	148				208				190
Commercial variants	717				1,802				827
New products	0	1	3	1	2	1	0	1	0

Note: A reconstructed product was one which had been developed and produced, but corrected for flaws. A modification, on the other hand, corresponded to a product with an incremental innovation such as a new spindle, a different type of handle or an additional speed. As the name implied, commercial variants were simply the number of variations possible for Iskra's products, needed to meet the different demands of Iskra's many markets and customers.

Source: Company Records

Manufacturing

Despite Iskra's product offenng of 200 power tools, most were variations of a common manufacturing mix of 10-15 models, all made in one factory using traditional batch production. Depending on the model, the array of products was manufactured on a monthly, quarterly, or annual basis. For example, Iskra had 70 variations of its drill, which was produced throughout the year in the same way as its angle grinders and circular saws. On the other hand, smaller volume products such as sanders and routers were made only on a quarterly basis.

Planning
At Iskra, batch sizes and sequencing were developed by a central planning department located in the Kranj factory. Typically, the planning department estimated the year's production and adjusted their forecast

quarterly. In addition, three planners prioritized the work at each factory workstation, based on the assembly plan which, in turn, was based on delivery promises. Prior to final assembly, the manufacturing department received figures for specific markets and attached the correct labels to the final package.

Differences between the batches produced and the amounts needed for assembly at any point in time (due to lead time variations) were stored in inventories until needed. In other words, purchasing of components and product fabrication at Iskra were always begun before the ultimate destination of a power tool was known, thereby limiting the ability to use dedicated machining in the first and last stages of the production process. From 1987-1989, Iskra Power Tools' inventory turnovers averaged 4.4, with the biggest inventories occurring at the beginning of the assembly process. By comparison, one manager estimated that Bosch's inventory turnover was in the range of 5-10 per year.

Milan Bavec, Manufacturing Manager, believed that parts inventories were too high because of difficulties in linking purchasing more closely to assembly. As an example, he explained that, on August 1, he might begin a series of 3,000 sanders, for which he ordered parts three months in advance. However, he said, when some parts took six months to arrive, one simply had to maintain the necessary inventory. All parts, he continued, were moved in and out of inventory. That is, whether Iskra produced or purchased its parts, all parts were stored in a warehouse until the full range was available to make a particular product. As an aside, Igor Poljsak, Financial & Accounting Department Manager, mentioned that the constant shifting of parts between Iskra's many buildings added 10-15% to production costs. Then, too, at 40-50% per year to borrow money, he estimated that the interest on working capital was 10-12%. Within manufacturing, some believed that if the individual market demands could be better coordinated with the manufacturing function, inventories could be reduced and more dedicated assembly implemented, thereby raising productivity.

Productivity

In terms of performance, productivity at Iskra Power Tools was somewhere between that of Eastern and Western power tool makers, with direct labor estimated at 10-12% of the cost of goods sold. *(See Table 5 for productivity figures, Table 6 for a breakdown of the manufacturing costs associated with a typical product, and Exhibits 5 and 6 for the Iskra income statement and balance sheets, respectively.)*

Table 5: Productivity Figures for Selected Power Tool Firms

Company or Location	No. Workers	Output(units/year)
Iskra	550	600,000
Bulgarian	5,000	40,000
Czechoslovakian	2,000	150,000
Western Firm	250	600,000

Source: Company Records

Table 6: Breakdown of Manufacturing Costs for Angle Grinders (%)

Purchased Materials	65.1
Machining & Diecasting & Molding	15.9
Motor Assembly	9.1
Final Assembly	9.9
Total	100.0

Source: Company Records

In discussing productivity, the management of Iskra acknowledged that labor costs were a serious burden and that the company probably had three times as many people as necessary. "And," commented one executive, "indirect costs are always too high, and we think that we have extremely high indirect costs for our production volume. For example, we have data indicating that Skil, with approximately the same number of people as Iskra, produces nearly one million pieces. Kress employs 400-500 people and produces around one million pieces. We have around 550 people, recently reduced from 760 without any strikes; however, I don't believe that will hold if we try to reduce further."

In addition to too many employees, Iskra's productivity was influenced by significant differences in production. Specifically, work was performed both in batch and in sequence, and, because all parts (except motors) were continually moved in and out of physical inventory, the flow of goods through the factory was complicated. *(See Exhibit 7 for the flow path of a typical item.)* On the third floor of the factory, where a dedicated motor assembly line was located, the situation was even more chaotic; there was little apparent continuity among work stations and, although the production machinery was only about 10 years old, the manufacturing process appeared much older. Lastly, the final assembly of tools was like a rabbit warren, with lots of discontinuities. As an example, newly finished goods often sat for several days waiting for complementary parts, such as chuck-keys, which had become stocked out.

Quality

The management of Iskra Power Tools was well aware that it needed to establish, improve and maintain quality in products and processes. In fact, the manager responsible for quality had organized statistical process control (SPC) procedures within the factory but, to date, had had only mixed success. Specifically, the level of quality was nowhere near that required to move to a production process – like JIT which could significantly reduce work-in-process inventories.

As of early 1991, incoming goods continued to be checked on arrival, according to prearranged contractual standards, using a standard acceptance sampling (Acceptable Quality Level – AQL) system. In fact, acceptance sampling was done at final production and final assembly, as well as with incoming items. In all cases, quality control (QC) was based on the first five pieces in a batch, followed by statistical sampling.

For the future, the quality manager hoped to integrate a quality attitude throughout the company. As part of the process, management had prepared a book containing quality standards, based on the International Standards Organization (ISO) 9000 series set of standards.[7] As of January 1991, management had not had much success implementing quality improvement. To do so, management believed, would require reshaping the attitudes of Iskra's workers.

The Production Workers

Iskra Power Tools' production process was characterized by low employee involvement, poor changeover performance between different models, and relatively poor maintenance performance. The assembly line workers were analyzed using modem time and methods analysis (Work Factor), and the analysis used to allocate labor staffing. However, since assembly was performed on a paced line, it was not possible for the employees to work faster. Thus, no pay incentives existed for higher output and workers were paid as a group. On occasion, quality bonuses were paid within the factory, despite the fact that some of the production being "rewarded" was not actually perfect.

Jakob Sink, Quality Assurance Manager, commented on the difficulties met in transforming the mindset of Iskra employees. "It is a new idea to send back a QC approval form within a few weeks. 'Why not do

---

[7] ISO 9000 was a technical standard that required the establishment of a complete system for monitoring quality standards.

it in a couple of months?' is still very much the attitude of those working in production." Then, too, Sink added, workers were concerned that identifying poor quality could cause either himself or a co-worker to be fired. Also, he mentioned that some employees might resist altering manufacturing processes, discussed by management in an attempt to deal with high variety manufacturing in a more efficient format. In defense of the workforce, Sink said that incoming materials played a key role in the quality problem and that, although Iskra controlled what it bought, it sometimes cost as much to control incoming materials as to produce a finished product.

The Supply Situation
Given that all major players in the power tool industry relied on suppliers for major components, it was not surprising that Iskra was also involved in such relationships. However, in Iskra's case, there was widespread agreement among the management team that the supply relationships were a competitive disadvantage. In fact, some thought that Iskra's manufacturing costs were 20-25% more expensive than for Bosch, for example, because of the supply situation. Then too, the company faced the added complication that one of its major suppliers was based in Serbia, a republic with which political tensions had been growing.

Within Yugoslavia, the manufacturing director distinguished suppliers according to raw materials or finished components such as gears and cables. He commented that, aside from having a lower quality, raw materials were also more expensive in Yugoslavia than in Western Europe. Furthermore, there were few finished component suppliers to choose from in Yugoslavia, and those that did exist did not possess a high quality standard. To use domestic components, Iskra would have to take what was available from several firms and remachine those components before assembling its power tools. In other words, the absence of quality suppliers and subcontractors added yet another step to Iskra's manufacturing.

As one remedy, Iskra forged close working relationships with its local suppliers. Generally speaking, these suppliers were able to respond to major design changes without any real problem, but efforts to upgrade the quality of the finished components had been unsuccessful. Despite the close relationships, it was highly unlikely that Iskra could put SPC into a supplier facility. According to Milan Bavec, "SPC is still too new, and even though we've held seminars, run films and the like, our results are still poor. At present, the real problem is getting the suppliers to comply with Iskra's own quality checklists. And that will take at least another two to three years.

Foreign Suppliers

Another manager pointed out that an obvious remedy to the problems encountered with domestic suppliers was to source from foreign firms. In general, sourcing at Iskra began after Iskra Power Tools had identified a potential supplier and negotiated the contract. Iskra Commerce then handled the commercial issues, such as invoicing and foreign exchange, for which it charged a fee of 4-6%. In addition, Iskra Power Tools paid an import duty of 4-5% on all items which it re-exported. For items sold on the domestic market, however, the import tax was 45%.

Another sourcing disadvantage for Iskra was customs delays. Typically, it took the company up to one month to obtain import clearance. To counter such delays, Iskra was obliged to order large stocks in advance. Additional factors that complicated Iskra's sourcing arrangements were premium prices because of small order volumes, payment problems due to foreign exchange availability, and the problem of Yugoslavia's external political image.

To summarize the above, one Iskra executive prepared a business system depicting the company's contribution to added value. For a customer paying a price of 100 (without VAT), distribution accounted for 50%, while parts, fabrication and assembly represented the balance (as summarized below).

The Iskra Business System

Parts	Fabrication	Assembly	Distribution	Customer
32.5	8.0	9.5	50.0	100.0
----------------------------- Value Added ----------------------------------				

Source: Company Records

Formulating a Strategy

In formulating Iskra's future strategy, Branko Suhadolnik believed the company should concentrate on less mature and less structured markets such as France and Italy. He reinforced his point by stating that the only way to succeed in these markets was to establish the Perles brand name and structure the distribution. Revamped manufacturing facilities, Branko added, would play a primary role in associating the company's image with quality products. Although he also supported the idea of serving as an OEM, he favored serving the niche players, provided Iskra could overcome what he believed was the company's inability to supply a requested volume of product at a competitive price.

On the other hand, Miro Krek believed the company's future lay in concentrating on becoming an OEM supplier to high volume producers, not trading under the Perles brand or worrying about distribution. As an OEM supplier, Krek felt that Iskra's inability to attract outside cooperation was due to a lack of price competitiveness, quality, and supply reliability. Consequently, special attention should be devoted to developing its price competitiveness and strengthening its ties with volume players such as Skil.

Then, too, a third group of Iskra executives believed that now was the time to attack Eastern Europe and the USSR. Specifically, these executives believed that Western suitors saw Iskra as a possible entryway into the Soviet Union.

Western Markets with Perles Branding

Based on the company's experiences through January 1991, Branko Suhadolnik felt that any activity in Western Europe required a concentrated focus on France, the second biggest market in Europe. Branko emphasized that with more than 8% growth in 1989 and five million power tools sold, France represented 20% of the total European market and warranted further attention. He went on to say that in France, there was no strong national producer of power tools. Secondly, the market was not nearly as developed as in Germany or the Netherlands and, therefore, customers bought more on price, less on quality and tradition. Third, the distribution channels in France were not well defined. "Then too," he added, "we believe the Latin way of life in France is closer to our way of life than the Germans, who are more formal and direct."

Like France, Suhadolnik also stressed the need for Iskra to target the Italian market. "Italy has a small power tool producer, but most of its production is exported; almost 60%. In value, almost 70% of the Italian market is imported. Bosch is number one, and Black & Decker number two with its own production through Star, a local company. Moreover, all the Japanese and other companies are minor, the market is close to Yugoslavia and, therefore, transport costs are low. Finally, Yugoslavia and Italy have a clearing agreement that allows unlimited import and export." One of Suhadolnik's colleagues added that the clearing agreement was one reason why Iskra entered the Italian market in the first place; Italy was the cheapest source of raw materials for cables, switches, plastic, and blades – almost half of Iskra Power Tools' raw materials.

In developing a strategy for the Italian market, Suhadolnik proposed to concentrate on that half of the professional segment which catered to specialty repair shops. "In Italy," one manager commented, "where the first thing for an Italian man is his car, there are an abundance of repair shops to service those cars." The manager then referred to a market research survey stating that Italy had about 100,000 known repair shops of all kinds; the unknown number was anyone's guess. The study also mentioned a trend in these shops toward building maintenance. "That's why," the manager concluded, "we believe Iskra can reach a 3% market share in Italy within two years, up from our present 1.3-1.5% share of market."

Western Markets as Volume OEM

It was no secret that one of Iskra's competitive- advantages in foreign markets was low price. In Germany, for example, Metabo sold one of its drills for DM 299, AEG sold a comparable drill for DM 199, and Iskra, under the Perles name, sold its drill for DM 139. A number of Iskra managers believed that a low price should be vigorously pursued. In their opinion, bolstered by favorable comments from foreign power tool manufacturers, Iskra's products possessed good value for money. Therefore, one executive added, he saw no reason why Iskra could not continue to use its low labor cost advantage and underprice the competition.

Western Markets as Niche OEM

During one meeting, Suhadolnik emphasized that Iskra was simply too small and had too few resources to offer a full range of products the way Bosch did. On the contrary, he added, Iskra should concentrate on angle grinders and drills, beginning with a new focus on R&D and production. In other words, focus on those products that represent Iskra's distinctive competence, beginning with design, followed by component sourcing and new manufacturing technology.

Taucher added, "Our output is 600,000 pieces per year. All our large European competitors are in the order of 1.5 to 2 million pieces per year. That is probably the threshold; we are much too small to compete on their terms. We are too small and we don't have a name like Bosch or AEG. That's the problem and, to be a niche manufacturer, you still need the name. We are not a Formula 1, but a Yugo on which we have put a Maserati label."

Eastern Europe

In Eastern Europe, Iskra management knew about power tool manufacturers in Poland, the DDR, Bulgaria, Czechoslovakia, and the Soviet Union. In three of these countries – Poland, Czechoslovakia, and the Soviet Union – Iskra had had some experience. In general, Suhadolnik explained that all these markets were virtually untapped and thus presented a tremendous opportunity for Iskra. Nonetheless, with the exception of the DDR, which was now part of Germany and where the one power tool manufacturer had been purchased by Bosch, none of the remaining countries could pay hard currency for Iskra's products. Therefore, Iskra was required to sell its products via counterpurchase agreements as it had done with Naradi in Czechoslovakia. Despite these countries' hard currency shortages, an executive pointed out that some of Iskra's competitors had not been discouraged from taking a further look at these markets. In particular, both Bosch and Black & Decker had planned to start manufacturing in the Soviet Union and were actively looking for personnel to run these facilities and market their products.

Exhibit 1: Iskra Power Tools Organization Chart

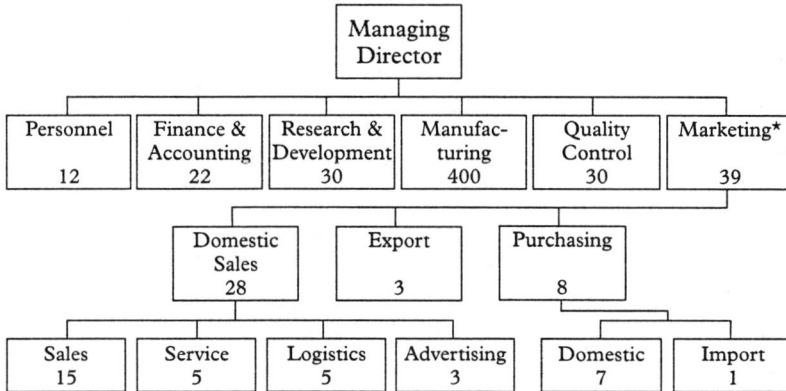

*Includes 10 people who also work in Iskra Commerce

Source: Company Records

Exhibit 2: Iskra's Main Competitors in Europe

Competitor	Location of Corporate Headquarters	Specialist (S) or Generalist (G)	Perceived Successful by Iskra
AEG	D	G	
Black & Decker	US	G	+
Bosch	D	G	+
Casals	E	G	
ELU	D	S, woodworking tools, esp. circular saws	
Fein	D	S, metalworking tools, esp. drills, and angle grinders	
Festo	D	S, same as ELU	+
Hilti	D	S, drills	+
Hitachi	J	G	
Impex	D	S,drills	
Kango	UK	S, percussion drills	
Kress	D	G	
Makita	J	G	
Metabo	D	G	
Peugeot	F	G	
Rockwell	S	G	
Rupes	I	S, table saws	
Ryobi	J	G	+
Skil	US,NL	G	
Stayer	I	G	+
Wegoma	D	S, same as ELU	

Notes:
D = Germany   USA = United States
E = Spain   J = Japan
UK = United Kingdom   F = France
I = Italy   NL = Netherlands

Source: Company Records

Exhibit 3: Competitor Positioning Diagram

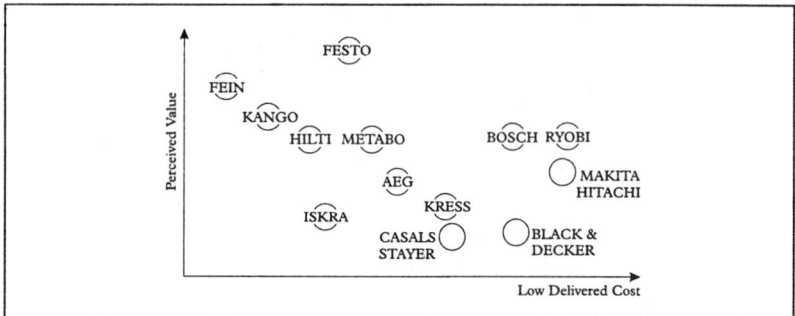

ISKRA POWER TOOLS

Exhibit 4

Overview of Iskra's Power Tool Offerings

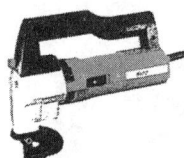

Iskra

orodje za vsake roke

ISKRA POWER TOOLS

Exhibit 4

Overview of Iskra's Power Tool Offerings

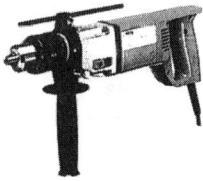

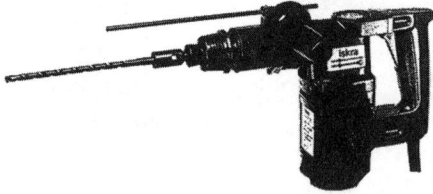

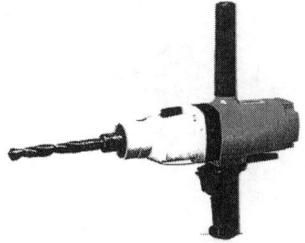

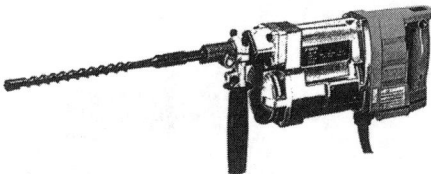

Exhibit 5: Income Statement for Iskra Power Tools

($US '000)	1986	1987	1988	1989	1990
Sales Revenue					
Domestic	25,362.9	4,842.5	18,196.4	20,658.6	24,886.9
Exports	7,559.2	12,311.6	11,882.3	10,204.6	12,815.1
Others	1,932.5	1,852.7	486.0	406.2	548.5
Total Sales	**34,854.6**	**39,006.8**	**30,564.7**	**31,269.4**	**38,250.5**
Cost of Sales	18,753.8	27,596.4	22,948.2	23,676.4	27,425.9
Gross Income	16,100.8	11,410.4	7,616.5	7,593.0	10,824.6
Selling and					
Administrative Expenses	10,065.4	8,226.5	5,032.3	5,191.8	6,020.4
Operating Income	**6035.4**	**3,183.9**	**2,584.2**	**2,401.2**	**4,804.2**
Other Income:					
Interest	58.3	3.3	36.6	**14,928.1**	797.5
Sundry Income	1,049.6	269.3	152.8	406.2	2,320.8
Total Other Income	**1,107.9**	**272.6**	**189.4**	**15,334.3**	**3,118.3**
Other Expenses:					
Interest	3,611.4	907.9	1,753.9	12,201.8	4,558.6
Sundry Expenses	1,380.5	583.0	482.5	13,664.8	4,781.7
Total Other Expenses	**4,991.9**	**1,490.9**	**2,236.4**	**2S,866.6**	**9,3403**
Obligatory Contributions					
to Community Funds	1,090.7	1521.9	507.6		
Net Income (Loss)	**1,060.7**	**443.7**	**29.6**	**(8,131.1)**	**(1,417.8)**
Allocation of					
Net Income (Loss):					
Business Fund	140.6				
Reserve Fund	269.7	292.8	26.6		
Collective					
Consumption Fund	557.2	128.6			
Joint Venture Partners	93.2	22.3	3.0		
Depreciation	1,109.7	1,402.7	1,269.9	1470.2	2,591.5
Net Income	1,060.7	443 7	29.6	(8,131.1)	(1,417.8)
Cash Generation	2,170.4	1,846.4	1,299.5	(6,660.9)	(1,173.7)

Fiscal Year Ending December 31
Source: Company Records

Exhibit 6: Iskra Balance Sheets

	1986	1987	1988	1989	1990
Current Assets:					
Bank Balances and Cash	68.2	71.9	13.7	29.0	24.3
Bills and Trade Receivables	6,068.1	6,851.3	4,954.3	5,791.2	10,257.3
Prepayments and					
other receivables	1,734.9	1,497.4	4,931.1	520.8	137.3
Current Portion of					
Long–term Receivables	29.1	1.8	0.5	408.6	184.1
Inventories:					
Raw Materials	4,104.0	3,506.8	2,289.7	856.8	3,367.0
Work–in–Process	1,538.8	1,367.4	957.8	245.9	1,148.0
Finished Products	1,367.9	1,211.4	640.0	802.2	1,750.0
Subtotal	7,010.7	6,085.6	3,888.4	1,904.9	6,265.0
Total Current Assets	**14,911.0**	**14,472.0**	**13,788.0**	**8,654.5**	**16,868.0**
Long–term Receivables	106.3	67.8	56.6	2,503.3	3,500.0
Investments	1,187.9	1,324.7	1,289.1	34.1	3,500.0
Deposits for					
Capital Expenditure	147.4	16.9	201.8	28.9	998.4
Fixed Assets:					
Land and Building	1,635.0	1,343.1	1,199.8	1,453.9	2,611.6
Equipment	12,571.4	12,804.9	11,697.2	17,554.8	32,520.9
Deferred Expenditure	0.2	15.8	14.0	188.0	
Construction in Progress	241.3	24.9	70.5	107.5	191.9
Total Gross Fixed Assets	**14,447.9**	**14,188.7**	**12,981.5**	**19,304.2**	**35,324.5**
Less: Accumulated					
Depreciation	7,238.1	7,495.2	7,542.2	12,363.5	25,093.6
Net fixed Assets	7,209.8	6,693.5	5,439.3	6,940.7	10,230.9
Intangible Assets			125.9		
Net Assets Allocated to Funds					
Reserve Fund	501.7	338.6	94.1	69.6	137.4
Collective Consumption					
Fund	1,328.1	847.3	466.1	169.6	380.6
Other Funds	43.9	21.4	9.6	21.3	168.5
Subtotal	1,873.7	1,207.3	569.8	260.5	686.5
Total Assets	**25,436.1**	**23,782.2**	**21,470.5**	**21,089.8**	**35,987.9**

Fiscal Year Ending December 31
Source: Company Records

Exhibit 6 (continued)

	1986	1987	1988	1989	1990
Liabilities and Funds					
Current Liabilities:					
Bills and Trade Payables	2,859.0	2,945.6	2,581.5	7,656.1	4,282.7
Payables for Fixed Assets	2.6	6.5	1.3		
Customers Deposits and Other Current Liabilities	4,231.5	2,648.2	2,689.5	0.9	3,836.9
Short-term Loans	3,224.9	5,381.4	5,981.1	4,325.3	7,188.4
Current Portion of Long-term Loans	1,503.3	889.5	511.1	502.7	263.2
Amounts Due to Reserve and Collective Consumption Funds	91.2	309.3	17.3		
Deferred Sales	2,158.8	1,355.9	1,111.5	172.1	4,207.3
Total Current Liabilities	**14,071.3**	**13,536.4**	**12,893.3**	**12,657.1**	**19,778.5**
Long-term Loans	3,024.2	3,362.5	3,345.4	2,788.3	5,001.0
Joint Venture Partner Investments:					
Domestic Partners	107.9	17.8	22.1	0.7	
Foreign JV Partners Business Funds	6,476.4	5,668.0	4,659.5	5,368.9	10,541.4
Other Funds:					
Reserve Fund	501.7	338.6	94.1	160.2	137.4
Collective Consumption Fund	1,236.9	847.2	448.8	69.6	380.6
Other Funds	17.7	11.7	7.3	35.2	149.0
Subtotal	1,756.3	1,197.5	550.2	265.0	667.0
Total Liabilities And Funds	**25,436.1**	**23,782.2**	**21,470.5**	**21,080.0**	**35,987.9**

Fiscal Year Ending December 31
Source: Company Records

Exhibit 7: Flowpath for Power Tool Gear Manufacturing

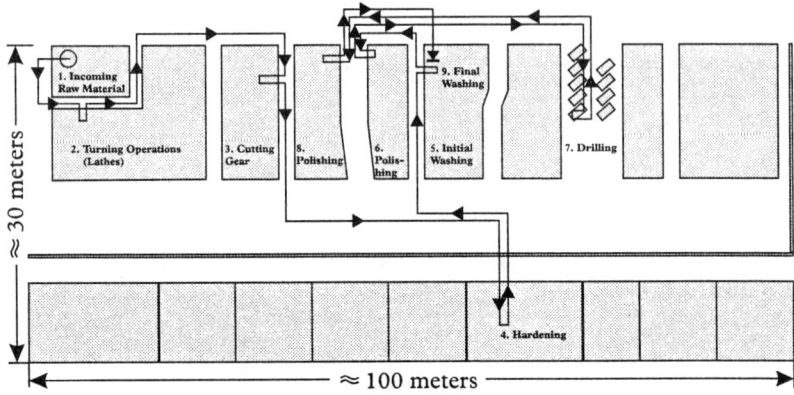

6. The Cochlear Bionic Ear

This case was prepared by Professor Sandra Vandermerwe and Research Fellow Marika Taishoff as a basis for class discussion rather than to illustrate either effective or ineffective handling of a business situation.

Creating a High-tech Market

"It's mystifying," he muttered, gazing out at the bright June light across the Rhine to Germany, which was just visible from the Basel-based European headquarters. "Our system works better than any other surgical procedure. We have a failure rate of 1%. No other kind of surgery offers that sort of result. Why aren't we selling more?" By June 1990 Mike Hirshom, CEO Worldwide, was getting increasingly concerned about the drop in sales of the Cochlear hearing implant device.

He had been with the Australian company since its inception, and had experienced all the ups and downs of getting regulatory approval and carving out an entirely new market. As one of the original members of the project team, Mike had helped take the ear implant invention of a university professor and transform it into a commercially viable product for the profoundly deaf.

"Look, "he declared, "we've managed to get rid of 3M, our biggest competitor. But still we've only succeeded in selling 3,500 units worldwide. Do you realize there are another 50,000 adults out there, if not more, who need us? Yet we can't seem to break through!"

After a brief silence Brigette Berg, CEO for Europe, responded. "Maybe we just have to face the fact that the market is smaller than we think. The only place we're still growing is in Europe, and that's only because new countries are finally beginning to include us in their health coverage schemes." Brigette had set up the Basel office in 1987 to market and distribute the Cochlear hearing system, the most technologically advanced in the world.

She went on. "Maybe we should stop worrying about volumes. After all, we've got 90% of the market in the US and 60% in Europe and the best product in the world. Why shouldn't the market be prepared to pay more for it? It makes more sense to me to consider raising the price."

She looked across at Dennis Wheeler, her American counterpart, for a reaction.

"Perhaps in Europe, where most countries just fix quotas and aren't that price sensitive," Dennis said quickly. "But then we'll risk losing the 25% of the US market which depends on government support. In my opinion, if we want to stay ahead of the competition, we've got to bring down the price even if it means finding ways to cut back on spending."

"We've got to be careful there, Dennis," Mike replied. "I would hate to hold back now. There's no way we can survive without opening up the market. Which means we must invest in marketing our implant better. At the moment, 95% of our potential customer base still doesn't even know we exist."

Cochlear's Background and Financial Profile

In 1979, after ten years of researching the possibility of implanting hearing devices into the cochlea, or inner ear, Professor Graeme Clark, head of the Department of Otolaryngology at the University of Melbourne, Australia, looked for an industry partner to help further his project. The Australian government, seeking to encourage high-tech development, called for tenders from companies able to perform a market study and write a development cost plan for commercialization. Nucleus Limited, a local company specializing in cardiac pacemakers and diagnostic ultrasound imaging equipment, won the tender.

Nucleus quickly put together a project team to engineer the product's evolution. This entailed three tasks: development of the product itself, filing the necessary patents, and developing a strategy. By September 1982, they were ready to perform the first implant which proved to be a huge success. The following year Cochlear Pty Limited was formed in Sydney to handle the new innovation's research and development, manufacturing, and sales. The first US implant took place in 1983 and, in the following year, the subsidiary Cochlear Corporation was established outside Denver, Colorado.

Real momentum began two years later when the US Food and Drug Administration (FDA) gave its approval. Only when this had been granted would US health insurers provide coverage for the product and the surgical procedure necessary to implant it. Unit sales in the US increased from 409 in 1987 to 596 the following year, although they decreased to 553 in 1989. In that same year, Cochlear produced and began clinical tests on the world's first inner ear implant for children.

Cochlear began to cultivate the European market in 1986, and in 1987 set up an office, Cochlear AG, in Basel, Switzerland. Although European countries did not have regulatory bodies such as the FDA for medical devices, the FDA's opinion was regularly adopted by the European medical authorities. By 1989, when the national health systems in certain countries began to reimburse patients in full or on a quota basis, the company's European position strengthened, with 198 units sold that year. This led to worldwide growth from 1988 to 1989 despite the decrease in US unit sales.

In an attempt to open up the Japanese market, a four-man operation called Niholl Cochlear was established in Tokyo in 1988; the company was the only player in that market. Clinical tests had been in progress since 1986 with 17 implants completed to date. However, FDA was not valid there and a governmental import license, which Cochlear was waiting for, had to be obtained. The Japanese trials cost $1.5 million. In order to get the import license, Cochlear had to provide implants free of charge.

The company reached financial break-even for the first time in 1986. Beginning in 1987 profits improved steadily, and in 1988 Cochlear became a cash generating unit for the parent company. In 1987, R&D expenditure increased significantly while operating expenses decreased as a percentage of sales. During this time, the sales and promotion expenses remained constant at 80% of general and administration expenses. The worldwide promotion budget was steady at half a million dollars a year.

The cost of goods was maintained at a relatively low level in order to fund research and clinical support. Sales force expenses were about 25% of the sales expense budget. The policy of allocating 15% of sales revenue to R&D was exceeded in 1989 due to the urgency of bringing out a new speech processor and a fall in anticipated sales volume. As a guideline, the company tried to spend 15% of its R&D budget on applications research for other developments. Any additional R&D expense had to be cleared by Nucleus, which insisted on a 20% return for all investments. *(Refer to Exhibit 1 for unit sales and financial data.)*

On Deafness and Being Deaf

There were two categories of deaf people, about equal in size: "postlingually" deaf (deaf as a result of illness, age or accident after having learned to hear) and "pre-lingually" deaf (deaf at birth). This hearing-impaired market was comprised of the *profoundly deaf* and the *severely deaf*. Severely deaf people could be helped, to a greater or lesser extent, by a hearing aid which amplified sound. Costing approximately 1,000 dollars, the customer bought this device after consulting a doctor or by going directly to a hearing aid retailer. These retailers, who were very commercialized, tended to regard Cochlear as a competitor and, therefore, a threat. Research showed that less than 20% of the people who needed a hearing aid actually bought one and, of those who did, only 50% used it. The rest put it in a bottom drawer either because it "failed to help", or because it "looked bad" and "made their handicap too evident".

People whose hearing problems were not being satisfactorily improved by hearing aids could have become a market for implants. But, as long as they could hear at all, such consumers were usually not prepared to risk surgery. In addition, they tended to mix frequently with profoundly deaf people and, thus, had an important influence on them as well as in the political arena.

Research was commissioned to assess the extent of the deaf phenomenon. It was estimated that approximately 500,000 adults worldwide were profoundly deaf, and that another 500,000 were severely deaf. Applying the rule of thumb for high-tech medical markets, it was assumed that the US accounted for roughly half of this amount.

Ordinary devices such as hearing aids were useless for the profoundly deaf, as the inner ear had become so damaged that surgical intervention was necessary. In ascertaining the real size of the profoundly deaf market, Cochlear took into account psychological and medical factors. Many people who became deaf early in life did not consider themselves "sick" and, therefore, saw no need for surgery. People with heart problems had no choice; without surgery they could die. But, typically, deaf people would try to live with their deafness.

Many potential users were wary of the concept of an ear implantation, especially of having an electronic device inside the body. One piece of research showed that over 40% of potential users were against the idea of "having wires in their head", "were afraid of doctors and hospitals", or "saw the procedure as far too risky to justify".

Cochlear therefore estimated that only about 10% of the profoundly deaf, or about 50,000 patients worldwide, were possible implant candidates. Apart from this backlog, the data suggested that another 3,000 new cases occurred each year worldwide. In 1990 there were about 10,000 profoundly deaf children in the Western world, with approximately 1,200 new cases per year. As of that time, only 50 children had been recruited to the clinical trials in the US. These trials showed good results, particularly for the postlingually deaf and for children implanted very early in life. While deaf children had to go to special schools, those who had had the Cochlear implant could often attend normal schools, although teachers had to be briefed and trained.

Generally, deaf people tended to be less well off economically than those with normal hearing; Cochlear assumed that about 10% were able to fund the implant themselves. Widely dispersed geographically, there were deaf people in all age categories, although 25% of the profoundly deaf were over 65 years of age.

Decision-making and Influences for Hearing Implants

The decision-making process for an ear implant could be complex, as there were many actors and influences well beyond just the end user. These included regulatory authorities, families, insurance companies, deaf associations and the media. Typically, patients would visit a doctor about a hearing problem. He would refer them to audiologists or ear-nose-and-throat (ENT) surgeons in hospital implant centers, where they would then be examined to see if they were suitable candidates for an implant operation.

The characteristics of patients and doctors differed in the US, Europe and Japan. American patients tended to be litigation prone and self-directed in their decisions. Although they were concerned about the implant's appearance, the prime consideration in their decision-making was whether and how much it would improve their earning potential. American specialists characteristically offered patients options rather than dictating what had to be done. European deaf patients were more influenced by the surgeon, were not as litigation minded, and the quality of life was more pivotal in their decision-making than were professional prospects. They were somewhat swayed by the look of the device, although less so than Americans. Since the main motive for Japanese patients was to cure the problem, they tended to do as their doctors told them.

To illustrate: an American doctor would typically say, "You've got three options – do nothing, have it although it's not great cosmetically, or wait till there's something better on the market." A European doctor's approach would have been more along the line, "I know it looks awful, but it's good for you." The typical Japanese patient would never have asked any questions. Doctors in America tended to adopt new medical technologies before anyone else, and so, despite the stringency of the FDA, the US was always considered the most important market. In fact, it was taken for granted that, in order to succeed worldwide, a firm first had to become established there.

Of the 7,000 American ENT specialists, who were predominantly self-employed or worked for free enterprise hospitals, 200 fitted Cochlear devices in the implant centers of which 100 did so at least once a year. The doctor was strongly influenced by the need to make a profit, while the hospital hoped to at least break even. Audiologists, a profession unique to the United States, would diagnose hearing loss as well as fit hearing aids and speech processors. The doctor and audiologist worked closely with the patient before, during, and after the operation diagnosing, fine-tuning the system, counselling and training.

Private or government insurance covered most Americans, with 60 private health insurers providing coverage for about 75% of those insured; the government welfare programs, Medicare and Medicaid, insured the rest. These reimbursement schemes invariably fell a few thousand dollars short of the average $30,000 necessary for the product and procedure. It was then either left to the patient to find the money, or for the hospital to agree to carry the shortfall. Of the 200 US hospitals which purchased the product, about half funded the shortfall either for reasons of prestige or for furthering medical research.

Because of the changes which were anticipated as a result of 1992, regulatory medical bodies similar to the FDA, but less well funded, were expected to emerge in Europe. After six years of lobbying by Cochlear, the UK's Department of Health and Social Security decided in 1990 to fund 100 units per year for three years. With Sweden beginning in 1983 and Norway in 1986, Scandinavia sponsored about 20 units per year. Workers' disability insurance covered relevant cases in Switzerland. Germany, which accounted for 60% of all European units sold, was the only country whose medical insurance system provided 100% coverage to anyone who needed the implant. In the remaining European countries, implants were funded by research and charity institutions, and were motivated on a case by case basis.

Most European surgeons, typically affiliated with state-run universities and hospitals, were not as profit oriented as the American doctors. Although held in high esteem, they were subject to "hospital politics" and were more conservative and slower to adopt new innovations. The more adventurous, who had sufficient decision-making experience and were influential politically, tended to be in their sixties. Since audiology was not usually a separate specialization in Europe, all diagnosis and fitting was done by the surgeons themselves. Of the 2,500 European ENT specialists, 40 regularly implanted and fitted the device.

In Japan, surgeons also worked primarily at state run hospitals, which were often poorly funded. These hospitals lacked audiologists, and only a small number of surgeons specialized in ear surgery. Ear surgeons were usually university professors with high status but conservative in outlook and slow to adopt innovations. The more aggressive doctors tended to be in their sixties, but those with political influence were the 80-year-olds. As of mid-1990, eight surgeons had been involved in clinical trials in Japan.

Deaf peoples' associations were organized on state, national and worldwide levels and although membership was limited to 10,000-20,000, their influence was widespread. In certain cases, Germany for instance, families were part of the lobby for government support. Some associations or charities, such as the Royal National Institute for the Deaf in the UK, were continuously lobbying on behalf of the deaf to obtain more funding from the national health system.

Encouragement from families and friends of potential patients to seek help and undergo surgery depended largely on whether those families and friends were also hearing impaired and part of the strong "non-hearing" communities which were growing worldwide.

The "deaf pride" movement had become a powerful force in the '80s with various factions. Extremists went so far as to suggest that Cochlear was experimenting with deaf peoples' brains. Mainstream members emphasized that deaf people constituted an ethnic community with their own languages and culture. Many were opposed to any pressure or opportunity for individuals to hear. They claimed it was better to have perfect communication with sign language than imperfect communication with an implant which they said relegated them to the status of second-class citizens in the "speaking" world. There were as many sign languages as languages and, because of increased mobility and the rapid internationalization of deaf associations, a move was on to develop a global version.

During the '80s, public awareness about deaf pride had grown. The film, *"Children of a Lesser God"* had raised public consciousness on an emotional level because it dealt with the philosophic issue as to whether profoundly deaf people should want to change. At that time, there was also widespread media coverage of the Washington-based Gallaudet

University exclusively for the deaf where students could follow a full university program in sign language. Public interest in this institution was enhanced when students protested over the nomination of a "non-deaf" president, forcing him to resign.

The Cochlear Hearing Implant System

The Cochlear implant was named after the *cochlea*, a part of the inner ear about the size of a pea and shaped like a snail shell. *Cochlea*, in fact, is the Greek term for "snail shell" which is what the product implant resembled. *(Refer to Exhibit 2 for a illustration of its technical characteristics.)*

People could become profoundly deaf either at birth or later in life due to injury or an illness such as bacterial meningitis or mumps. The inner ear has a multitude of sensory cells, or hair cells, each one connected to the hearing nerve which transmits sound in electrical messages to the brain. Profoundly deaf people lack or lose such sensory cells.

Hearing aids amplified sound. This instrument was only adequate for the "hard of hearing" or, in some cases, the severely deaf. The Cochlear "Bionic Ear" was for the profoundly deaf who could not hear at all. Micro-electronic engineering had been adapted to the latest research on hearing physiology to produce a high-tech system which consisted of five parts, all of which were necessary to enable the deaf person to hear:

> The *directional microphone* (fastened onto the ear) picked up sounds, converted them into electrical energy impulses which were sent to the speech processor;

> The *speech processor* (resembling a Walkman and worn externally on a belt, shoulder pouch, or in a pocket) was a computer that selected the most important electrical impulses needed for hearing noises and words, coded them and sent them to the transmitter;

> The *transmitter* (placed behind the ear) relayed the coded noises and words through the skin to the receiver/stimulator in the implant;
> The *implant* itself (surgically placed in the bone behind the ear) consisted of a *receiver and electrodes*. The receiver, comprised of an integrated circuit with more than 1,000 transistors (similar to those in a pacemaker), converted the codes into electrical signals and sent them to the electrodes. The electrodes, which substituted for the damaged sensory "hair cells", electrically stimulated the hearing nerve fibers, and thus allowed individuals to

hear a variety of high and low sound pitches which were subsequently transmitted to the brain to be deciphered. *(Refer to Exhibit 3 for illustrations of the product in use.)*

Cochlear was the only company to have a 22-channel electrode. Unlike its earlier 1-channel unit, the multichannel device enabled more sounds to be heard and could be fine-tuned for a particular pitch and loudness by the surgeon, thereby catering to the individual hearing needs of each patient. But, no matter how much customizing was done, people who had become deaf could not hear in the same way as before the impairment. They would hear new sounds which had to be correlated with ones they had heard in pre-deaf years. This process was like learning to speak a foreign language, and it took, on average, three months of training and practice. For children, this process was even longer. It could take years for those who were born deaf to be able to hear and speak.

Despite Cochlear's technological superiority, it remained impossible to predict before a surgical operation how each individual patient would respond. Research showed that about 50% of patients who had the operation were eventually able to understand speech without lipreading, and could even use the telephone. The remaining 50% benefited as well, but to significantly varying degrees – from the worst cases, where only noises and warning signals were audible, to those who could follow speech only by lip reading. The result depended on each individual – the state of the ear as well as the brain's learning capacity – neither of which could be assessed at the outset.

All R&D in Australia was done by 25 people. R&D was grouped into three areas: implant technology, electronic engineering and mechanical design. Aware that many patients would be hesitant to undergo successive surgery because of improvements in technology, Cochlear's R&D team deliberately designed its first implant version in 1982 with much more capacity than the speech processor could then handle. The idea was to enable the patient's hearing ability to be improved at some future date, without having to undergo further surgery, by updating and modifying the speech processor.

Since then, most R&D efforts had gone into improving the speech processor, with rewarding results. In the first six months of 1990, the firm sold $4 million worth of upgrades and modifications to its existing customer base. Every new model or improvement of an existing model had to go through the FDA approval procedure. New product developments could not be heavily publicized because users would put off any buying decision when they anticipated a model change, which caused serious inventory problems.

All manufacturing was done in Sydney. Using a manual process with extensive computer testing, the 50 highly skilled and specially trained plant workers produced approximately 1,400 systems annually, but there was capacity for twice that amount. The components used were very specialized and tended to come from single-goods suppliers worldwide. A constant stock was kept to eliminate delays in the event of problems in the suppliers' market and in order to get bulk prices.

There were two main areas in Cochlear's factory: the section where the implant was made under "clean room" procedures, and the non-environmentally controlled area where the speech processor "externals" were made. For the implant, subassembled parts were first manufactured and then put together in small batches of 20-30 units. The entire cycle, which required using microscopes, would take at least three months. Discrete electrical components and custom integrated circuits were soldered onto circuit boards. The external parts of the system were made using standard assembly techniques similar to those used by any small volume, high-tech electronics equipment manufacturer. Staff turnover in the external area was very low whereas in the implant section it was high.

Improving reliability of the units and the performance of the system were key priorities. It required ongoing upgrading of the electrode manufacturing methods. Although the staff generated many ideas, 99% of them could not be used because of the difficulties of working with an item as small as 0.6 mm in diameter.

Over the years, Cochlear looked at three other applications for its technology: implantable hearing aids, tinnitus, and functional electrical stimulation (FES). In 1986 it seemed that hearing aids had considerable synergy with its product. However, after having spent $1 million up to 1989, the company decided that the technology, marketing, manufacturing and profit margin formula were too different to warrant further investment. In 1989, Cochlear started work on the treatment of tinnitus ("ringing in the ears" syndrome), a condition experienced by 1 in 7 people. By mid-1990, half a million dollars had been spent. A large investment would have been necessary to perfect an FES device, an implant which electronically stimulated the nerves of paraplegics. Cochlear carried out some R&D, but decided, after losing a tender to supply the US Department of Veterans Affairs, to give the FES only low level research support.

Overview of Cochlear's Competitive Position

The American multinational 3M had entered the market at approximately the same time as Cochlear, with a lower technology product that the company believed would yield a similar hearing benefit. As 3M's price was one-third lower than Cochlear's, 3M initially dominated the market. Once Cochlear entered, however, the US firm gradually lost market share and faded from the scene late in 1989.

Although there were five major players in the worldwide market, Cochlear was the only one with FDA approval. The others – Hochmair, Hortmann, Symbion, and Minimed – were all developing similar devices and intended to get the required approval. Because some European doctors protested that Cochlear was making too much money, one or two university medical schools in Europe, including the University College of London, developed their own low budget version of the implant. Although such hearing systems, distributed only through the universities' clinics, were only one-tenth the price of Cochlear's device, they were not regarded as sufficiently reliable to pose a serious competitive problem.

While Cochlear was confident, given its 3,500 satisfied patients worldwide and the FDA stamp, that it had a clear competitive advantage, the company constantly monitored the competitive strength of the main manufacturers, using four criteria: *1) organization size and professionalism; 2) technology; 3) clinical benefit and effectiveness; and 4) safety.*

Neither the Hochmairs, an Austrian team, nor Hortmann of Germany were considered serious opponents by Cochlear, given their lag in the important categories of clinical benefit, effectiveness and safety. However, the two American firms, Symbion and Minimed, were both perceived as potential threats to future sales.

Symbion, a firm associated with the University of Utah, was in the clinical trial stage. It had managed to produce a unit which, while using a much lower level of implant technology, nonetheless achieved the same hearing performance, and at the same price, as Cochlear's device. Symbion's accomplishment was due to putting considerably more effort into the speech processor than into the implant. A plug which connected the microphone headset to the implant by penetrating the skin created both an aesthetic and a safety disadvantage as the passageway could permit infection to enter the inner ear and the brain. It was considered a flexible product, however, because any kind of stimulation could be used whereas the Cochlear device only allowed radio wave transmission.

Affiliated with the well-known University of California at San Francisco medical school, Minimed began its research in 1966. Although its device had only 16 channels, Minimed's performance could potentially be as good as Cochlear's due to its capacity to better represent certain non-speech sounds. Because of problems with its micro-chip technology, the company had not yet been able to begin clinical trials, needed to receive FDA approval and medical coverage. There were rumors that the problem would soon be solved and by 1991 Minimed would be making clinical trials.

The company annually analyzed market share. With doctors eager for more players to enter the field, Cochlear had, in making its projections for 1990 and 1991, factored in the entry of Minimed and a growth in market share for Symbion. *(Refer to Exhibit 4 for market shares from 1982-1989 and projections for 1990.)*

Cochlear's Marketing Strategy

Cochlear treated the ear implant market as a single one. The logic was that the medical profession and deaf associations were linked internationally through medical conferences and medical journals.

The product was identical worldwide. All units and promotional material clearly identified the Cochlear brand name and logo, and the 22-channel feature was used extensively to differentiate the product as the one with maximum clinical benefits.

Cochlear decided early on that it could not devote equal time and resources to both aesthetics and performance. Convinced that the latter would be the more important criterion for the market, the company decided to position itself as the most technologically sophisticated and clinically superior.

In early 1990, market research confirmed what top management had suspected: performance was more important than either price or appearance. This survey, which was intended to gain a better understanding of the needs and wants of the implant market, was conducted among 14 Cochlear implant patients, 11 audiologists, a surgeon and the director of an implant center in one of the US hospitals which fitted Cochlear devices. The results revealed that implant patients considered performance to be the most important factor. In fact, on a scale of 1-10, performance was ranked 8 out of 10, price 5, and appearance 3.

These people were extremely happy to be able- to hear and, if given a choice, would have opted for an implant system that allowed them to hear speech, music, and environmental sounds over one where the external units were either cordless or worn behind the ear, but offered lower performance. Nevertheless, the patients did acknowledge that a segment of the deaf market would consider a Cochlear implant if a behind-the-ear system became available, and would probably accept a lower performance level to get a device so small and unobtrusive.

Cochlear had given some thought to the cosmetic appeal of its external units, particularly the speech processor. Initially, it had been made from plastic pipe, then from stainless steel and, in September 1989, a more contemporary design was developed using molded plastic.

For three months after surgery, patients had to return to the hospital or the doctor for training; check-ups were then repeated annually. The non-usage rate of all implant patients worldwide was 1%. For the very few patients who experienced a problem with their unit, there were doctors trained by Cochlear to "troubleshoot". If a unit proved faulty, it was sent back to the regional office for repair. While the implant was guaranteed for five years, it was expected to last a lifetime. The speech processor had an average breakdown time of three years, and each system had a three-year warranty. Hospitals had to maintain adequate supplies of spare units at all times to avoid any risk that the patient could be incapacitated due to a faulty product.

A premium price strategy was deliberately used and strictly maintained in order to highlight the Cochlear system's unique technology. The average $30,000 cost to patients included the Cochlear system as well as all hospital and surgical expenses. On average, the Cochlear device was priced at $17,000 for both adults and children, although it was slightly more in Europe and even higher in Japan. The figure was three times the price of the 3M model when it had been on the market. Symbion's price was equal to Cochlear's, and it was rumored that Minimed would enter clinical trials at the same price level. Hochmair and Hortmann were priced in the middle range.

Cochlear distributed its products directly in three regions – Denver, Basel and Tokyo – each one headed by its own CEO reporting to the Sydney head office. The salespeople, clinically trained audiologists and engineers, called on doctors and hospitals. They were supported by a team of clinical experts who advised, counseled and handled any problems that arose, using clinical support centers in each region. These support centers would also work with patients who wanted an implant but were unsure how to handle the finances or apply for insurance. Every office also maintained a technical service team, reimbursement specialists, and 2-3 marketing people to organize conferences, handle PR and prepare brochures.

In the US, some private audiologists who had fitted and tested hearing devices would leave their own practices and, on a part commission basis to help cope with the workload, sell Cochlear implants. Some extra audiologists in hospitals were funded by Cochlear. In Europe, where the ENT surgeon was also the audiologist, the Basel-based European headquarters oversaw all sales except for the UK, Scandinavia and Israel, which were handled in London. Any direct selling by doctors would have been regarded as unethical in Europe. In Germany, Cochlear managed to persuade one of the largest healing aid retailers to stock its cables and spare batteries.

Upgraded units became an important part of Cochlear's marketing activities. The $4 million in sales in 1990 was achieved by reaching users through doctors and offering a special reduction in price (from $6,000 to $4,000) if a decision were made by a particular date. The upgrade was introduced and launched at a promotional event hosted on a river boat. This event was followed by direct mail and by papers presented at conferences by doctors who had experienced improved performance during clinical trials. Most patients paid for their own new units in the US because the insurance companies refused to pay. In Europe, they were funded by the national health systems.

Publicity was aimed at patients and doctors. Initially, the novelty of the implant innovation made it relatively easy to get media attention and, on the whole, newspapers, radio, magazines and TV provided reasonable coverage, particularly of successful cases. Although no formal market research had been done, the Cochlear top team estimated that company awareness worldwide was 70-80% amongst ENT surgeons, and around 5% amongst potential users.

The company encouraged medical and scientific journal articles about its product and occasionally paid doctors' travel expenses when they delivered papers at conferences. The system was exhibited at major worldwide medical conferences, while local community forums and meetings with education departments and school authorities were routinely organized. Because it could be considered unethical to directly approach such supporting charities as the Rotary Club, Cochlear only provided information when needed.

Promotional material was distributed to doctors, hospitals, audiologists, and hearing aid retailers to enable them to respond to queries. Post-operative instructional booklets were provided for patients, and a newsletter was sent out from each sales office to doctors, to the existing patient base as well as to local family self-help events. *(Refer to Exhibit 5 for examples of promotional material)*. Lectures were given to any deaf association on request, and papers were presented at conferences on deafness whenever possible. Inevitably, though, these activities engendered a certain amount of antagonism, such as walk-outs or other forms of protest from "deaf pride" members in the audience.

Mike Hirshom continued talking. "The FDA is on the verge of giving us the go ahead for children. That's a market worth another 10,000 units provided we do the job right. Parents will do anything to help their children, so I expect that market to be much easier and quicker to penetrate than it was for adults."

He stood up and walked to the window watching the last rays of sunshine disappearing over the horizon. "For a start, we could increase our sales force. That way, we could break into new territories and increase the call rates with existing doctors."

"What about the additional costs?" Brigette inquired.

"It's not a big deal," Mike answered. "Even if we doubled our sales force worldwide, we would only have to sell 15% more units. The Sydney factory can easily handle the extra volumes."

"We could, of course, use the capacity to make a cheaper second model instead," Dennis Wheeler suddenly suggested. "Maybe then we could get into some new countries like Turkey, Greece, the Middle East and Southeast Asia. Come to think of it, that could also push up our numbers in the States and maybe even in Europe."

"That would ruin our image," Brigette responded. "If we want to keep our position, we have to stick to making the highest performance quality even if it means raising our price. Isn't there a section of the US market that could take a price hike, Dennis?"

"Yeah, maybe 10%, max 20% but of the privately insured market," Dennis replied hesitantly. "Don't forget, though, that this may be exactly what Symbion and Minimed are waiting for – to grab market share."

Mike listened carefully. He knew that he would soon have to recommend to his board ways to maintain profitability despite sagging sales and more threatening competition. He agreed that Cochlear's future hope was its hearing technology. But, somehow the company had to get that technology used and appreciated...

Exhibit 1: Unit Sales and Financial Data

Unit Sales	1987	1988	1989
(including clinical trials)			
USA	409	596	553
Worldwide	574	798	839

Dollar Sales*			
(excluding upgrades)			
Worldwide	8.7	13.0	14.2
R&D	1.1	2.3	3.2
General and administration expenses	6.9	7.1	7.0
Promotion expenses	0.6	0.6	0.6
Cost of goods sold	constant	constant	constant

* *in $ millions*

Exhibit 2: Technical Characteristics

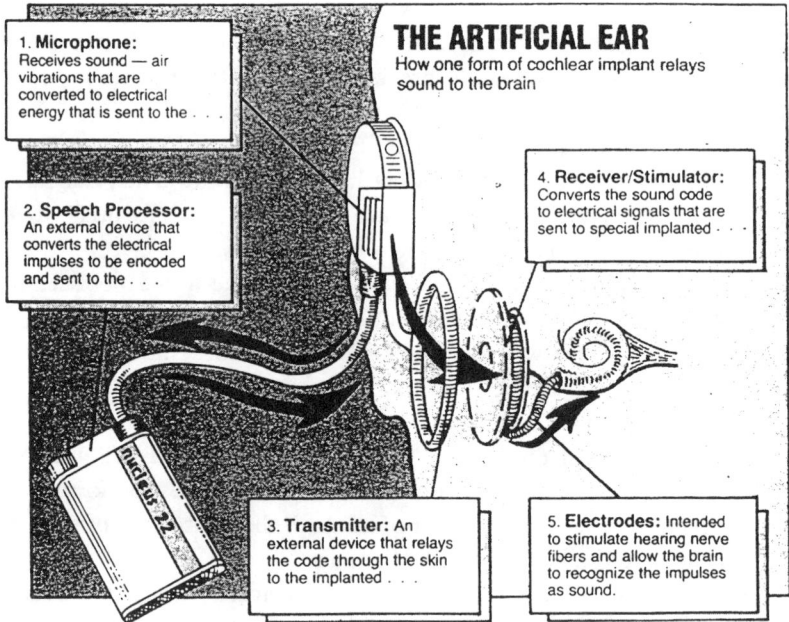

THE ARTIFICIAL EAR
How one form of cochlear implant relays sound to the brain

1. **Microphone:** Receives sound — air vibrations that are converted to electrical energy that is sent to the . . .

2. **Speech Processor:** An external device that converts the electrical impulses to be encoded and sent to the . . .

3. **Transmitter:** An external device that relays the code through the skin to the implanted . . .

4. **Receiver/Stimulator:** Converts the sound code to electrical signals that are sent to special implanted . . .

5. **Electrodes:** Intended to stimulate hearing nerve fibers and allow the brain to recognize the impulses as sound.

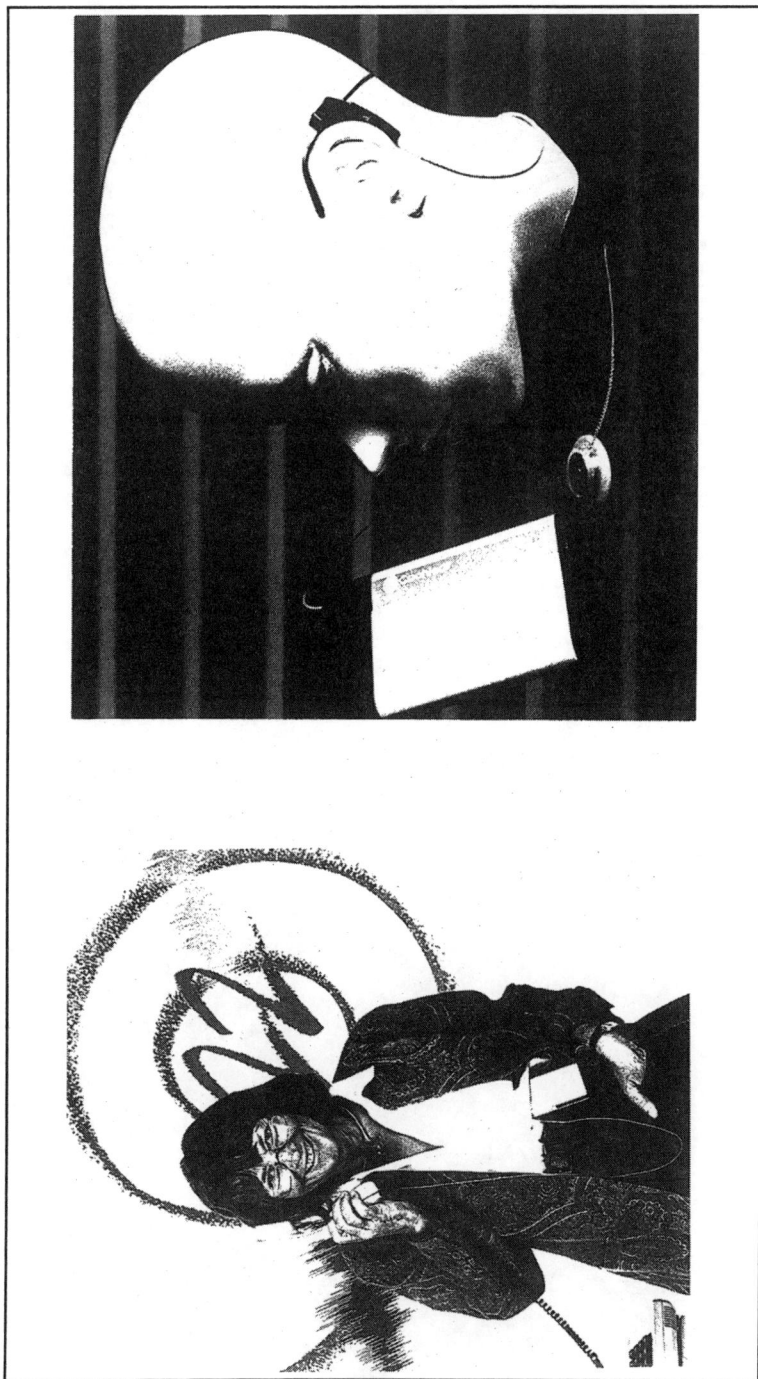

Exhibit 3: Illustrations of Products in Use

Exhibit 4: Market Share and 1990 Projections

%Market Share

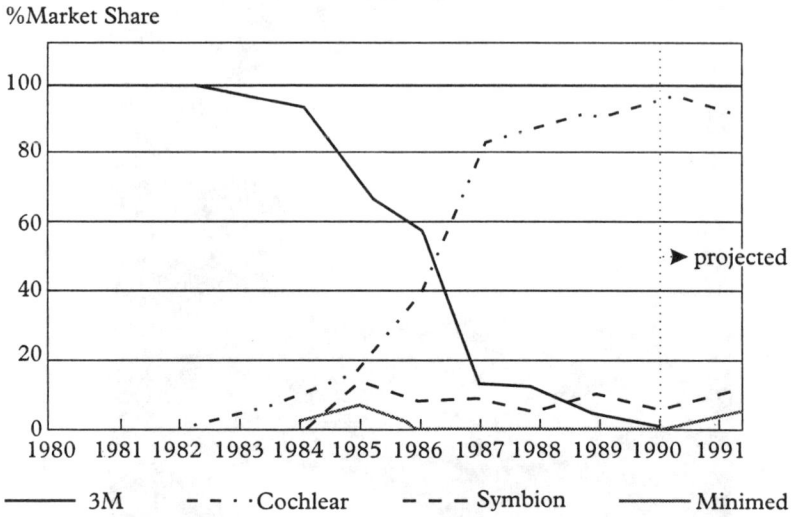

```
———— 3M        – – ··Cochlear      – – – Symbion        ———— Minimed
```

Exhibit 5: Examples of Promotional Material

OTOBRIEF

from ©Cochlear
a member of the nucleus *group*

EDITION 4, JULY 1989

RESEARCH NEWS

In this edition of Otobrief we highlight a few of the research studies based on the Nucleus Cochlear Implant System that are proceeding world-wide. We extend our thanks to those people contributing articles on their projects for inclusion in Otobrief.

Another Option For The Profoundly Deaf

As the cochlear implant becomes the treatment of preference for postlinguistically deafened adults, attention has been turned to this previously somewhat neglected population and research into developing devices to benefit the severely and profoundly deaf has taken new directions. In collaboration with the University of Melbourne, Cochlear is developing yet another potential world beater originating from the University of Melbourne. The technology is an 8 channel electrotactile device affectionately known as the "Tickle Talker".

In contrast to vibrotactile devices which provide a pattern of vibrations on the skin surface (usually on the wrist or sternum depending on where they are worn) and other electrotactile devices which electrically stimulate superficial nerve endings, the Tickle Talker electrically stimulates the digital nerve bundles of one hand to provide information which will augment lipreading. Auditory information provided by hearing aids (if they are worn) can also be enhanced. Melbourne University is currently conducting a trial of a second stage prototype and early results with the device have demonstrated significant improvements in the communication abilities of a small group of severe-to-profound and profoundly deaf adult and pediatric patients.

The project initially began in 1985 when Professor Graeme Clark and Dr Peter Blamey developed the first prototype Tickle Talker at the University of Melbourne. The Tickle Talker has a

handset and connecting cable, a stimulator unit, a speech processor (a modified version of the current WSP) and a microphone. The handset provided eight electrodes positioned on either side of four plastic rings. When in place, these electrodes were situated over the digital nerve bundles on the four fingers of one hand. The electrodes were connected to the stimulator unit by way of cables, joining at a wrist band. The wrist band also contained a common (or return) electrode which made contact with the skin on the underside of the wrist.

Results of a pilot study (Cowan et al, 1988) involving four hearing impaired subjects and seven normally hearing subjects greatly encouraged the Melbourne University team. The results demonstrated that the prototype Tickle Talker was able to provide users with prosodic and spectral information which significantly aided speech understanding.

Bob Cowan, who heads the Tickle Talker clinical programme has found that a minimum period of forty hours is necessary to train a person to use the device effectively. His results, however, show that performance continues to improve with additional training.

Continued on page 2

Case History
1st Deaf and Blind Person who Received a Cochlear Implant

On June 5, 1985, Jo Helen Mann became the first deaf and blind person to receive the Nucleus 22 Channel Cochlear Implant System. Surgery was performed by Dr. Jack Hough at Baptist Medical Center, Oklahoma City, Oklahoma. Blind from birth, due to agenesis of the optic nerve, Jo Helen had also experienced a gradual hearing loss beginning in her teenage years. The etiology of her hearing loss is unknown. At the age of 17, she began wearing amplification and continued the use of hearing aids for 20 years. In 1977, Jo Helen lost all her hearing in her better ear and could perceive only noise on the poorer side. She could no longer understand speech. Jo Helen had to quit her job and give up her home. She experienced a divorce and lost her daughter in a custody case. "It was a horrible time for me," Jo Helen says, "I wallowed in self-pity. Finally, I realized there were some positive steps for me to take to begin adjusting to life as a deaf/blind person".

Jo Helen found a way to communicate with people using the Tellatouch, a device with a typewriter plus a braille writer keyboard. She spent 15 months at the Helen Keller Center learning daily living skills, mobility, communication, speech, and preparing to be a teacher's aide. As a result, Jo Helen found a job at the Oklahoma School for the Deaf and Blind.

Continued on page 2

Jo Helen, Cisternas et Perez Porch, Baptist Medical Center, Oklahoma City

Brochure for audiologist, doctors, children an their families, sent during clinical trials

Exhibit 5b: Example of Promitional Material

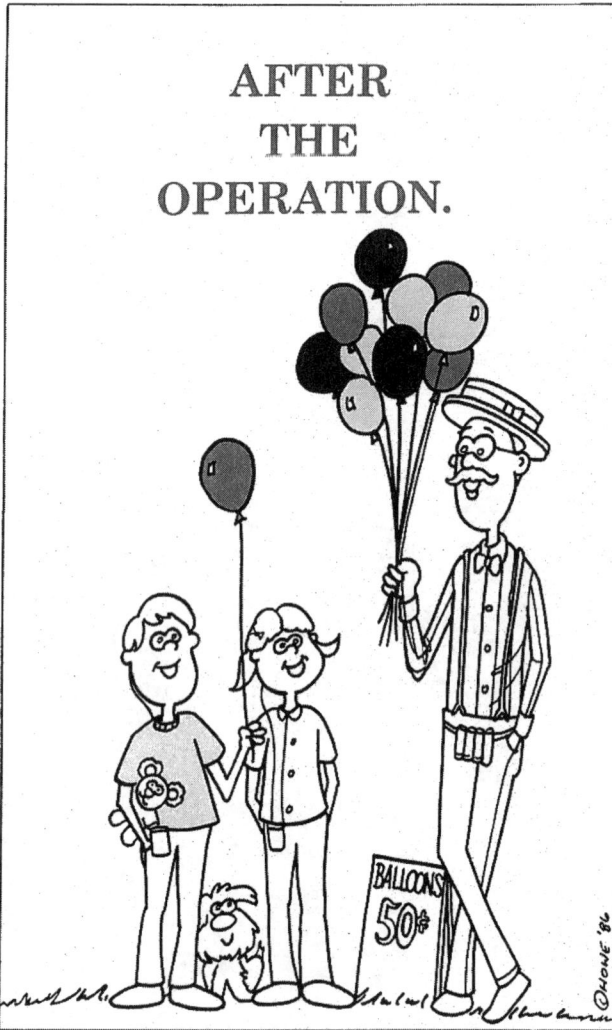

Idea by Dianne J. Mecklenburg

Information newsletter sent to hospitals, doctors and audio-logists

7. Jac Jacobsen Industrier A/S

This case was prepared by Professor Per V. Jenster and Research Associate Bethann Kassman as a basis for class discussion rather than to illustrate either effective or ineffective handling of a business situation. This case was developed as an Institutional Project on the Management of Internationalization and conducted in collaboration with the Industrial Development Authority of Ireland.

Acquiring a Competitor

On a rainy Monday in May 1990, Alv Inge Karlsen, chief executive officer of Jac Jacobsen Industrier (JJI) A/S of Oslo, Norway, looked around the meeting room at the group of managers from the firm's Luxo division. He had just introduced and welcomed his successor, Lars Harlem, and was about to announce the unexpected acquisition of Ledu, Luxo's fiercest competitor for the past 20 years.

The look of surprise on the faces of the country managers and functional executives quickly changed to satisfaction as they thought of the agonizing hours, tapped energy and scarce resources expended on this competitor in the European and US sectors. The managers were not slow to volunteer their comments: "One down, and one to go!" "No more bickering with distributors over margins *vis-à-vis* Ledu!" Others said, "Why spend money buying Ledu when you could have given it to marketing and R&D; we could have beaten them in the market with better budgets!" "What are our distributors going to say, how are we going to respond? How are we going to manage the channel conflict?"

Alv Karlsen and Lars Harlem exchanged glances as each thought about the issues of growth and control which the acquisition strategy raised. They had anticipated some of these reactions, but so many opinions was more than they had bargained for. Nevertheless, the Ledu organization had to be dealt with. Alv Karlsen leaned back in his chair and said, "Gentlemen, these are all valid concerns. However, I would very much like to hear how you propose we deal with the international integration of Ledu and Luxo?"

History

Jac Jacobsen was founded in 1934 as a textile machinery company. Over the years, the focus of the company had changed to lighting, with all subsequent growth based on the phenomenal success of its Luxo Lamp.

The Luxo lamp, one of the world's more original designs, was a parabolic lamp with a flexible arm, developed by an Englishman. Mr. Jacobsen had found the lamp in a case of textile machinery. After receiving a manufacturing license to produce the Luxo lamp in Scandinavia, he subsequently redesigned it and gave it a new look.

The first Luxo lamps were produced and sold in Norway in 1937. During the war, the operation in Norway had to close. However, in 1939, a manufacturing company was established in Sweden. This company operated at full capacity during the war years and was highly profitable. When the war ended, the Swedish company represented a solid financial base for the international expansion in the years to come.

The company had started with a single product model. Over the years many new models were developed, all based on the original Luxo arm principle. Currently, the product portfolio included lamps for a number of applications for the office environment, health care sector, industrial segments, etc. By 1990, the original Luxo lamp accounted for no more than 1% of total sales.

When the patents for the original lamps expired in the late '60s, extensive copying took place throughout the world. Consequently, the company gradually upgraded its products and changed its strategy. It began producing asymmetric light for the high end of the modern office market – for premium offices and high profile locations where the quality of light was important. With the acquisition of Ledu in late 1990, that strategy was under evaluation.

In the USA, Jac followed a dynamic acquisition policy. Beginning in 1981, 11 companies in the lighting field were acquired over a seven year period. These acquisitions enabled the company to become the eighth largest producer of lighting in the US, and one of Norway's most internationally active manufacturing companies.

In 1989 the company was organized into three divisions, with two of them in lighting (these two divisions were Jac Jacobsen International A.S. Europe, and USA Lighting). The Group Holdings also included Jac Jacobsen Industries, Inc., USA, an American division, comprising the companies that had been acquired (in which Jac Jacobsen owned a 47.5% interest), and Jac Jacobsen Enterprises, Inc., Canada, a holding company which owned Luxo Lamp Ltd., Canada. *(Refer to Exhibit 1 for further details of Group Holdings and Exhibit 2 for the Consolidated Balance Sheet for December 1988 and 1989.)*

International Growth

The first phase of Jac Jacobsen's internationalization process occurred in the late 1940s. The company located distributors and sold lamps in England and on the Continent. It was also during this period that the company made its first approach to enter the US market, but the results of these efforts were not impressive. The company realized that it had to get around the heavy trade barriers that existed at that time by establishing its own companies in the local markets. During the 1950s, therefore, new companies were established in Denmark, Germany, the US (New York) and Canada (Montreal), and a period of significant sales growth commenced.

In the mid-1960s, clear signs of what a company official termed "volume disease" became apparent – rapid sales growth, high costs and deteriorating profits led to frequent and serious liquidity problems. When Alv Inge Karlsen was hired as managing director in 1964, he started to reorganize the company and build up the management control systems. Decision-making was centralized in Norway, where much of the production was also concentrated. Over the next five years, profitability improved significantly and, toward the end of the 1960s, the company appeared to be in good financial condition. These years, however, were a period with only modest sales growth because the focus was on planning and budgeting.

At the beginning of 1970, Norway found oil in the North Sea. Fear that this discovery would lead to higher labor costs and a strengthening of the Norwegian currency led Jac Jacobsen to a decision to contract out a major part of the production from Norway to subsidiaries in the US and Canada. (At that time, the US dollar had started to "float", and the dollar/krone rate changed significantly over a short period of time.) Because Norway was not a member of the EEC, the company also found it necessary to establish a production unit within the EEC, thus a new plant was built in northern Italy in 1971.

Along with the transfer of production outside Norway, the company saw the need to strengthen the organizations of the subsidiary companies. A number of new key local people were hired, most of them with a strong marketing background. Nearly all of these people were successful and, within a few years, the management – the old "entrepreneurs" – in the various subsidiaries had been replaced. Again, reorganization took place. Decision-making that had been centralized in Norway was, to a high degree, delegated to frontline managers. The group was organized into divisions, and it became a profit center where responsibilities were clearly defined and substantial profit-sharing possibilities were available to key employees. The parent company became, in effect, a holding company. Fast growth and solid profitability followed.

In the late 1970s, extensive numbers of counterfeit Luxo products made by Far East manufacturers began to flood the US market. Jac Jacobsen's high market share and premium price were particularly vulnerable to copying. In response to this threat, Jac Jacobsen decided to change the strategy of the US division. Instead of fighting the Far East competition, it was decided that the US division should enter new fields in the lighting market, while securing its growth through acquisitions. At the same time, the European division would concentrate all its efforts in traditional areas in order to balance this risk. When the first acquisition was made in 1981, Jac Jacobsen had one company in the US (Luxo Lamp Corporation) with sales of $15 million. By 1988 that one company had become a division comprising 12 companies with sales close to $100 million. At that time, almost 70% of the group's total sales were being generated by the US division.

The acquisition strategy in the US was a great success. However, continued diversified growth in the US would, management feared, tie up too many resources, thus preventing the company from making the most of even greater opportunities which were emerging in Europe. The company also realized that the technical expertise and knowledge gained through the US acquisitions achieved little added value for the European organization; the anticipated synergies did not occur because American companies were not able to meet the local requirements of European markets.

The company had originally planned to launch a public issue in the United States to raise funds needed for US operations. For various reasons, this approach proved impractical. Instead, it was decided to carry out extensive restructuring. The aim was to reduce the exposure in the United States and enhance the core business. Through this restructuring, the two original Luxo companies in the United States and Canada were "bought back" by the parent company. The remaining companies (the acquired companies) became the objects of a Management Buy Out (MBO), in which a group of investors, headed by the American division's former management team, acquired a majority of the shares. These companies continued to operate under the name Jac Jacobsen Industries Inc. The parent company in Norway remained the largest shareholder, but its holdings were reduced to 47.5%.

Acquisition Strategy

The basic concept underlying the acquisition strategy in the US was to establish new business in other areas of the lighting market in order to compensate for the expected loss of market share within the traditional segments of the market, due to the heavy Far East competition. A detailed, long-term strategy for this new venture was developed including a set of criteria to evaluate potential acquisition candidates. These criteria identified the following:

1. Companies which were profitable in their own right;
2. Companies whose products were already commercial;
3. Companies which were niche players;
4. Small companies which were either in a complimentary area of lighting or with products that could expand Luxo's offerings.

The company also made it clear that it was not interested in "turn-around projects" or "bargain opportunities".

The acquisition strategy was further enhanced by establishing a holding company (Jac Jacobsen Incorporated) in the US, which was used as a vehicle for identifying and acquiring suitable candidates. The company recognized the importance of separating the acquisition related tasks from those of the operating companies. A small professional staff was responsible for identifying and evaluating acquisition candidates, overseeing the "due diligence" process, analyzing staff and organizational issues, and supervising external consultants brought in for specific analytical tasks. This was a costly process that included management reviews, and interviews with end users and distributors to determine the market perception of the potential acquisition candidate.

With few exceptions, Jac Jacobsen's strategy included assimilation of the acquired company. Following the purchase, a JJI team was sent to the new company to educate the staff about corporate philosophy, personnel and reporting requirements, financial accounting practices, and other steps necessary to insure immediate alignment. At the same time, Jac Jacobsen tried to keep the original management team in place whenever possible, and to maintain the purchased company's identity and products.

Market Strategy: The Luxo Division in Europe

The Luxo companies were the market leaders in "task lighting" for offices in major markets in Europe, and also a major supplier to the hospital/health care sector. Other competitors were not as broadly based within the product ranges or as internationally positioned as Jac Jacobsen. As the company entered the 1990s, its main focus was the modern office environment, especially lighting systems that interfaced with computers and ones that were energy efficient.

The marketing strategy for Europe called for quick market penetration by concentrating on the end user directly. The niche strategy of the "modern office" was to be expanded by broadening product offerings with "uplighters", both freestanding and wall-mounted. The industrial sector was receiving more emphasis than the health care sector, but both areas were being targeted as growth areas.

The hospital segment presented a challenge because the market was dominated by German suppliers; however, Jac Jacobsen produced for hospital wards, outpatient centers and physicians' offices, rather than specifically for the hospital industry.

Product Strategies: The Luxo Division in Europe

The stated product strategy emphasized "international" products that looked the same and were sold throughout the Western industrial world. However, local market preferences differed among the major markets in Europe. Thus, the product development and marketing strategies of the production units in Norway and Italy continued to vary greatly.

In northern Europe, Jac Jacobsen was the leading international supplier of ergonomic/asymmetric lighting. The trend toward ergonomic awareness was very strong in Sweden, and Jac Jacobsen believed Norway and Denmark would follow that trend in the early 1990s. Although the trend was expected to spread to Germany and England also, Luxo, as the leading supplier, intended to stimulate this market demand.

In southern Europe, the preference was almost entirely for design and halogen lighting, which continued to be the driving force of Luxo Italiana. Its strategy was to expand the product range further into the lighting sector for projects and specifiers with indirect lighting systems.

These differences between northern and southern Europe led to difficulties in having uniform pricing, brochures, sales material, etc. Because of these dissimilarities, distribution was tailored to the needs of each market. Marketing and sales strategies also differed among markets and between the two Luxo product lines.

On the other hand, this "dual" Luxo product strategy also created increased opportunities, as all major markets could be attacked with two different Luxo product lines, thus expanding the Luxo total business growth and market position.

European Trends

Total sales growth in Europe for 1987-1989 had been positively dominated by sales companies in Sweden and Germany, which respectively had sales increases of 20-25% and 15-18% per year. Sales projections indicated that both markets would continue to grow, with Germany identified as the market having the strongest real growth potential. Sales in Norway and Denmark had stagnated in the late 1980s, due to difficult national economic situations, but increased sales growth was expected through new product offerings in the early 1990s.

Australia and England, both new subsidiaries, were affected by recession-like economies that had high interest rates. Industry experts felt that England would bounce back in the early 1990s, but Australia would have to fight recession for a longer period of time.

Italy, Spain and France all experienced slow growth in 1989, and it was anticipated that 1990 would also be slow, but that growth could be expected through new product introductions in i991. *(Refer to Exhibit 5 for the total sales growth per market.)*

Sales Organization

Luxo felt that a strong sales organization in major markets was its backbone. Thus, with the exception of Italy and Spain, where multi-company agents were used, most of the European market was served by Luxo's district salespeople. To compete in the project market, it became increasingly necessary to educate the sales personnel on a more technical level to enhance their communication with lighting consultants and architects. The 1991 budget added project salespeople to the sales organization to provide this knowledge on specific, new product introductions. *(Refer to Exhibit 3 for details of the sales organization.)*

The European distribution channels used by the company varied greatly depending on the markets served, as summarized below *(refer also to Exhibit 4)*:

Norway	53.8% through wholesalers
Sweden	59.5% direct to office retail
Italy	56.0% direct to lighting retail
England	25.5% through medical supply houses
Germany	22.0% direct to end user

These local/national differences in distribution patterns had a strong influence on marketing strategies and tactics, which consequently differed from market to market.

Major Competitors in Europe

The European lighting industry was very fragmented and, as Luxo Europe moved into new market segments, its competitors multiplied and became less well defined. In design and tube lighting, competitors were numerous and diffused, while the industrial market had few competitors. In the area of office lighting, the competition was consistent on a year-to-year basis. The economy market continually flourished with an infinite number of suppliers but with little real impact on Jac Jacobsen.

The task light market was divided into two standard categories; Consumer and Professional/Industrial task lighting. Consumer task lighting for private homes, was of little interest to Luxo, due to low prices and low margins. The exception was the high-priced design lighting from Luxo Italiana.

Of more interest to Luxo was Professional/Industrial task lighting for the work environment – for modern offices and industrial workplaces, particularly computer workstations, which required better quality ergonomic lighting.

In the modern office market segment, Ledu and Waldmann were the major competitors for ergonomic task lighting. In the interior design (task lighting) area, Luxo competed with Italian companies like Artimede, Targetti, PAF and Iguzzini. Most of the competitors had narrow geographical penetration of their product lines with large market share within their defined market segments.

In the indirect lighting systems area, Luxo competed with Ledu, Fagerhults, Concorde and Waldmann, in the tube systems area with

Siemens, Philips, Staff, Erco and Hoffmeister. The Luxo introduction of the "Cornice" and a new range of uplighters was designed to place Jac Jacobsen in a better position against these competitors. In this project market, competitive price and ability to fill technical specifications were of crucial importance.

In the "industrial" market, Waldmann was the major competitor. Much of the strategy developed in the industrial area was designed to allow Jac Jacobsen to enter the market against Waldmann.

The "medical" market was quite diffused; however, the dominant players were Hanau, Verre et Quartz, Dr. Mach and Fagerhults. (Refer to Exhibit 6 for a product/mix trend analysis.)

In the "medium to low price" market, Luxo competed with companies like Ledu, Lival, Massive and Fase. Lival had moved away from producing inexpensive task lighting towards a more comprehensive range including spot and track lighting. Both Massive and Fase had a wide range of products suitable for consumer segments. The latter two dominated the lower end category and had a firm grip in the department store market. There were also a number of smaller producers who sold primarily to department stores. Luxo's strategy was to de-emphasize this end of the market. However, the less costly products were the largest product group, in terms of volume, and provided products to use against competitors.

Research & Development

Jac Jacobsen saw a future in "well-designed functional lighting". To that end, it devoted 5-7% of the ex-factory budget to research and development, emphasizing electronic assembly and new products in the medical, office and industrial segments. Although R&D was originally focused totally in Norway, over time some research was delegated to the US and Italy. R&D in the recently acquired Ledu was to be coordinated to some extent with R&D in Luxo. Continual knowledge transfer amongst all divisions was a priority, although this was a difficult process because electrical standards differed from one country to another. 1992 was seen as a positive development in facilitating technical exchanges among divisions.

Jac Jacobsen's marketing strategy called for the development of new quality concepts in lighting and achieving a sustainable competitive advantage in the industry. In order to reach these objectives, R&D had to be strengthened and resources committed to assure success in the development of new products. Additionally, R&D would concentrate on unique product development and bringing new products to market before the competition. Thus, it was critical to shorten the new product approval process in order to enter the market in a timely fashion.

To shorten the time frame between development and the market, Jac Jacobsen needed to reevaluate its production process. If the firm wanted to serve more than 10 different markets with "international" or "global" products, whether produced in Norway or Italy, restructuring was necessary. However, the factory in Norway continued to develop Scandinavian models based on ergonomic/asymmetric lighting technology and functional lighting needs, while the factory in Italy maintained development of high quality design products, basically for the Italian market. The production of "global" products required that each factory make a more thorough evaluation of the demand for each type of lighting and have a greater sensitivity to the needs of the international marketplace. In order to meet the time factor demands of entering the market quickly, better market analysis communication in the early stages of development had to be achieved. In addition, the market research had to extend beyond the sales organizations and deeper into the markets in cooperation with the Luxo sales companies. To facilitate this process, an Italian-speaking engineer was hired for the R&D department in Norway and more funds were allocated for hiring outside competence when needed. A lighting expert, whose tasks were to educate the sales personnel and agents in general lighting concepts, and to increase technical information about lighting throughout the companies was also added to the staff.

Using outside designers was an accepted practice in Italy, coordinated by Luxo, Italiana. The Italian designs were highly innovative and consistently won a number of design awards, elevating Luxo's image.

Acquisition of Ledu

Ledu and Jac Jacobsen's history went back a long way. Not only had Ledu and Luxo been major competitors for 40 years, but the founder of Ledu had also previously been a general manager for Luxo's Swedish subsidiary. Although the European strategy was one of organic growth, Jac Jacobsen was very interested when Ledu became a potential acquisition candidate. It was felt that the JJI Group would be more strongly positioned in the international market segments of task lighting with a combined Ledu-Luxo ownership.

As perceived by Jac Jacobsen, Ledu's strengths were in its aggressive marketing and organizational flexibility. In 1990 Ledu's turnover was 148 million Norwegian kroner. The company had a history of adjusting quickly to changing market conditions and was very strong in the French market where Luxo had limited presence. Moreover, Ledu had a firm hold on the residential lighting market and was believed to have a number of new products in the "pipeline". The R&D budget had been used innovatively and well to develop competitive lighting products in a variety of product lines. Ledu's weakness was seen as its sales and volume focus, at the expense of a profit orientation.

In September 1989, Mr. Hasse Larsson, Managing Director of Ledu International AB, initiated informal contact with Jac Jacobsen Industries, Inc. USA to explore the possibility of close collaboration between the two North American companies. Both companies had experienced a drop in US and Canadian profitability due to increased competition with small Far Eastern importers, and Ledu felt that its North American position would be enhanced by an alliance with Luxo. As the discussions progressed, the possibility of a worldwide merger between Jac Jacobsen and Ledu became realistic. Negotiations between the CEOs of the two companies were described as simple, open, honest and uncomplicated, thus providing a good starting point for future growth.

The purchase of Ledu was accomplished through a direct issue of shares to Saksinvest, an investment company which owned Ledu. Saksinvest retained a 15% share of Jac Jacobsen Industrier A/S, and one person from Saksinvest joined the board of Jac Jacobsen Industries. *(Refer to Exhibit 7 for the Ledu International Group Balance Sheet.)*

Ledu's Sales Organization

Ledu's sales organization was heavily dependent on distributors, while Luxo worked predominantly with salaried sales people. Ledu used distributors in 10 countries, with company sales teams only in Canada, Germany, Sweden, the UK and the US. (Refer to Exhibit 8 for details of the Sales Organization.) The sales teams often sold through office supply buying groups or through wholesalers and catalogue houses. As the wholesalers and buying groups became multinational, Ledu was able to supply them from many locations throughout Europe. However, the role of distributors and sales teams was changing as the buying groups became more sophisticated. As an example, five years earlier, Germany had been served by one sales manager and 12 independent manufacturers' representatives, whereas currently the same structure was augmented by 15 salespeople to call on individual members of the buying group.

Price compatibility among countries was also of concern as 1992 approached. Price variations of more than 5% created problems for the sales teams of both Luxo and Ledu, and was an issue which needed to be addressed quickly.

Ledu's Market

In the 1970s, Ledu's market focus had been in low- to medium-priced residential products. Survival required expansion beyond this market niche. Thus, beginning in the mid-1980s, Ledu gradually expanded into the mid-range industrial and office segments of lighting products. This expansion was later to create problems for Jac Jacobsen in that both companies were in similar channels of distribution with similar product ranges. In other areas, the companies were complimentary to each other. Ledu was strong in merchandising and in penetrating different markets from those of Luxo – such as warehouse clubs. Moreover, Ledu was strong in Southern Europe – particularly France – where fashion orientation was important, while Luxo was strong in northern Europe – primarily in Scandinavia – where ergonomic lighting was important. (Refer to Exhibit 9 for the Ledu International Group sales.) Many of Ledu's products were successfully manufactured in the Far East, whereas Luxo had had little positive experience in this region.

Ledu's Reaction to the Purchase

The initial discussions centered around a merger between the North American companies of Ledu and Luxo, a strategy which received the full support and enthusiasm of Ledu management. However, as the discussions expanded to focus on a worldwide merger, many Ledu executives experienced less positive feelings toward a Ledu acquisition by Jac Jacobsen Industries. There was concern that a worldwide merger would weaken Ledu's market position and that JJI management, which was unknown to Ledu's staff, would impose different work standards from the current ones.

As seen by Ledu, JJI's strengths were its well-developed product range in high end lighting and its strong management continuity. Unlike Ledu, which had experienced a succession of management changes over the years, JJI's weakness was perceived to be its inability to move quickly. Although not a major disadvantage previously, as the industry became more fashion oriented, an inability to move could quickly hamper market entry and penetration.

The strengths that Ledu would bring to JJI included a number of new, fashion-oriented products which were already in the "pipeline" and the ability to move quickly through the new product development phase. Ledu's negatives included its lack of both profitability and management continuity. The strengths and weaknesses of both companies appeared to fit well together. Jac Jacobsen Industries could provide a secure financial position, a well-managed organization and knowledge of the lighting industry, while Ledu could bring quicker access to new products and markets.

Alv Karlsen was pleased about the purchase of Ledu and the way it had been accomplished. He and Lars Harlem exchanged glances as they waited for suggestions from their managers.

Exhibit 1

Jac Jacobsen Industrier A/S, Norway

USA ◉	Europe ○	USA ●	Canada ●	Norway ●
Jac Jacobsen Industries, Inc.	Jac Jacobsen International A.S.	Lighting	Jac Jacobsen Enterprises, Inc.	Non-lighting
47.5%	64%	100%	100%	100%

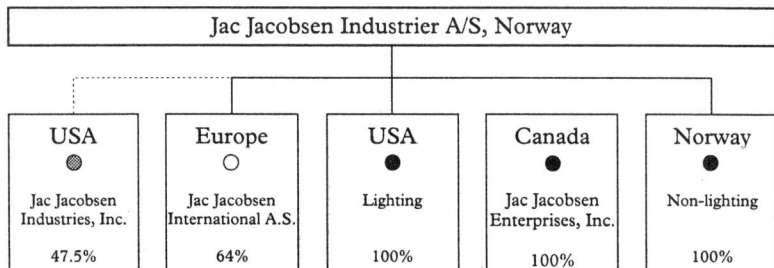

◉ Alkco Lighting Franklin Park, IL

◉ Burton Medical Products Corp. Van Nuys, CA

◉ Lam Lighting Systems Inc. Wakefield, MA

◉ Guth Lighting St. Louis, MO

◉ Nessen Lamps Inc. Bronx, NY

◉ South Coast Lighting Santa Ana, CA

◉ MWC Lighting Systems, Inc. Fountain Valley, CA

◉ Specialty Lighting Inc. Shelby, North Carolina

◉ Quality Lighting Inc. Guernee, IL

◉ High Lites, Waterbury, CT

◉ Troy/Trak Lighting, Inc. City of Industry, CA

○ Luxo-Leuchten GmbH Hildesheim

○ Luxo 1001 Lamps Ltd., London

○ Luxo Lamper A/S, Copenhagen

○ Jac Jacobsen AB Gothenburg

○ Luxo Lamp of Australia Pty.Ltd. Sydney

○ Luxo Italiana S.p.a. Bergamo
◖ Luxo Española Barcelona

● Luxo Lamp Corp. Port Chester, NY

● Luxo/Sverige Inc. Quebec

● Jac Jacobsen Vental A.S.

Board of Directors:
Knut Rasmussen (Chairman)
Alv. I. Karlsen
Truls Krogsrud
Jens Chr. Krogsrud
Pal Angell-Hansen

Source:
1989 Annual Report

Exhibit 2: Consolidated Balance Sheets December 31, 1989 and 1988*

ASSETS (NOK in Thousands)	1989	1988
Current assets:		
Cash	80,477	27,879
Investments	82,461	30,084
Accounts and notes receivable	68,702	147,242
Inventory	68,096	188,238
Other short-term receivables	16,584	17,370
Total current assets	316,320	410,813
Investments in bonds and shares	18,567	7,715
Intangible assets	30,659	25,694
Machinery and equipment	24,574	88,794
Land and buildings	20,930	36,709
Total other assets	94,730	158,912
Total assets	411,050	569,725
Liabilities and Shareholders' Equity		
Current liabilities:		
Bank overdraft	24,966	19,370
Accounts payable	31,987	59,721
Accrued income taxes	11,932	17,387
Other current liabilities	38,322	58,786
Total current liabilities	107,207	155,264
Long-term debt	34,159	157,473
Deferred taxes	4,292	9,493
Untaxed reserves	57,595	46,348
Minority interests	32,089	43,263
Stockholders equity:		
Share capital (3000 shares of NOK 1000)	3,000	3,000
Other funds	172,708	154,884
Total stockholders' equity	175,708	157,884
Total liabilities and stockholders' equity	411,050	569,725

*These figures include all majority-owned companies

Exhibit 3: Business Plan 1991-93 Jac Jacobsen International. Sales Organization 1991 Domestic Market

	Sales Manager	District Sales-Men	Project Sales-Men	Order Receiv./Inside Sales	Customer Records	Tele-Mark	Total Empl	Agents Single Company	Agents Multi Company
Norway	-	4	1	2 1/2	-	-	7 1/2	-	1
Sweden	1	5	1	4	-	-	11	-	-
Denmark	1	4	1	3 1/3	-	-	9 1/2	-	-
Germany	-	4	2	4	1	6	17	-	2
England	-	6	-	5	3	-	14	-	3
Italy	1	-	1/2	4	1	-	6 1/2	2	22
France	-	3	-	2	-	-	5	-	1
Spain	-	2	-	3	-	-	5	-	12
Australia	1	2	-	2	-	-	5	-	-
Total	4	30	5 1/2	30	5	6	80 1/2	2	41

Exhibit 4: Jac Jacobsen International Business Plan 1991-93. Distribution Channels 1991 - % Split

	N	S	DK	G	UK	I	ES	FR	AUS
Office Retail	17.5	59.5	42.0	39.0	7.9	21.3	27.9	20.0	10.0
Office Wholes.	27.7	-	-	-	18.5	-	-	10.0	38.0
Total Office	45.2	59.5	42.0	39.0	26.4	21.3	27.9	30.0	48.0
Lighting Retail	3.2	4.2	2.0	5.0	4.5	56.0	43.8	32.0	5.0
Lighting Wholes	26.1	4.7	23.0	23.0	3.1	-	-	18.0	5.0
Total Lighting	29.3	8.9	25.0	28.0	7.6	56.0	43.8	50.0	10.0
Government	8.0	25.6	10.0	3.0	2.4	-	-	3.0	21.0
Medical	5.3	-	8.0	6.0	25.5	-	-	-	14.0
Industrial	-	-	-	-	4.7	-	-	-	6.0
Mass Merchand.	-	-	-	-	4.5	14.4	14.1	-	1.0
Direct (End-User)	10.5	4.4	8.0	22.0	19.4	7.8	14.2	8.0	-
Other	1.7	1.6	7.0	2.0	9.5	0.5	-	9.0	-
Total	100.0	100.0	100.0	100.0	100.0	100.0	100.0	100.0	100.0

Exhibit 5: Jac Jacobsen International. Total Sales Growth per Market 1991-93 Compared to Last 3 Years and Estimate 1990

Markets	A-87	A-88	A-89	Est-90	B-91	B-92	B-93
Norway	21.7	20.1	18.0	19.4	25.4	29.2	33.6
Denmark	31.0	30.0	31.3	32.7	34.6	40.6	47.5
Sweden	29.2	35.9	44.5	48.3	52.5	58.8	68.2
Germany	27.2	32.6	38.1	44 4	49.5	56.8	63 9
England	–	–	26.4	26.3	33.9	38.4	43.5
Australia	–	13.1	15.2	13.1	14.4	15.8	17.8
Italy	26.5	33.9	32.2	32.5	40.0	45.0	50.0
Spain	–	–	13.2	13.8	16.5	19.0	21.8
France	–	–	–	10.3	12.3	14.2	16.3
Sum Direct							
Luxo Sales Co.	135.6	165.6	218.9	240.5	279.1	317.3	362.6
Dir. Exp. USA/CA	3.8	1.8	1.8	2.2	1.6	2.0	2.0
Dir. Exp. Norway	18 4	15.4	10 5	11 8	13.2	14.5	16.0
Dir. Exp. USA/CA	3.1	4.4	3.0	1.5	1.5	2.0	2.0
Dir. Exp. Italy	27.6	35.2	20.0	26.1	24.8	23.7	30.0
Sum Dir. Exp.	52.9	56.8	35.3	41.6	41.1	44.2	50.0
Total Direct Sales	188.5	222.4	254.2	282.1	320.2	365.0	412.6
Increase	29.1	33.9	31.8	28.0	38.1	44.3	47.6
Increase %	18.3	18.0	14.3	11.0	13.5	14.0	13.0
Interco. Exp N	38.0	51.8	70.1	67.6	80.9	91.4	103.3
Interco. Exp I	13.1	16.1	24.5	33.7	31.0	28.7	30.0
Sum Interco.	51.1	67.9	94.6	101.3	111.9		133.3
Annual Cons.							
Sales JJInt.	189.0	229.2	255.4	280.3	318.4		

Mill. NOK (91-currency)

Exhibit 6: Growth Strategies 1991-93
Major Products for Jac Jacobsen International Consolidated

Product-Mix Trend

Even if the product-mix varies greatly from market to market, we still have our *"LUXO-brand" product line* concentrated on two different product lines from our factories in Norway and Italy, with different product-mix concepts:

A. *Luxo product-mix from Norway (units)* show the following sales trend
   from our Luxo sales companies (in total units):

Product Group	E -90	B -91	B -92	B -93	Growth % 93/90
Asy-lamps	91,400	98,000	107,800	116,800	+ 28
Magnifiers	49,600	52,600	56,200	60,200	+ 21
Industry	21,000	21,000	21,500	21,500	
Medical	4,800	7,400	8,200	10,000	+ 107
Total Norway	166,800	179,000	193,700	208,000	+ 25

We plan a careful "real" growth average of 25% in units for all products from Norway, including the stagnation of the old lamp FL-101, now classified as "industrial product".

B. *Luxo product-mix from Italy (units)*

Product Group	E -90	B -91	B -92	B -93	Growth % 93/90
Economy lamps (incandesc.) Economy	222,000	215,200	222,500	230,900	+ 4
(FL)/ T-80/T-88	91,600	90,600	97,300	104,900	+ 15
Design lamps	19,200	21,500	23,600	24,800	+ 30
Total Lamps	333,000	327,300	343,400	360,600	+ 8
Total Systems (via Lattea + Cornice)	17,400	23,200	26,600	28,900	+ 66

	E -90	B -91	B -92	B -93	Growth % 93/90
C. Uplighters from Italy + Norway	1,700	5,300	7,000	8,500	+ 408

Exhibit 7: Ledu International Group Balance Sheet*

Assets	
Cash & Bank	3177
Acc. Receivables, Group	0
Acc. Receivables, Ext.	24395
Prep. Costs & Accr. Inc.	1915
Tax Receivables	0
Other Short-t Rec Group	0
Other Short-t Rec Ext.	2064
Inventories	28790
Total Currents Assets	60342
Blocked Acc Swe C. Bank	30
Shares In Subsidiaries	0
Other Shares	0
Long Term Rec Grp	0
Long Term Rec Ext.	497
Brands, Pat., Leasehold.	1
Development Costs.	1277
Goodwill	700
Machinery and Equip.	4035
Buildings	0
Land and Land improvement	0
Total Fixed Assets	6539
Total Assets.	66881

* in Swedish kronor

Exhibit 8: Ledu's Sales Force

Country	Organization
Australia	Distributor
Austrian	Distributor
Belgium	Distributor
Canada	Represented by Luxo Canada
Denmark	Distributor
Finland	Distributor
France	Distributor
Germany	Own sales company 1 managing director, 1 sales manager, 2 customer service plus 15 agents
Holland	Distributor
Norway	Distributor
Spain	Distributor
Sweden	Own sales company 1 managing director, 4 salesmen, 2 customer service
Switzerland	Distributor
United Kingdom	Own sales company 1 managing director, 1 customer service
USA	Own sales company (JJI) 1 managing director, 1 sales manager, 2 customer service and a lot of reps.

Exhibit 9: Ledu International Group - Sales 1989

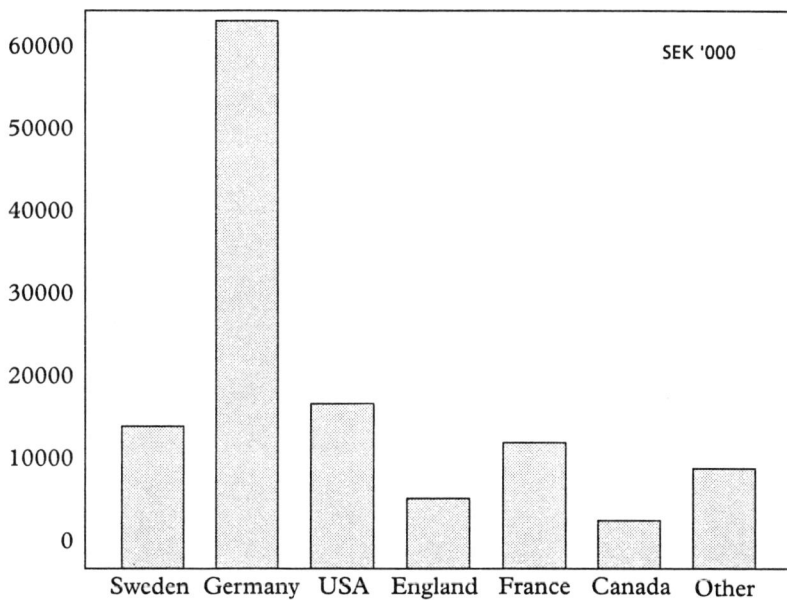

8. Jordan A/S

This case was prepared by Research Associate David H. Hover, under the supervision of Professors Per V. Jenster and Kamran Kashani, as a basis for class discussion rather than to illustrate either effective or ineffective handling of a business situation. The case is partially based on research by IMD Research Associates Dana Hyde and Mark E. Brazas and Peter O'Brien of the Industrial Development Authority of Ireland, and is part of IMD's Institutional Research Project: Managing Internationalization.

Mr. Knut Leversby, Managing Director of Jordan A/S, took a good deal of pride in the certificate on his office wall in Oslo. In Norwegian, it proclaimed Jordan "Company of the Year 1986" - as judged by a broadly composed jury and the journal Næringsrevyen. The jury had stressed Jordan's ability to conquer market positions, especially in an international context. Four years later, in January 1990, Mr. Leversby remained proud of the award, but his internal compass guarded against pride turning into complacency. As Jordan's CEO, he knew better than anyone the strategic challenges that his company was facing. Jordan was a small company among multinational consumer goods giants like Unilever and Colgate Palmolive. And consumer goods was, more and more, a game that turned on volume, threatening to overwhelm smaller competitors.

Jordan had prospered by focusing its foreign strategy on mechanical oral hygiene products – mainly non-electric toothbrushes, but also dental floss and dental sticks (toothpicks). By combining high product quality with an innovative distribution strategy, Jordan had successfully defined and defended its niche to become the largest toothbrush maker in Europe, and the fourth largest in the world. But, Mr. Leversby was not sure that the tactics of the past would carry Jordan into the future. Increasingly, competition came from trade retailers and major multinationals, both of which had significantly greater resources than Jordan.

Jordan's retailers, mainly food-based mass retailers, were becoming increasingly concentrated to achieve economies of scale in purchasing and logistics. Larger scale also increased the bargaining power of retailers with suppliers on prices and trade terms. More and more, these trade terms included on-time delivery of increasingly smaller order lot sizes, as retailers implemented and refined just-in-time ("JIT") systems.

Retail chains were also increasing their cross-border activity, often via acquisitions or strategic alliances, as they prepared for the "single European market" – the elimination of trade barriers between the 12 members of the European Community – due to be implemented in 1992. Consequently, they tended to favor pan-European brands for volume and ease of handling. Larger retailers could also contract production of "own label" products to compete with manufacturers' brands. In fact, about 13% of Jordan's sales came from contract production of these private labels. Mr. Leversby was concerned that Jordan's private label business might be cannibalizing name-brand sales and/or diluting the carefully built Jordan-brand image.

Concentration was also underway among European toiletries manufacturers, who performed contract distribution for Jordan. Mr. Leversby was especially concerned about the recent acquisitions of some of these distributors by multinational consumer goods companies. For example, in 1985 Procter & Gamble had acquired Richardson-Vicks, which distributed Jordan products in Italy and several other European countries. Quality distributors, like Richardson-Vicks, were difficult to replace.

Company Background

Jordan was founded by Wilhelm Jordan, a man familiar with hard times. Born in Copenhagen in 1809, he was the eldest of 11 children raised by his widowed mother. Leaving home at an early age, he apprenticed himself to one of the master combmakers of Hamburg. In 1837, Wilhelm Jordan moved to Christiania, Norway, with two fellow combmakers, starting a modest workshop destined to become the largest brush factory in Europe.

During the late 19th and early 20th centuries, the Jordan company distinguished itself as a social pioneer. Despite frequent labor unrest in Norway, the Jordan factory never experienced a strike. In 1910, the company set up a pension fund wholly financed by profits. Considering the conditions of the time, Jordan was a good place to work, a fact reflected in the long-term employment and loyalty of its workers. Throughout Jordan's history, advancement from the shop floor was common; Per Lindbo, Knut Leversby's predecessor as Managing Director, began his career with Jordan as a 15-year-old on the production line. A Jordan publication issued in 1987 to commemorate 150 years of company history referred to the internal "culture", strongly influenced by the founder's faith in the individual human being. For the employee with skill and the will to make the effort, the opportunity was there to accept the challenges, irrespective of formal education and qualifications.

Another continuous thread in Jordan's history was its commitment to product excellence. Brushmaking was a skilled worker's trade, and in 1989 Jordan still produced handcrafted "jewelry brushes" as nostalgia items. More importantly, the company continually invested in advanced technologies to maintain its competitive ability.

Jordan began producing toothbrushes in 1927 under the leadership of Hjalmar Jordan, grandson of the founder. By 1936, the company had captured half of the Norwegian market. In 1958, Jordan began to take a serious interest in exports, realizing that the oral hygiene field was largely underdeveloped. Jordan's subsequent success was evident. By 1988, foreign sales of dental products provided over 60% of Jordan's revenues. *(Financial information on Jordan is shown in Exhibit 1, and an organization chart in Exhibit 2.)* The company's sales for 1989 reached NOK 330 million[1]; 44.6% of sales were made in Norway, 32.2% in the balance of Europe, and 10.0% in the rest of the world. The remaining 13.2% consisted of private label sales to other markets.

Management Challenges

In the early 1980s, Jordan suffered a period of reduced earnings. The success that Jordan achieved in increasing exports led to overemphasis on marketing and sales at the expense of financial performance. Steps were taken to re-emphasize the importance of financial results. Company-wide financial targets were set at 18% return on assets with 16% return on sales and were communicated directly to employees. In addition, efficiency measurements were established for the individual foremen to help them identify their contribution to the overall profitability objectives of the company. Monthly reports and annual reviews for production looked at labor hours per unit, scrap rates, absentee rates, energy usage and other measures of efficiency. Other reports for general distribution included weekly sales figures, profitability analysis, and accounts receivable.

The renewed emphasis on financial and efficiency measures made

---

[1] Exchange rates had fluctuated widely in recent years. Approximate values for the Norwegian krone were: NOK 1.00 = FF 0.88 = US $0.16 = £ 0.09.

employees at all levels realize that the company was dependent on the successful interaction between production and marketing. This re-orientation of company values had a direct impact on performance. Sales more than doubled between 1979 and 1989, while employment stayed flat at 450 after falling from 700 between 1979 and 1982. The workforce reduction resulted from Jordan's policy of increasing produc-tivity through mechanization. The reduction was, however, achieved without major employee displacement. With government aid, older workers were retired and approximately 80 workers were pensioned. Manufacturing efforts achieved productivity improvements of 6-8% per year.

Downsizing remained a priority in 1989. The personnel department spent a considerable amount of time helping people leave the company. New people, however, were hired occasionally as needed, particularly in marketing. Jordan had achieved the reputation of being a good com-pany for international marketing. A few individuals took advantage of Jordan, staying with the company only long enough to learn its methods and techniques before leaving and joining another company. Interna-tionally-minded employees were in high demand in Norway.

The Competitive Environment in 1989

Jordan's products were marketed in more than 85 countries worldwide; 1.4 billion toothbrushes were bought in 1989. Market size and tooth-brush replacement rates varied considerably among countries *(refer to Exhibit 4)*. Japan was the largest consumer of toothbrushes both in total volume and on a per capita basis. Whereas Japanese consumers pur-chased an average of 3.2 toothbrushes per year, Irish consumers, for example, replaced their toothbrushes about once every two years. *(Jor-dan's market share in major markets is given in Exhibit 3. Information on major competitors is given in Exhibit 5. Key brands are listed in Exhibit 6.)*

During the 1930s, Jordan had competed on quality, and its success had made Jordan-style quality an industry standard for toothbrushes. The company recognized that, as producing brushes was not a very dif-ficult process, the battle of the future would not be about product devel-opment or production technology. As a result, Jordan shifted its focus toward product presentation and being responsive to end-user de-mands. Jordan concentrated its efforts on developing marketing tech-niques that reached the customer in the store, where most toothbrush purchase decisions were made. Through careful attention to point-of-sale promotions, packaging and product design, Jordan was able to establish and maintain a strong market presence.

In the increasingly competitive consumer product market, volume was a precondition for survival. Consequently, during the mid-60s, Jordan considerably reduced its product lines (which included brushes, combs, toys and wooden soles for footwear). The slimmed-down product portfolio concentrated on products with volume-related potential. From that time onward, oral hygiene products became increasingly important to Jordan's success.

Jordan's cost structure was probably not typical for the industry, for two reasons. First, Norwegian labor costs were high. Hourly wages in Holland and Scotland, for example, were 70% and 30%, respectively, of the Norwegian rate. Manufacturing labor accounted for about 20% of the ex-factory sales price for toothbrushes. Second, as a small company with a niche strategy, Jordan did not have the financial or personnel resources for marketing and distribution that its large competitors had. Marketing expenses were generally allocated evenly between Jordan and the distributors in each country. Still, Jordan was limited in its ability to compete in some areas.

Jordan's experiences in the United Kingdom illustrated the problems Mr. Leversby expected to see develop in the rest of Europe. Although the UK had been one of Jordan's first export markets, the company's success there had been uneven. Despite repeated attempts, Jordan had been unable to secure ongoing distribution in several of the large retail chains. It was a perplexing problem. Retailers demanded that manufacturers support their products with advertising, which Jordan management felt was unnecessary given the impulsive nature of toothbrush purchases. In one case, a retailer wanted Jordan to spend £ 2 million on advertising, almost twice the company's annual budget for promotions in the UK. The 1988 toothbrush advertising budgets in the UK for several of Jordan's competitors were estimated as follows: £ 2 mn for Johnson & Johnson's "Reach" brand; £ 1.5 mn for Gillette's "Oral B;" and £ 1 mn for Unilever's "Mentadent P Professional. "

Because Jordan would not meet their advertising demands, British retailers frequently placed Jordan products on lower shelves where the company's point-of-sales promotions were less effective. Under these conditions, sales could not meet expected levels, and so retailers would pull the line off the shelves entirely. Because of these difficulties, Jordan had only 4% of the UK market in 1987. *(Exhibit 7 shows a comparison of the leading brands and distributors in the UK.)*

Some large retail chains increasingly demanded listing fees before they would stock a particular item.[2] For example, one large French chain required FF 150 per store per variant for a similar product. The total listing fee for an initial introduction of 10 product variants in 1,200 stores would cost FF 1,800,000. On the other hand, Jordan's relative scarcity of resources had led to the creative (and highly successful) use of marketing and distribution alliances, a key factor in the company's success.

By contractual agreement, most transactions between Jordan and its distributor and licensee partners were dominated in Norwegian kroner. The few exceptions included transactions with affiliates in developing countries and in Holland, which used US dollars and Dutch guilders, respectively. The policy was a convenience. It was not Jordan's intention to push the foreign exchange risk onto its overseas partners. If its affiliates or distributors stopped making money due to exchange rate exposure (or any other reason), Jordan would soon lose them as partners. Jordan did not make currency denomination an issue in contract negotiations. Experience had shown that it was better to avoid involving the finance managers of the distributors, since "they would start to make all kinds of funny arrangements".

Retail Distribution

Toothbrush distribution varied from country to country. In France, for example, 83% of 1987 volume was accounted for by the grocery trade and 17% by pharmacists, while in the Netherlands the comparable figures (1986) were 62% and 38%, respectively. Overall, however, pharmacists were losing ground to food-based retailers.

A second significant industry trend was the increasing concentration of the European grocery trade. Hypermarkets were getting a growing market share along with organized retail groups, which pooled their member stores' purchases and supply. European supermarkets were more likely to be chain members, and retail outlets were generally getting larger, although there continued to be some variation amongst countries, the share of food turnover by the top 10 food buying organizations in West Germany had reached 81%; in the UK, the figure was 66%; for France 62%, compared to only 36% in the US.

---

2 Listing fees were a one-time fee, usually paid by the manufacturer or distributor at the time of new product introduction.

For the end-user, a larger sized retailer meant not only lower prices but a wider range of product choices. For the retailer, size meant more bargaining power with suppliers on prices, packaging and other product characteristics, as well as payment terms, order lot sizes and delivery times. The size of the new stores was a significant factor in managing distribution; one Euromarche hypermarket in France, for example, sold the same volume of toothbrushes as 260 Norwegian stores.

The retail price of toothbrushes also varied from country to country for a number of reasons, including distributor and retailer margins. For the product category, retailer margins across Europe averaged 35% of the final consumer price.

Country differences, however, could be significant; margins in France were about 25% whereas UK retail margins reached 60% in some cases. Large retail chains and hypermarkets considered 30% the target margin in the product category. Wholesaler and distributor margins averaged 10-15% although country differences could also be substantial. In Spain, distributor margins ranged as much as 20-25%, while margins in the UK averaged about 10%. Manufacturers' coverage of sales, marketing and overhead expenses were approximately 30% of the final retail price.

Jordan management expected that after 1992, European integration would further concentrate the European retail distribution trade. As competition rose, closures, acquisitions and strategic alliances would accelerate. Carrefour, the leading French hypermarket chain, had already allied with Castorama, the leading French do-it-yourself chain, normalizing relations after a previous Carrefour takeover attempt. Cross-border activity was also increasing in retail distribution, in contrast to the previous tendency of retail multiples to operate entirely within their domestic markets.

Coinciding with retail concentration was the increasing sophistication of retailers in obtaining and using market information. Retailers were highly aware of consumer preferences, competitive products and market opportunities. Processing this market information had been enhanced by point-of-sale scanner systems which evaluated product contribution per increment of shelf space. Armed with analytical data closely tied to their own bottom line, retailers were increasing their demands on suppliers' sales representatives for changes in packaging, pricing and other product attributes. As retailers became more aware of the changing market, product and package life cycles were getting shorter. Also, retailers were increasingly using JIT, which reduced their inventories but put a heavier logistical burden on suppliers to deliver smaller orders with less lead time.

Jordan's Export Development

Jordan began to take a serious interest in exports in 1958 when the EFTA and EC were in their formative stages. According to Leversby, the primary motivation for developing exports was that "...four million Norwegians did not consume enough toothbrushes to keep the company moving!" Jordan's initial exports, however, were vacuum cleaner brushes rather than toothbrushes. Choosing Great Britain as its first market because "they spoke the language", Jordan was disappointed with the results. The company realized that building a profitable business as a subcontractor was a difficult task.

The company, however, saw toothbrushes as an underdeveloped market, characterized by low usage rates and an increasing awareness of dental hygiene, with clear volume related potential. With toothbrushes, Jordan could also take advantage of its dominant domestic market position to support developing overseas operations.

The strategy adopted by Per Lindbo, who was then Managing Director, and Mr. Leversby, was simple and inexpensive. Jordan asked distributors to cover product launch expenses in return for sharply discounted prices on toothbrushes. Because the toothbrushes were of good quality and supported by Jordan's marketing acumen, distributors found this offer attractive. It also allowed Jordan to enter new markets without substantial cash commitments.

Exports of toothbrushes were first made to Denmark, where Jordan entered into a distribution contract with the pharmaceutical company Astra. Denmark was chosen because of its physical proximity, cultural similarities and the small size of the market. Later, due to Danish import restrictions, a factory was established in Copenhagen. The Danish factory assembled parts supplied by the Oslo factory. Jordan continued to diversify its export markets by expanding the Astra partnership to include Astra-Wallco in Sweden and Finland. Jordan toothbrushes were introduced in the Netherlands in 1963, with 240,000 units sold in two and a half months. In 1964, Switzerland, Belgium and France were added to the export map as Jordan became more confident in working with distributors and new markets.

A major boost to Jordan's initial export moves was a partnership with the large German consumer goods company, Blendax Werke, started in

1961. A license contract allowed Blendax to produce and market Jordan-designed toothbrushes in West Germany under the Blend-A-Med name. This arrangement with Blendax was still operational in 1989, making Germany the only country in Europe where the Jordan brand name was not used. The relationship with Blendax was very important to Jordan in the competitive West German market. Mr. Leversby did not relish the idea of having to go it alone if something should happen to Blendax.

Export Strategy

Jordan's international strategy had a number of key elements. First, the company consciously and persistently pursued a niche policy, sticking to mechanical oral hygiene products. Shortly after Jordan went international, it selected one product only – toothbrushes – for export. Since then, the company had enlarged its foreign product line to include dental floss and dental sticks (interdental cleaners made from wood), but mechanical dental care remained Jordan's export business focus. The company's sales budget for 1989 estimated that 97% of dental product volume would be exported.

Jordan deliberately shunned the toothpaste market. Entering it would put Jordan into a larger and, therefore, more visible competitive arena, inhospitable to companies of Jordan's size. (About 80% of all oral hygiene sales were toothpaste.) Moreover, Jordan did not have either experience or any particular strength in this arena.

Second, international expansion was conducted step by step, one country at a time. Jordan's *modus operandi* involved getting to know the culture of a particular target country and making an assessment of the market. If conditions looked promising, the company would begin to search for a local distributor, possibly collaborating with a local advertising agency. This process could take between one and two years. Given the right "chemistry" with a distributor, marketing would begin, with Jordan being introduced as an international rather than a Norwegian brand.

Third, Jordan fielded its own sales force only in the Norwegian market. Foreign sales were entirely handled by local distributors. There were several reasons for this policy. Overseas sales forces would overstretch Jordan's resources. Moreover, with only a limited product range to offer retailers, Jordan had no real distribution strength. Finally, an independent sales force would challenge well-developed distributors on their own ground. Instead, as Mr. Leversby put it, "Company management traditionally viewed limited marketing resources as an advantage. We continued to think small by gradually building all new export markets through distributorships and working arrangements with established, successful firms." The development of local distributors as active partners was crucial to the success of this strategy.

Resources

Similarly, Jordan tried to conserve its resources by limiting its capital expenditures. In 1988, 30% of Jordan toothbrushes sold were produced by licensed subcontractors in eight different countries, including Venezuela, Thailand, and Syria. Relative to direct foreign investment, licensing was an efficient way for Jordan to avoid tariff barriers. Even the high perceived value of Jordan products did not allow the company to remain profitable when import duties were as high as 60-80%, as was the case in some countries.

Direct foreign investment was made only when market factors dictated it. Jordan opened a factory in Holland in 1988 as a manufacturing bridgehead within the EC, anticipating the abolition of intra-EC trade barriers scheduled for 1993. (Norway was not an EC member.) The Dutch plant was also used to separate private brand production from Jordan brand. Private brand production ran in small lots, requiring many changeovers. To optimize the volume-based manufacturing technologies available at the Norwegian plants, private label production was done almost entirely in Holland. The proximity of the Dutch plant to the major private label customers also facilitated integration with the JIT requirements of these companies. The decision to manufacture in the Netherlands was heavily influenced by the Dutch government's offer to provide 35% of the plant cost. Other important factors included the sales volume available in the Dutch market as well as tax, culture and language issues.

Despite Jordan's successes, the company had not been able to enter markets at will. In Great Britain the changing nature of the retail industry had disproportionately increased buyer power for the time being. High listing fees demanded by mass retailers exceeded the returns Jordan believed could be achieved. The situation in the US was different; in Leversby's words, it was "a big black hole". Despite the attractiveness of its size, the US market presented more risks than Jordan management was willing to undertake. Jordan, however, had not excluded the market and had actually begun working with an American company. In general, Jordan's managers believed that more attractive opportunities existed in countries with low toothbrush usage rates and limited penetration by competitors. Finance Director Erik Foyn emphasized, "We cannot succeed in all markets, we must be selective."

Private Label

Jordan management also faced the problem of how to balance the Jordan brand and private label parts of the company. Although the private label business provided only 13% of Jordan's sales, there was considerable debate about how this business fit into the company's future.

The private label business was organized as a separate company, Sanodnet, under the leadership of Mr. Juliussen, a member of the General Management team. Toothbrush designs used for the private label were not the same as those used by the Jordan brand to distinguish the two. The private label business had a diverse customer base, including Colgate-Palmolive and Safeway, the American retail chain.

Jordan's management was acutely aware of the problems associated with having two similar competing brands in one company. Cannibalization of the carefully built branded sales by the private label products was one such problem. It was possible to have two Jordan products next to each other on shelves, one Jordan brand and the other Jordan designed and manufactured, but private label. For retailers and distributors, this could cause a conflict of interest between Jordan – made private label products with their name and the Jordan brand. As one distributor commented, "I don't mind Jordan's private label business, but why do they have to be so good at it?".

International Management Issues

Control over the operations of licensees was also a major issue for Jordan. Because the company operated under the Jordan brand name throughout the world, it was felt that quality had to be uniform. Engineers were dispatched from Norway annually to inspect licensee plants, and product samples were sent to Oslo on an ongoing basis to insure that standards were being met. Production volumes were controlled by supplying at least one part of the final product from Norway, usually the back of the package. Foreign accounts were relatively easy for Jordan to track as there was usually only one distributor per country.

Expansion into Greece

By the summer of 1988, Greece was one of the few European countries where the Jordan brand name was not known. Management felt that entering the Greek market was a logical step toward consolidating the company's position in Europe.

Preliminary market research, using readily available sources such as government statistics, trade journals, country reports and Nielsen data, confirmed original suspicions that Greece was an attractive opportunity characterized by low usage rates and underdeveloped competition. More comprehensive research, including extensive discussions with various distributors, retailers and consumers was carried out before securing a distributor. The interviews, besides giving Jordan management a first-hand account of local business practices, also allowed management to evaluate numerous potential in-country partners.

In Greece, as in many markets, it quickly became apparent that Jordan would have to work closely with the retail trade to create a new selling environment. Traditionally, Greek retailers kept toothbrushes behind the counter, forcing customers to ask for assistance, thus giving the store clerk a significant role in product selection. Jordan's competitive strategy relied on the impulsive nature of toothbrush purchases, which dictated that the products be readily visible to the customer.

To introduce the trade to Jordan's marketing concept, the company held two presentations for interested distributors. More than 250 representatives attended these meetings. The concept behind point of purchase displays was explained, samples were demonstrated, and results in similar countries were outlined.

After selecting a partner, Jordan made a successful launch in the Greek market. Jordan's first year target was for 5% of the market. The company's first shipment, (equal to 1.6% of total annual market sales volume) sold out in less than a month.

The Future

During 30 years of exporting, Jordan management had consistently relied on its knowledge of country markets and its ability to develop relations with experienced and qualified distributors. This had not always been easy. The changing European retail and economic environment implied that Jordan would face many more challenges in the future.

The consolidation of competitors in the industry, including the purchase of Jordan's local distributors by large multinationals, was straining the company's resources. The Jordan family, however, wanted to keep their company. Despite a number of attractive offers, the company was looked on as the family inheritance as well as a prestigious institution in Norway for well over 150 years. The greater financial and distribution power that would come from a merger would be beneficial, but "after 12 months the spirit would be gone," Mr. Leversby explained.

Despite the challenges facing his company, Mr. Leversby was optimistic about the future. "Fortunately, we have a long way to go."

*Exhibit 1: Selected Financial Results**

Income Statement	1986	1987	1988
Operating revenues	265.0	307.0	321.0
Operating expenses:			
Depreciation		(14.0)	(15.6)
Other		(240.0)	(257.5)
Total op. expenses	(226.4)	(254.0)	(273.1)
Net op. revenues	38.6	53.0	47.9
Net financial income (cost)	(8.3)	(2.0)	1.2
Extraordinary items	1.3	(8.7)	2.2
Profit before allocations			
to funds and taxes	31.6	42.3	51.3
Allocations	(15.8)	(11.8)	(12.6)
Taxes	(7.4)	(15.4)	(21.2)
Net profit	8.4	15.1	17.5
Balance Sheet			
Cash	31.9	55.2	81.5
Accounts receivable	42.8	35.8	52.9
Inventory	23.6	24.4	28.3
Total current assets	98.3	115.4	162.7
Long-term investments	10.8	12.9	14.2
Property, plant and equipment	124.1	129.6	144.5
Total fixed assets	134.9	142.4	158.7
Total assets	233.2	257.9	321.4
Current liabilities	71.1	75.0	98.4
Long-term liabilities	61.1	57.0	66.2
Untaxed reserves	79.7	91.5	106.7
Minority interests	-	-	0.8
Shareholders' equity	21.3	34.4	49.3
Total liabilities and			
shareholders' equity	233.2	257.9	321.4
Return on assets	18.0	23.4	18.2
Cash ratio	14.6	20.2	28.0
Equity ratio	43.3	48.8	48.5

**(Millions of Norwegian kroner)*
Source: Jordan

Exhibit 2: Organization Chart, June 1989

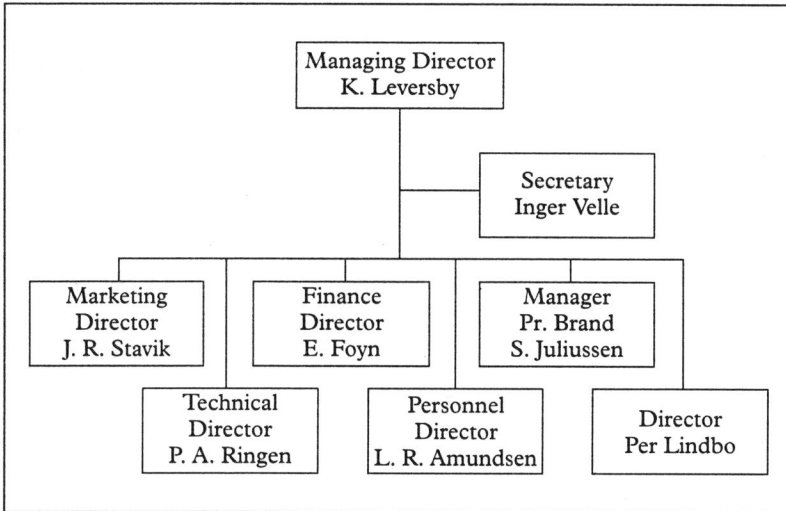

```
                    ┌─────────────────────┐
                    │  Managing Director   │
                    │    K. Leversby       │
                    └─────────────────────┘
                              │
                              │        ┌──────────────┐
                              │        │  Secretary   │
                              ├────────│ Inger Velle  │
                              │        └──────────────┘
     ┌──────────────┬─────────┴────────┬──────────────┐
┌──────────┐  ┌──────────┐      ┌──────────┐
│ Marketing│  │ Finance  │      │ Manager  │
│ Director │  │ Director │      │ Pr. Brand│
│J. R.     │  │ E. Foyn  │      │S.        │
│Stavik    │  │          │      │Juliussen │
└──────────┘  └──────────┘      └──────────┘
    ┌──────────┐   ┌──────────┐   ┌──────────┐
    │ Technical│   │ Personnel│   │ Director │
    │ Director │   │ Director │   │Per Lindbo│
    │P. A.     │   │L. R.     │   │          │
    │Ringen    │   │Amundsen  │   │          │
    └──────────┘   └──────────┘   └──────────┘
```

Exhibit 3: Jordan Market Share by Country, 1987

Country	Market Share
Norway	90
Finland	70
*Netherlands	50
*Denmark	48
*Belgium	30
*Ireland	28
Sweden	20
Iceland	20
*Spain	16
Canada	15
*France	15
*Portugal	13
*Italy	3
Switzerland	4
*UK	4

Member countries of the European Community (1990)

Source: Company Records

Exhibit 4: The World Market for Toothbrushes, 1985[1]

Country	Total (millions)	Unit sales Per capita
Japan	360.0	3.2
North America:		
US	300.0	1.4
Canada	25.0	1.1
Western Europe:		
*UK	53.0	0.9
*Italy	38.1	0.7
*France	36.0	0.7
*Spain	15.8	0.4
Sweden	15.0	1.8
*Netherlands	12.4	0.9
Switzerland	11.0	1.7
*Denmark	7.2	1.4
Norway	5.8	1.4
Finland	4-3	0-9
*Belgium	4.2	0.4
*Ireland	2.0	0.6
South America:		
Brazil	90.0	0.7
Colombia	21.0	0.7
Argentina	10.0	0.4
Venezuela	6.8	0.4
Chile	4.2	0.3
Australia	10.0	1.5

[1] *Data unavailable for some countries*

*Member countries of the European Community (1990)

Source: EIU/Trade sources

Exhibit 5: Major Competitors in Toothbrushes, 1987.
Selected Financial and Operating Statistics

Company/ Nationality	Sales ($millions)		Net Income	Return on Assets (%)*	Employees
	Total	T/brush			
Lion Corp. (Japan)	2,451	20.3%	41	4.8	4,892
Gillette (US)	3,167	4.0%	230	19.5	30,100
Unilever (NL/GB)	31,279	0.002%	1,407	7.6	294,000
Johnson & Johnson (US)	8,012	.5%	833	19.2	78,200
Colgate-Palmolive (US)	5,648	1.6%	204	16.5	24,700
Anchor Brush Co. (US	50	+50%	N/A	N/A	1,150
Jordan	46	69.7%	2	23.4	475
Procter & Gamble (US)	17,163	.01%	327	3.6	73,000

*Operating profit/total assets
Source: Company records, Advertising Age, Annual Reports.

Exhibit 6: Major Competing Brands of Toothbrushes, 1987

Manufacturer	Major toothbrush brands
Lion	Lion
Gillette	Oral-B, Dr. West
Unilever	Gibbs, Signal, Mentadent, Pepsodent, DX, FSP
Johnson & Johnson	Micron, Reach, Prevent, Tek, Alcance
Colgate-Palmolive	Colgate, Dentagard, Defend, Tonigencyl
Anchor	Various private labels
Jordan	Jordan, private labels
Procter & Gamble	Blendax
Addis	Wisdom

Source: Jordan, Annual Reports.

Exhibit 7: British Toothbrush Market, 1989

Brand	Jordan	Wisdom	Mentadent	Oral B	Reach
Distributor	Alberto Culver	Addid/ Wisdom	Elida Gibbs	Oral B (Gillette)	Johnson & Johnson
Number of Salespeople	10	20	N/A	11	15
Market Share	2.5%	26.3%	1.9%	22.4%	7%
Average Consumer Price	99p	99p	£1.19	£1.09	99p

Source: Jordan

9. Cochrane S.A.

This case was prepared by IMD Professor Carlos Jarillo, with Professor Jon I. Martinez of the Universidad Adolfo Ibáñez, as a basis for class discussion rather than to illustrate either effective or ineffective handling of a business situation.

"Our target is to be a multinational graphics company, the leader in Latin America. We want to export to all parts of America and, to do that, we need at least two plants. Our only facility in Santiago, Chile. at the end of the world, is insufficient and presents many logistics problems. We need two plants geographically located at strategic points, so that shipping charges will be equally convenient for exporting both to Argentina and the United States."

With these words, Ramiro Urenda, Executive Vice-President of Cochrane S.A., summarized, early in March 1991, the current strategy of his company, the largest magazine catalog and fascicle printer in Chile, and one of the industry's largest exporters in South America. With sales of more than US $35 million in 1990, Cochrane had to make a final decision regarding the creation of a joint venture with the Brazilian group O'Globo, one of the largest communication conglomerates in the world, whose sales were over $1 billion.

The projected "Globo Cochrane Gráfica Ltda." corporation represented an initial investment of $19.5 million on a plant which would have 235 people on the payroll, to be built in Sao Paulo, Brazil. The project offered, according to Cochrane's managers, several advantages for the company, However, it was also a venture that involved significant risks, especially considering that the company had recently invested almost $6 million to expand the Chilean plant's capacity, in response to a similar investment made by its main competitor.

Company Background

Cochrane's History

The beginnings of Cochrane S.A. went back to 1956, when El Mercurio S.A.P., the main newspaper chain in Chile, decided to renovate its rotary printing presses. Rather than selling the old presses and thus creating potential competitors, it was decided to set up a different kind of printing house, one that would offer its services to third parties in the field of general publishing and printing. Roberto Edwards, the youngest son of the family owning the newspaper chain, took charge of this print shop. Thus Cochrane S.A., named after Lord Cochrane – the English sailor who had a decisive part in the independence of Chile and several other Spanish American countries – became one the 1,300 print shops then existing in the country. Soon afterward, the company rapidly began to expand into every area of the printing business, purchasing new machinery and venturing into the publishing area as well.

In the 1960s, the printing house originated a company that became a leader in the publishing field in Chile, introducing a series of important Chilean magazines – such as *Eva, Mampato, Paula,* etc., along with franchises from Walt Disney and other international publications (e.g. *Vanidades, Buen Hogar*). The growth in the publishing area was accompanied by the purchase of new rotary presses, which immediately increased the production capacity considerably. As the new level of capacity far exceeded the internal demand, Cochrane decided to print for other publishing houses as well. But, then, the company began to suffer from conflicting interests, as it was printing for third parties whose magazines competed with its own. This situation inhibited growth of Cochrane's publications, as the company could not compete aggressively against its own customers. As a result, after 1975 Cochrane reduced its focus on publishing and concentrated on increasing the printing business for third parties.

In 1980, Cochrane was the second largest printing company in Chile, only slightly behind the leader, Gabriela Mistral. But, by the end of that year, there was a serious market recession underway, and the two companies – both of which had production capacity in excess – engaged in a price war that ended in bankruptcy for Gabriela Mistral. At that point, Cochrane, which had been bordering on failure, was left as the absolute market leader, though its financial position was still precarious. To overcome this situation, the management had to rationalize the company's operations and sell part of the assets, among them the machines for printing labels, a business in which Cochrane had had the largest share in the country. After achieving this financial relief in 1981, the company was able to invest heavily in technology and, in this way, consolidate its leading position for a full decade.

The Cochrane Enterprises

During the '80s, Cochrane formed a company group which included numerous businesses, such as publishing, pre-printing, printing, distribution, photography, television and video production, publication of telephone guides, importing and distribution of office equipment and computers, etc. In all, in 1990 the group had a consolidated total sales of $72 million, and net profits after taxes of $587,000. *(Refer to Exhibit 1 for Consolidated Financial Statements.)*

In a comprehensive restructuring carried out in 1989, the different businesses were grouped into four areas. Mr. Roberto Edwards, head of the Corporation and President of the Managing Board, was the only owner. The Board included six other members, one of them from outside the group. Of the five internal members, all at the Executive Vice-President level, one was in charge of the group's corporate finances – which were centrally managed, while each of the other four was responsible for one business area. The general managers of each business area then reported directly to the Vice-President of that respective area *(as described below)*.

Publishing

All publishing was done by Editora de Publicaciones S.A. (EPSA), which produced high-quality periodicals on feminine, scientific, international, and other subjects. The group also owned Editorial San Telmo in Argentina, as well as some small firms devoted to video production and to sponsoring special events, such as beauty contests, etc.

Pre-printing

This area included Taller Uno Ltda. in Chile, Cromoscan S.A. in Argentina, and Photoprint in Brazil. Taller Uno Ltda. the leader in Chile, offered integrated pre-printing services: i.e., taking and producing photographs, photo composition, color selection and photomechanics. The companies in Argentina and Brazil newer and smaller, specialized in color selection and photomechanics.

Printing

The printing area included two companies: Cochrane S.A. and a company formed in partnership with third parties to give ultraviolet varnish services. Cochrane S.A., the parent company of the group, specialized in printing magazines, books and catalogs using high-speed rotary presses. The company employed 800-1,000 workers, depending on the season of the year. It had a 70% share in the Chilean market and exported about 55% of its sales, which in 1990 reached $35.4 million *(refer to the financial statement in Exhibit 2)*. Cochrane S.A. had increased its sales by 22% relative to the previous year, but the company's net profits had decreased from $2.4 million to $654,000.

Related Businesses

Finally, this area included another four companies. One very important business was a contract held by Impresora y Comercial Publiguias S.A. to produce Chile's telephone guides and yellow pages for the Compania de Telefonos de Chile. This company was a joint venture with the Carvajal Group, located in Colombia, a leader in this business in South America. Another very important company was Sociedad de Distribuciones Alfa S.A., which distributed 90% of the magazines in the Chilean market to newsstands (*kioskos*). Another member of this group was Distribuidora Bertran S.A., one of the leaders in magazine distribution in inland Argentina. Finally, this area also included Ditempo Ltda., a company importing and distributing office machines, furniture and computers.

The Printing Industry in Latin America

The Printing Industry in Chile

Experts usually divided the printing industry into four basic businesses: magazine printing using rotary presses, packaging printing, printed matter, and continuous forms. Cochrane competed only in the first area.

The magazine and catalog printing market using high-speed rotary presses included 75 important titles, which meant, early in 1991, a total monthly volume of 4.4 million copies. More than half of this material was devoted to department store catalogs and credit card magazines. Cochrane printed 46 of those titles – i.e., 3.36 million copies *(refer to*

Exhibit 3). There were 25 imported titles and 20 domestic titles printed in minor shops also sold in the Chilean market (but available data was lacking). Though the Chilean market had typically been growing roughly 10% a year, experts estimated that in 1991 the market would grow 5% relative to the previous year, which was basically due to an increase in the number of copies printed. It was expected that the few new introductions that year would be catalogs for trade companies and institutions.

With the failure in late 1981 of Gabriela Mistral – its traditional competitor, Cochrane S.A. had become the industry leader. In the experts' view, Gabriela Mistral had made several mistakes, particularly its purchase of a high-quality "rotogravure" press, too big for the South American market. This press had been greatly used in Europe, where magazines typically issued over 300-400 thousand copies, an amount that would rapidly absorb the high start-up costs. Cochrane bought some of these machines when Gabriela Mistral went bankrupt, taking them off the market and thus ensuring that no other print shop would be set up. At the same time, the company acquired an M-200, the state-of-the-art "offset" high-speed rotary press at the time.

However, early in the '80s, a new print shop appeared: Antártica, which – having started in 1961 as a book and magazine importer and distributor – became a small booklet printer in 1977. This company took a big step in 1983, when it bought the same M-200 that Cochrane had. Thus, again there were two companies in the market: Cochrane, with a 70-75% market share, and Antártica, with the remaining 25-30%. Cochrane's managers described Antártica as a good quality print shop, with low prices and very personalized service, though it did not have a developed management structure.

The competitive struggle with Antártica forced Cochrane to invest continuously in new machinery in order to respond to its rival's growth, and thus maintain the company's leadership position in the Chilean market. Late in 1990, Cochrane had a total printing capacity of 90,000 paper sheets (each containing 16 pages) per hour, while Antártica's capacity was 45,000 sheets per hour. Then, Antártica suddenly bought a high technology offset rotary press, raising the capacity to 85,000 sheets per hour.

Cochrane, whose management was studying the Brazil project, decided to maintain the company's leadership in the Chilean market at all costs. They reacted by purchasing the M-1000B, a high-speed offset rotary press with a capacity of 150,000 sheets per hour, much faster than

Antártica's press. This machine, with its complementary investments, cost almost $6 million, roughly the same amount that Antártica had paid for its press.

The Printing Industry in the Rest of Latin America

The magazine printing industry in Latin America showed significant differences from one country to another. With the exception of Cochrane and Antártica, which operated in more than one country, virtually all the rest were local printers. Most of them reflected the economic crisis that had afflicted Latin America throughout the '80s. They had not invested in technology and new equipment for years, and thus their production tended to be inefficient and of low quality. A description of the main competitors in each country is given below. Unfortunately, most of these countries had no reliable statistics about the printing and publishing markets.)

Brazil

This market was, undoubtedly, the most important one in the region, not only because of the population size, but the development of the magazine publishing industry was also greater. (The following table shows its evolution over recent years.)

Year	No. of Copies	$ millions
1989	316 million	158.0
1990	305 million	152.5
1991 (est.)	325 million	162.5

An important share of this market was concentrated in two publishing companies, Abril and O'Globo. In 1990, the distribution was:

Publishing House	Market Share	Units (millions)	Number of Publications
Abril	40%	122.0	150
O'Globo	28%	85.4	50
Bloch	7%	21.4	16
Azul (Abril)	6%	18.3	15
Editora Tres	6%	18.3	8
Medium publishers	7%	21.4	20
Small publishers	6%	18.3	100
Total	100%	305.1	359

Among these publishing companies, Abril, Azul, Bloch and Tres had their own print shops. The others hired printing services from third parties. Increasingly, there was a shortage of good quality printing services being offered, particularly using offset rotary presses. Brazil could not even cover its internal demand. The main magazine printers were:

Abril, the biggest print shop in South America, mainly served its own publishing house, while idle capacity was sold to third parties. The shop's quality patterns and commitment fulfillment were excellent. There were three photogravure and four offset rotary presses, and ten flatbeds – with a monthly capacity of 150 million 16-page sheets.

Bloch also mainly served its own publishing house and sold the idle capacity to third parties. Service was poor. This shop had been an important supplier to O'Globo. There were three rotogravure and two offset rotary presses, and 11 flatbeds – with a monthly capacity of 78 million sheets.

Cly served third parties only and did not have a publishing house of its own. O'Globo Publishing represented 50% of sales. The shop did not have a very good image until it purchased new machinery. Service to customers was only fair. Its monthly production capacity was 30 million sheets.

W. Roth centered its printing services on the Atica publishing house, serving also a pool of small publishing houses and handling some orders from O'Globo. The shop's equipment was inferior. There were two offset and two flatbed presses – a monthly capacity of 12 million sheets.

Marprint served O'Globo and various advertising agencies. The shop's image in quality and service was good. There were two offset presses and ten flatbeds – a monthly capacity of 12 million sheets.

Brazil imposed no tariffs on books and magazine imports, but had a 22% tariff on catalogs and like material. Air shipping cost was only $0.6 per kilo, while land shipping was $3,730 per truck of 24 tons. Paper, which amounted to 60-70% of printing costs, was normally supplied by the publisher.

Argentina

There were no reliable data available regarding the size of the Argentinean market for magazine printing. The most important local printers were:

> *Morvillo* had an offset rotary press with a capacity of 15,000 sheets per hour. The printing quality was good, but capacity was limited by its small rotary presses.

> *Mundial* had flatbeds, low technology, medium quality of services, and high prices. Capacity was high, but overall quality was low.

> *Perfil's* capacity was all devoted to its own publishing house, which had experienced a large growth in recent years. The shop's size was 40% that of Cochrane in Chile.

> *Antártica,* Cochrane's only real competitor in Chile, exported to the Argentinean market as well. The shop had flatbeds and rotary presses, good technology and quality, good service, personalized attention, and low prices. Since 1991, when new machines were installed, capacity had been high.

Argentina imposed a 22% tax on printing imports. Air shipping costs between Santiago and Buenos Aires was $0.35 per kilo, and $2,208 for a 24-ton truck.

Other Countries

In Mexico, a market 4-5 times bigger than Chile's, there was a large service printing house, whose production capacity was about 50% that of Cochrane's in Chile, as well as 4-5 smaller print shops, each one about 25% of Cochrane's size.

Colombia had a large printing industry, specializing in hardback books and publications and stamped products, all of which were more sophisticated than magazines. However, in the rotary press industry there were two important service printers, though neither of them compared to Cochrane's size. Printer was about 50% and Carvajal 25% of

Cochrane's size in Chile. The latter was the largest book printer and exporter from South America to the United States.

Venezuela had only one moderately important service printer: De Armas, whose size was about 30% that of Cochrane Chile. In addition, there were three other smaller printers, all of medium quality. Ecuador and Peru had small service print shops, the largest being 15% that of Cochrane Chile, using technology that was 15-20 years behind. In Uruguay and Bolivia, there were no service printers using rotary presses. Throughout most of Latin America, there were virtually no tariffs on books and magazines due to the mutual agreements of ALADI and Pacto Andino.

Cochrane's Internationalization

International Expansion

From 1983 onwards, the combined production capacity of Cochrane and Antártica extensively began to surpass internal demand. The only possible way to avoid repeating the same kind of price war as the one between Cochrane and Gabriela Mistral was to export printing services. The growth of exports by both companies, mainly to neighboring countries, was dramatic. In 1985, exports had reached $7 million, and it was expected that in 1991 they would surpass $30 million.

However, at the beginning, it had been very difficult, because the business of exporting magazine printing services had been nonexistent. There had been some exporting in the book sector, but that business was very different, as it was not constrained by time or technology. Many publishers, for instance, sent their art books to be printed in Japan or the United States. The magazine business, in contrast, was weekly, fortnightly or monthly. Usually, publishers wanted to be near the print shop to make last-minute changes. The printing of weekly magazines could not take more than 24-48 hours. Thus, it was very difficult to sell printing services outside national borders.

Cochrane's first international experience was with the Reader's Digest, late in 1983. This magazine circulated in different Latin American countries, and its printing was contracted out in each country. In Argentina, *Reader's Digest* had a serious problem: determining how to send money to the parent company in the US, while overcoming the restraints on converting the local currency into dollars, as well as high tax payments and a strong devaluation due to the large inflation prevailing at the time. Cochrane, which had been printing the *Reader's Digest* for the Chilean market for years, proposed a clever solution. The company would print the magazine in Chile, would then export it to Argentina, collecting and remitting the profits from Chile to the US, after discounting the printing services. Cochrane had no problem collecting from the Argentinean customers, because it was a matter of paying for imports, not of remitting profits abroad. The triangular operation was accepted by the American company, and the experience was a big success. Though this process did not involve a large business, it was useful for Cochrane as a means of learning to export, manage shipping logistics problems, etc. Later, the arrangement with the *Reader's Digest* extended to include Uruguay, Paraguay and Bolivia.

In 1985, Cochrane was able to take a big leap. Ramiro Urenda, who was then Commercial Manager, managed to get the executives from Planeta, one of the great publishing houses in Spain, interested in printing Spanish products in South America, which until then had been imported from Spain with high shipping costs. They created the Cochrane-Planeta corporation to publish and print fascicles in Chile. Ramiro Urenda remembered:

> "They sent us the films, transferred their rights to us, and we gave them 50% of the profits we obtained. We did fairly well. The next step was to do this same business in Argentina in the following year, with the printing being done in Chile."

This arrangement allowed Cochrane to demonstrate that exporting printing services was feasible. Urenda added:

> "The partnership with Planeta gave us credibility. We began to issue better quality fascicles in Buenos Aires, using the same amount of time as the local printers did, and a myth was shattered On the other hand, we found that the way to open up these markets was to get involved in the customers' businesses, that is, not to be merely graphic exporters. It was very difficult to go into countries like Argentina and Brazil and offer to print their magazines. We had to enter the publishing business and take risks and, in that way, show the other publishers that all this was feasible."

Later on, another very important milestone in Cochrane's international expansion was reached. Before joining Cochrane, Ramiro Urenda had been General Manager of the Chilean magazine *Ercilla*. While working there in 1983, he had the idea of giving a book with each copy of the magazine. These books, which were printed on Cochrane's rotary presses, and not on flatbeds as had been traditionally done, had a minimum cost if they were printed in large quantities. The idea was a tremendous success. *Ercilla's* sales went from 10,000 copies a week to 200,000 units over a period of several years. The books were collections: Chilean great novels, Chilean history, encyclopedias, etc. Later, when Urenda became Cochrane's Commercial Manager, he realized that this idea could also be exported to other countries, particularly for publications needing more volume in sales. Like Planeta, Cochrane did not confine itself to offering printing services. Ramiro Urenda elaborated:

> "During a meeting with the Argentinean publishers, we told them that we were going to deliver the books with rights included and would charge them according to their sales. We agreed to arrange the advertising campaign, but we would do the commercials jointly, with all of this included in just one price: book printing."

The Chilean success was repeated in Argentina, and later Cochrane introduced its idea in Brazil, Peru, Venezuela, Ecuador and Paraguay. Cochrane's exports grew explosively. From the $500,000 received for the *Reader's Digest* in 1984, the company grew to a level of $14 million from exports in 1987. As a result, the company's total sales doubled between 1985 and 1987.

However, 1988 was a time for decision. Cochrane's sales were roughly divided among Argentina (40%), Peru (10%) and Chile (50%). All of them were completely focused on fascicles and promotional books because, until then, they had not exported magazines, Cochrane's core business. Peru fell into a complete economic crisis, which virtually closed down the Peruvian market. The Argentinean economic crisis became more serious, and the fascicles business began to disappear in Latin America, because of its high sensitivity to the income level of the population. The decline in Argentinean .and Peruvian exporrts forced Cochrane to make a thrust into the Brazilian market. The strategy used was to set up a pre-printing company, Photoprint, whose business covered a range of activities – from text diagramming to color selection.

With Photoprint, Cochrane intended to learn about the Brazilian market in depth, including training some personnel as specialists in this market. The company sent three Chilean employees to Brazil and supplied them with state-of-the-art pre-printing equipment. Little by little, they began to get to know the Brazilian publishers. They became involved in a weekly magazine and introduced the book promotion scheme. Using that source as a means of introduction, they made contact with the big publishing houses, among them O'Globo – the largest in Latin America. Though Photoprint was losing money, the effort did bear fruit, and Cochrane began to print between 20-25% of O'Globo's magazines in Chile. Thus, the growth of exports to Brazil counteracted the decline in the Argentinean and Peruvian markets.

In Argentina, however, Cochrane employed an opposite strategy. After the company had been exporting significant volumes, it decided to set up a pre-printing facility there – as a means of giving one more service to customers – in order to get closer to them, which was particularly important in the pre-printing phase. Customers liked to see a printed proof of photographs and text before the final printing. Thus, in 1988, Cochrane created Cromoscan S.A. in Argentina.

Parallel to that operation, Cochrane opened two commercial offices in the United States: one in Miami and the other in New York. These subsidiaries were looking for jobs with fewer discontinuation problems and of a more long-term nature, such as booklets or handbooks with enough volume to be printed on the rotary machines that Cochrane had in Chile. In 1988, Cochrane won an open bid in New York to print almost a million copies of "The Leading Hotels in the World" catalog, which was distributed throughout the world. Early in 1991, exports to the US represented 3-4% of the company's total sales.

International Strategy Development

Cochrane's achievements in the Latin American market encouraged the company to allocate resources for an international strategy. Management's positive attitude was reflected in the 1988 annual report in the remarks of Roberto Edwards, Board Chairman, as he commented on the decline in the Argentinean and Peruvian markets.

> "In the year just ending, Cochrane S.A. has had to confront some difficult commitments. However, that challenge has served to confirm our will and the goal we intend to achieve: to be the leading company in the printing industry, not only in Chile, but also in Latin America."

The strategy that Cochrane adopted at the time was to create an efficient print shop in Chile that, through exporting, would supply the rest of the countries in the region. However, early in 1991, this strategy changed. Ramiro Urenda elaborated:

> "Some time ago, Cochrane's mission was to conquer South America through its exports. Now, this approach has changed; we want to be a multinational company in Latin America, with investments in other countries, because we feel that that is the only way we can go on capitalizing on our know-how and our management advantages. Our idea is to have two complementary facilities, conveniently located in countries with good investing conditions, to export from them to the rest of the Latin American countries. Given the fluctuating exchange rate and the instability of economic policies in the various countries, it is sometimes better, for instance, to export to Argentina from Chile and, on other occasions, to do it from Brazil. Besides, it is necessary to consider the bilateral agreements between countries. Currently, there is a bilateral agreement to have no tariff whatsoever on exports from Brazil to Argentina, while the tariff from Chile to Argentina is 22%."

Indeed, Cochrane's objective was not limited to the Latin American market; it was even more ambitious. Urenda explained:

> "In the near future, we will assess the possibility of decisively entering the markets of the United States, Canada and Mexico. In the United States, graphics services imports reach $5 billion, with a significant number of them coming from Asia. Those countries are farther away than we are, yet they enter the US market competitively. If, for instance, we have a facility in Chile and another one in Brazil, we can offer more reliability and have a better introduction for entry into those markets. Investing in Brazil with an important partner would give our project credibility in developed countries. In this business, demonstrating effectiveness and establishing trust are absolutely necessary."

The Partnership with O'Globo
O'Globo Group

O'Globo was the biggest communications group in South America and one of the most important in the world. With sales of more than $1 billion, it owned the most popular newspaper, television channel and disk recording brand in Brazil, besides filming studios, broadcasting chains, independent television broadcasting stations, and a publishing house. It also owned one half of an Italian television channel; it shared a satellite, and was associated in Brazil with NEC, the Japanese multinational telecommunications company. Finally, it had investments in hotel chains, haciendas, banks, insurance companies, building firms and food manufacturing companies.

Its only owner, Roberto Marinho, was one of the richest men in South America and one of the most influential in Brazil. It was said that his influence had been decisive in electing Fernando Collor de Melo to the Presidency. His three sons also worked in the group companies. All of O'Globo's executive staff were considered to be top of the line, with excellent professional training.

Beginnings of the Cochrane-O'Globo Relationship

As previously stated, Cochrane's small investment in Photoprint was not profitable but, by providing pre-printing services to the big local publishers, it enabled the company to gain an insight into the Brazilian market. Later, Cochrane offered to supply printing services from Chile. The company then proposed this idea to the O'Globo publishing house, which spent two years examining the pros and cons of having their magazines printed in Chile before deciding to proceed with the plan in 1989. By the end of 1990, Cochrane was printing a third of O'Globo's magazines, fascicles and books in Santiago.

O'Globo, which had growing printing needs, printed the remaining two thirds in Brazil, but complained about the quality and service given by the local printers. Thus, being satisfied with Cochrane's job as supplier, O'Globo then offered to set up a print shop as a joint venture. O'Globo had had this project in mind for years, but had been putting it off because of lack of experience in the printing business and the fear of losing money. Observing the inefficient operations experienced by Editora Abril and other publishing houses that owned print shops had led

O'Globo's management to believe in the advantages of retaining an independent relationship between publisher and printer.

O'Globo was Cochrane's largest customer, accounting for roughly 20% of the company's total sales. The continual instability of Latin American export markets, and a fear of losing the important Brazilian market, enhanced Cochrane's interest in the O'Globo project. Management was aware that it was not possible to centralize everything in Chile.

Jorge Encina, Cochrane's General Manager commented:

> "In Chile, we are at the limit of our business capacity, because there are no more economies of scale to capitalize on. Investing in Brazil would allow us to be near our customers, particularly Editora O'Globo. In this business. nearness gives flexibility, and it is as important as costs. Publishers – from a journalistic perspective – want to publish the very latest news while – from a commercial standpoint – they want to sell advertising until the last moment, because that's what provides their living. So much last-minute pressure means that the printer must develop a vastly flexible structure. If you are rigid, you drive away the customer and destroy yourself."

The Partnership Project

The managers of both companies met on countless occasions throughout a full year, examining the scope of the partnership and designing a specific project. The project's objective was to create the "O'Globo Cochrane Gráfica" corporation; it would have limited liability and be subject to Brazilian law. A graphics facility would be located in the outskirts of Sao Paulo, containing two rotary presses and one flatbed, capacity that would eventually be doubled in the second phase. The rotary presses would have a capacity of 60,000 and 30,000 (i.e., a total of 90,000) printings an hour, which would equal 60% of the total capacity of the Chilean facility. Initially, the new company would have 235 employees: 58 white-collar employees and 177 workers divided into three shifts. The project would start up in April 1991 and, by June 1992 – 14 months later, the plant would be completely finished and would begin to operate.

The target for quality would be based on the US standard – that is, a balance between high productivity and good printing quality. At the same time, the joint venture would benefit from having lower internal costs in Brazil. In order to reach the proposed target, the plant would need to purchase the most advanced technology in the world: a Harris M-1000B machine – like the one Cochrane had recently bought for the Chilean facility. In addition, there would be several other lower grade machines, imported and domestic, both new and second-hand. The total machinery cost would be almost $9.7 million. The new facility would require 6,513 m^2 on a 20,000 m^2 site.

The total project investment would equal $19.5 million, which would be funded in the following way: $6 million would be supplied by the partners on equal terms over a 16-month period; $6 million for new machines would be funded directly by suppliers, with a payoff period of 5-6 years and an interest rate between 12% and 13% a year; finally, $7.5 million would come from local business development loans, with payoff terms of 5-6 years and an interest rate of 12% a year. As to the finance policy, the partners planned to reinvest profits in order to finance the new company's growth. Fixed assets would be funded by long-term credits, while the working capital and start-up would be funded using the partners' own capital. Cochrane's technical and commercial know-how would be considered for the start-up, which would include training specialized personnel at the Chilean facility.

The management of the new company would be independent from the partners. The General Manager would be a Brazilian, given his better knowledge of that market, though he would not necessarily come from O'Globo. Both the Marketing and Technical Managers would be Chilean, and they would be appointed by Cochrane. The Finance and the Human Resources Managers would be Brazilian nominated by O'-Globo. Ramiro Urenda explained the reason that the Marketing Manager should come from Cochrane.

> "It is very important because it will definitely be to our best advantage in the middle term. We have to link the marketing activity in the Chilean facility with the Brazilian one – in order to do business jointly, to export to the United States, to offer printing services from either Brazil or Chile, etc. It is the only way that we can have really integrated plants."

The company's management would report to a Managing Board, which would control the company's global performance and decide on strategic issues, as well as manage the relationship between the partners.

This Board would be composed of three representatives from O'Globo and three from Cochrane.

Lastly, one aspect which the parties took more time to agree upon was setting a marketing policy for the new company. The partners wanted the print shop to be highly competitive in both the domestic and the international markets; it especially wished to develop the latter. O'-Globo publishing house would use a maximum of 60% of the productive capacity, which meant that the remaining 40% could be offered to third parties. And, during the start-up period, O'Globo would be able to contract an even bigger percentage. This restraint was set due to the fact that, in the first phase, the plant's total capacity would be only 50% of O'Globo's magazine printing demand early in 1991, not considering fascicles and books.

Pricing would be based on a clear, long-term market-focused policy. Given the instability and volatility of market prices in the highly inflationary Brazilian economy, the partners were proposing that the print-shop should charge O'Globo publishing house a price that would generate a profitability of 20% on the investment, after taxes. To this effect, they would establish long-term costs and prices, with the understanding that they should match the going market rates, in order to prevent any company from subsidizing another. Consequently, whatever figure yielded that rate of profitability on the investment would be used as the *reference point*, while the actual price would be the prevailing competitive market-fixed price. If application of these prices resulted in a higher profitability than the reference level, there would be a markdown for work volume contracted by O'Globo. Temporary price fluctuations would not affect the prices charged by the print shop, in order to maintain a stability that was not dependent on occasional internal market fluctuations.

Final Considerations

In March 1991, the Managing Board of Empresas Cochrane had to make a final decision about the association with O'Globo so that, if the project were approved, it could start up in April, as scheduled. Any delay in the final decision would not only hold back the work on construction of the new Sao Paulo facilities, but could also alter some basic parameters in finance assessment.

Ramiro Urenda, who was responsible of the Printing Area of Empresas Cochrane, was in charge of presenting the Board with the project's final features and a corresponding financial assessment, which his team had been calculating over the last weeks. It showed that, for the first project phases, the return rates would fluctuate between 17.8% and 30.3% after taxes, depending on the price assumptions adopted, given the instability of local industry and the Brazilian exchange policy fluctuations *(refer to Exhibit 4 for the financial assessment results)*. Using this approach, the investment could be recovered in 3.6 to 4.8 years. The most probable scenario would be one where the expected return rate would exceed 20%, with a long-term income tax actual rate lower than 50%. The Board would be asked to approve the project based on these figures.

Using the figures, Urenda and his team were convinced that the project was fully consistent with Cochrane's international strategy. As their goal was to become a leading multinational in Latin America, with strong inroads into North America, they believed that the project offered important advantages.

Nevertheless, several aspects were troubling them. First, in recent years, Cochrane had experienced strong growth, which had resulted in corresponding financial restrictions for the company. In addition, it was necessary to consider the financial pressure due to the recent acquisition of new machinery for the Chilean plant, in response to their main competitor's investment in similar machinery. On the other hand, the increased production capacity in Chile occurred simultaneously with the proposed plant construction in Brazil, which expanded Cochrane's overall production capacity even more. Although the Chilean plant would continue to export printing services, O'Globo was nonetheless troubled by the risk implied with such a big production volume, since the new facility in Sao Paulo could meet only part of the company's demand.

Cochrane's managers were also concerned about the significant difference in size between the partners. For the Brazilian group, the investment needed for the joint building project was not considered especially large, while it meant a substantial financial effort for Cochrane. In fact, O'Globo had proposed a plant with capacity that was double what was ultimately agreed upon for the project. To offset the obvious size difference between the parties, Cochrane proposed that the partner not be the entire O'Globo group, but only the publishing house, whose size was more comparable to the Chilean company. However, the size of O'-Globo publishing house relative to that of the new company, O'Globo Cochrane Ltda., was also troubling, because it would be buying 60% of its printing services and, therefore, would have inevitable monopsonistic strength. Cochrane's managers were aware that resisting the publisher's temptation to lower prices, in order to improve the publishing business – of which they were 100% owners, would be a complex issue regardless of the full agreement to charge market prices.

Finally, Brazil's economic instability worried the management, as did the possibility of labor trouble. Regarding the first issue, it was very difficult to make a prediction about the Brazilian economy. Collor de Melo's economic policy had been confusing. Regardless of his statements about economic liberalization in order to become a market economy, he had fixed all the bank deposits, prices and wages *(refer to Exhibit 5 for some economic and demographic indicators for Brazil and other Latin American countries)*. Brazil was a country with an inflation rate of over three digits and, because of difficulties paying its huge foreign debt, it had no international funding. Regarding labor problems, the graphics industry was especially sensitive about this issue. Trade unions were powerful and workers in the new plant at Sao Paulo would undoubtedly be union affiliates.

So many factors related to the decisions determining the final joint-venture agreement. Each one had to be weighed and evaluated for its ultimate risks and benefits in order to optimize the chances of success for "Globo Cochrane Gráfica Ltda.".

Exhibit 1: Empresas Cochrane Consolidated Financial Statements

Cochrane Companies Consolidated									
(US$* 1000)	1982	1983	1984	1985	1986	1987	1988	1989	1990
Assets									
Cash	1,436	1,833	1,503	854	712	1,109	1,355	905	1,039
Receivables	9,116	8,506	5,690	5,950	7,983	9,750	11,749	15,266	17,617
Related Comp	645	0	0	0	0	407	74	540	2,013
Inventory	3,693	2,540	2,577	3,277	3,778	4,949	6,348	6,791	7,311
Other current assets	567	155	128	307	689	1,074	988	931	977
Total current assets	15,457	13,034	9,898	10,387	13,162	17,290	20,515	24,432	28,958
Land & Buildings	2,195	2,432	2,120	2,374	3,403	4,303	4,920	5,045	6,972
Equipment	6,447	6,935	6,322	6,193	6,842	9,927	11,824	12,614	17,255
Other fixed assets	1,200	1,483	1,536	976	1,232	1,709	1,968	2,272	3,249
Depreciation expenses	-518	-560	-494	-455	-556	-698	-1,102	-1,207	-1,704
Depreciation reserves	-2,066	-2,634	-2,440	-2,340	-2,853	-3,394	-4,120	-4,850	-6,635
Net property & Equipment	7,258	7,656	7,044	6,748	8,066	11,847	13,490	13,875	19,136
Investments	0	0	0	0	0	0	0	0	0
Other	269	223	288	377	60	174	552	457	251
Total other assets	269	223	288	377	60	174	552	457	251
Total Assets	**22,984**	**20,912**	**17,230**	**17,513**	**21,290**	**29,311**	**34,558**	**38,763**	**48,345**
Liabilities									
Short-term banks	4,042	1,817	1,213	2,305	3,225	6,871	10,788	14,616	14,303
Long-term portion	1,824	986	780	633	1,243	1,282	1,301	826	476
Notes payable	3,230	3,526	3,931	3,264	4,190	4,419	5,759	6,675	11,125
Related comp.	0	237	266	437	145	0	0	0	0
Other	2,188	1,059	805	789	938	1,555	1,637	1,702	2,186
Total current debt	11,285	7,624	6,995	7,428	9,741	14,127	19,484	23,818	28,090
Banks	3,060	3,074	2,091	2,891	2,514	2,606	1,831	937	455
Other	2,745	3,330	1,571	1,220	567	903	997	836	1,953
Total long-term debt	5,805	6,404	3,662	4,111	3,080	3,509	2,828	1,772	2,408
Total debt	**17,090**	**14,028**	**10,657**	**11,539**	**12,821**	**17,636**	**22,313**	**25,591**	**30,498**
Net Worth									
Common stock	4,401	4,438	3,619	3,141	3,612	3,707	3,911	4,011	4,532
Reserves	3,136	6,032	4,953	3,992	4,316	5,248	4,850	8,036	10,585
Retained Earnings	87	-3,521	-2,774	-1,704	-1,341	-684	1,963	-920	2,143
Yearly Earnings	-1,730	-65	776	545	1,881	3,404	1,522	2,044	587
Total Net Worth	5,894	6,884	6,573	5,974	8,468	11,875	12,245	13,172	17,847
Liabilities & Net Worth	**22,984**	**20,912**	**17,230**	**17,513**	**21,290**	**29,311**	**34,558**	**38,763**	**48,345**

* not audited

Exhibit 1 (Continued):
Empresas Cochrane Consolidated Financial Statements

Cochrane Companies Consolidated

(US$*1000)	1982	1983	1984	1985	1986	1987	1988	1989	1990
Income Statement									
Net Sales	25,686	24,145	21,473	27,861	37,145	47,054	50,306	55,950	72,056
Cost of Sales	-15,383	-15,389	-13,405	-18,975	-24,925	-30,221	-33,352	-36,217	-48,130
Gross Profits	10,303	8,756	8,068	8,886	12,220	16,833	16,954	19,733	23,926
Sales & Adm. Expenses	-6,611	-4,918	-4,447	-5,275	-7,214	-9,934	-12,319	-12,511	-15,956
Operating Income	**3,692**	**3,838**	**3,622**	**3,611**	**5,006**	**6,898**	**4,636**	**7,222**	**7,970**
Income from Other Companies	0	0	0	0	0	0	0	0	0
Interest Expenses	-3,886	-2,184	-1,409	-974	-1,227	-1,505	-1,810	-4,140	-6,275
Other Income	1,812	295	167	212	200	195	186	212	260
Other Expenses	-1,419	-819	-815	-1,064	-1,288	-533	-1,200	-1,115	-1,116
Inflation Adjustment	-1,712	-1,046	-583	-946	-534	-1,290	-279	-72	-94
Earning B/Taxes	-1,514	85	982	838	2,157	3,764	1,532	2,107	744
Income Taxes I	-216	-149	-207	-294	-276	-361	-11	-63	-157
Net Income	**-1,730**	**-65**	**776**	**545**	**1,881**	**3,404**	**1,522**	**2,044**	**587**
Financial Analysis									
Acid Test	0.94	1.36	1.03	0.92	0.89	0.77	0.67	0.68	0.66
Current Assets	1.37	1.71	1.42	1.40	1.35	1.22	1.05	1.03	1.03
Debt/Net Worth	2.90		1.62	1.93	1.51	1.51	1.82	1.94	1.71
Sales/Total Assets	1.12	1.15	1.25	1.59	1.74	1.61	1.46	1.44	1.49
Oper. Income/ Total Assets	0.16	0.18	0.21	0.21	0.24	0.24	0.13	0.19	0.16
Net Income/ Total Assets	-7.5%	-0.3%	4.5%	3.1%	8.8%	11.6%	4.4%	5.3%	1.2%
Net Income/ Net Worth	-29.3%	-0.9%	11.8%	9.1%	22.2%	29.2%	12.4%	15.5%	3.3%

*not audited

Exhibit 2: Cochrane S.A. Financial Statements

Cochrane Companies Consolidated (US$*1000)	1982	1983	1984	1985	1986	1987	1988	1989	1990
Assets									
Cash	1,290	1,538	1,312	294	136	279	748	381	227
Receivables	7,261	6,350	4,140	4,294	5,630	6,568	7,664	10,175	11,236
Related Comp.	961	268	133	95	871	1,510	2,232	3,813	4,089
Inventory	3,392	2,284	2,204	2,569	3,195	3,909	4,706	4,868	5,557
Other current assets	416	74	98	231	244	897	686	448	717
Total current assets	13,320	10,513	7,887	7,482	10,075	13,163	16,037	19,685	21,826
Land & Buildings	2,169	2,257	1,915	2,162	3,161	3,522	3,941	4,195	5,161
Equipment	5,495	5,798	5,178	4,856	5,234	7,149	8,653	9,629	12,863
Other fixed assets	637	870	1,170	734	899	980	1,064	1,223	1,354
Depreciation expenses	-451	-393	-331	-291	-334	-349	-456	-538	-651
Depreciation reserves	-1,931	-2,247	-2,197	-1,987	-2,338	-2,710	-3,066	-3,283	-3,998
Net property & Equipment	5,919	6,084	5,735	5,473	6,622	8,591	10,136	10,227	14,448
Investments	1,643	1,727	1,124	1,869	1,794	2,166	3,577	4,245	5,762
Other	2,620	1,520	1,642	304	13	16	20	21	30
Total other assets	4,263	3,246	2,766	2,173	1,807	2,177	3,598	4,266	5,791
Total Assets	**23,501**	**19,844**	**16,389**	**15,129**	**18,504**	**23,931**	**29,771**	**34,178**	**42,066**
Liabilities									
Short-term banks	4,031	1,738	1,024	1,806	2,756	5,170	9,066	11,865	11,548
Long-term portion	1,555	674	610	522	1,064	1,130	1,137	736	368
Notes payable	2,794	3,133	3,604	2,348	3,014	2,809	3,822	4,693	7,935
Related comp.	203	258	277	413	379	301	441	598	553
Other	1,827	664	528	413	482	973	931	1,197	1,348
Total current debt	10,410	6,512	6,044	5,501	7,695	10,382	15,397	19,089	21,752
Banks	1,860	1,833	1,133	2,154	1,923	1,624	1,106	495	263
Other	4,611	4,574	2,692	1,064	509	189	70	39	44
Total long-term debt	6,471	6,407	3,825	3,218	2,432	1,813	1,176	534	307
Total debt	**15,551**	**12,920**	**9,589**	**5,719**	**10,127**	**12,195**	**16,574**	**19,623**	**22,069**
Net Worth									
Common stock	3,706	3,845	3,207	2,830	2,976	3,144	3,359	3,382	3,860
Reserves	2,328	4,859	4,017	3,544	4,073	5,258	5,966	8,811	12,795
Retained Earnings	2,368	-1,849	-1,485	-622	-309	0	2,374	0	2,697
Yearly Earnings	-1,782	69	779	658	1,637	3,334	1,498	2,362	654
Total Net Worth	6,6Z0	6,924	6,519	6,410	8,377	11,735	13,197	14,555	20,006
Liabilities & Net Worth	**23,501**	**19,844**	**16,389**	**15,129**	**18,504**	**23,931**	**29,771**	**34,178**	**42,066**

* not audited

Exhibit 2 (Continued): Cochrane S.A. Financial Statements

Cochrane Companies Consolidated

(US$*1000)	1982	1983	1984	1985	1986	1987	1988	1989	1990
Income Statement									
Net Sales	15,291	14,320	13,236	13,432	20,266	26,385	26,184	29,046	35.392
Cost of Sales	-9,442	-9,288	-8,153	-8,073	-12,351	-14,804	-15,654	-16,890	-20,892
Gross Profits	5,848	5,032	5,083	5,359	7,915	11,580	10,530	12,156	14,499
Sales & Adm. Expenses	-5,402	-3,635	-3,450	-3,427	-4,837	-6,578	-7,827	-7,946	-8,858
Operating Income	**446**	**1,397**	**1,633**	**1,931**	**3,078**	**5,002**	**2,703**	**4,210**	**5,642**
Income from Other Companies	2,340	1,837	1,440	1,615	1,46S	1,505	1,713	2,380	1,984
Interest Expenses	-3,481	-1,865	-1,153	-985	-1,153	-1,513	-1,621	-3,361	-5,849
Other Income	1,600	250	109	42	122	104	55	90	132
Other Expenses	-1,233	-790	-612	-1,011	-1,244	-472	-857	-861	-1.018
Inflation Adjustment	-1,427	-759	-548	-758	-416	-1,005	-411	-74	-232
Earning B/Taxes	-1,755	69	869	835	1,852	3,622	1,583	2,385	659
Income Taxes	-27	0	-90	-177	-216	-288	-85	-22	-5
Net Income	**-1,782**	**69**	**779**	**658**	**1,637**	**3,334**	**1,498**	**2,362**	**654**
Financial Analysis									
Acid Test	0.82	1.21	0.90	0.83	0.75	0.66	0.55	0.55	0.53
Current Assets	1.28	1.61	1.30	1.36	1.31	1.27	1.04	1.03	1.00
Debt/Net Worth	2.55	1.87	1.51	1.36	1.21	1.04	1.26	1.35	1.10
Sales/Total Assets	0.65	0.72	0.81	0.89	1.10	1.10	0.88	0.85	0.84
Oper. Income/ Total Assets	0.02	0.07	0.10	0.13	0.17	0.21	0.09	0.12	0.13
Net Income/ Total Assets	-7.6%	0.3%	4.8%	4.3%	8.8%	13.9%	5.0%	6.9%	1.6%
Net Income/ Net Worth	-26.9%	1.0%	12.0%	10.3%	19.5%	28.4%	11.3%	16.2%	3.3%

* *not audited*

Exhibit 3: Financial Assessment for the First Phase of the Cochrane-O'Globo Partnership Project

	After Taxes	Before Taxes
Option 1		
VAN 20%	US$ (1,084,000)	US$ 2,201,000
TIR	17.8%	23.7%
Normal Annual Sales	US$ 11,710,000	US$ 11,710,000
Invest. Recover Period	4.8 years	4.7 years
Net Annual Flow	US$ 3,417,000	US$ 4,805,000
Option 2		
VAN 20%	US$ (8,000)	US$ 4,162,000
TIR	20.0%	26.9%
Normal Annual Sales	US$ 12,350,000	US$ 12,350,000
Invest. Recover Period	4.5 years	4.3 years
Net Annual Flow	US$ 3,706,000	US$ 5,437,000
Option 3		
VAN 20%	US$ 5,408,000	US$ 14,545,000
TIR	30.3%	42.3%
Normal Annual Sales	US$ 15,738,000	US$ 15,738,000
Invest. Recover Period	3.6 years	3.2 years
Net Annual Flow	US$ 5,237,000	US$ 8,785,000

Option 1: US$ prices paid by O'Globo Publishing House to its suppliers early in 1991. This level was considered as the lowest in the long term, given that the large increase in the exchange rate over the last few months had not yet been transferred to prices and there was a strong recession in the local graphics industry. Prices to third parties were increased by 12.1% in order to correspond to market prices.

Option 2: Average export prices from Cochrane-Chile to O'Globo Publishing House. They matched competitive prices in several countries around the world, with normal market tax margins. Prices to third parties were increased by 10%.

Option 3: Both to O'Globo Publishing House and to third parties. These prices would correspond to those charged to O'Globo Publishing House by its Brazilian suppliers early in 1990. This option allowed prices to reflect any strong changes that had occurred in the domestic market during the year.

Income Tax Rate: All three alternatives considered using a 50% tax rate.

Exhibit 4: Economic and Demographic Data in some Latin American Countries

Economic Performance of Latin American Countries

	Gross Domestic Products			Inflation	Investment		Foreign Trade		Foreign Debt		
	GDP total 1990 (billions US$)	GDP per capita 1990 US$	Average annual % Real growth rate, 1988-1990	Average annual % rate of inflation, 1988-1990	Average annual rate of gross inv. as % of GDP 1988-1990	Average annual rate of foreign inv. as % of GDP 1988-1990	Total exports, 1990 (billions US$)	Total imports, 1990 (billions US$)	Total foreign debt, 1990 (billions US$)	Average annual % change in foreign debt, 1988-1990	Price of foreign debt swaps %, June 1991
Argentina	93.3	2,887	-2.6	1,423.3	9.2	1.8	12.3	3.8	65.0	3.7	25.1
Bolivia	5.3	738	2.8	18.7	13.3	n.a.	0.8	0.8	3.8	-3.2	n.a.
Brazil	383.4	2,550	-0.6	1,443.5	16.4	0.4	31.4	20.6	122.2	0.3	32.9
Chile	27.2	2,066	6.4	20.3	16.6	4.9	8.3	7.0	18.6	-3.4	88.3
Colombia	44.4	1,345	3.9	28.9	15.4	0.8	7.1	5.1	16.7	2.2	72.8
Costa Rica	5.9	1,946	4.1	20.6	21.2	1.8	1.4	1.8	3.7	-5.5	46.4
Ecuador	11.5	1,087	5.4	62.4	14.4	0.8	2.7	1.7	11.2	3.0	22.3
Mexico	220.1	2,485	2.8	33.1	17.7	1.3	26.8	29.8	98.2	-1.4	55.1
Paraguay	4.5	1,043	5.2	29.4	20.4	n.a.	1.2	1.5	1.8	-4.8	n.a.
Peru	34.1	1,526	-8.3	3,336.1	17.2	0.0	3.3	2.9	17.3	4.1	6.6
Uruguay	8.9	2,890	0.4	94.2	10.8	0.3	1.7	1.3	7.4	7.8	n.a.
Venezuela	46.0	2,328	1.1	49.6	16.5	0.2	17.3	6.5	33.0	-1.8	60.2

Source: CEPAL for columns 1,7,8 and 9. Own elaboration of data from CEPAL for columns 2,3,4,5 and 10 and from Latin Finance for column 6, U.N. DIESA for column 11.

Exhibit 4 (continued): Economic and Demographic Data in Some Latin American Countries

Economic Performance of Latin American Countries

	Population		Urban% 1989	Life expectancy at birth 1989 (years)	Infant mortality rate 1989 (per 1,000 live births)	Adult literacy rate 1985 (%)	Level of Development			
	Total 1990 (millions of inha- bitants)	Average annual increase 1988-1990					Real GDP per head 1987*	Inhabitants per passenger car 1989	Inhabitants per telephone 1989	Inhabitants per TV set 1989
Argentina	32.2	1.3	86	71	30	96	4,647	7.5	8.1	4.8
Bolivia	7.2	2.5	51	54	106	75	1,380	95.9	37.1	13.5
Brazil	150.3	2.1	74	66	59	78	4,307	15.5	10.5	5.4
Chile	13.2	1.7	85	72	19	98	4,862	19.4	15.0	4.1
Colombia	33.0	2.0	69	69	38	88	3,524	48.4	12.5	9.9
Costa Rica	3.0	2.6	47	75	17	93	3,760	36.2	7.2	4.9
Ecuador	10.6	2.6	55	66	61	83	2,687	152.0	15.2	12.8
Mexico	88.6	2.2	72	69	40	90	4,624	15.4	9.0	7.2
Paraguay	4.3	2.9	47	67	32	88	2,603	69.3	37.1	12.3
Peru	22.3	2.5	70	62	79	85	3,129	55.1	29.6	10.7
Uruguay	3.1	0.6	85	73	22	95	5,063	18.4	5.8	4.8
Venezuela	19.7	2.6	84	70	35	87	4.306	12.0	11.0	5.6

* Purchasing power per capita according to United Nations Human Development Report 1990. Sources: United Nations, World Bank, BID, CEPAL.

Source: "Don't Forget Latin America", from Jon I. Martinez, John A. Quelch and Joseph Ganitsky, published by Sloan Management Review, Winter 1992.

10. Fundación Chile

This case was prepared by IMD Professor José Carlos Jirillo, with Professors Jon I. Martínez and Gastón Galleguillos from the Escuela de Negocios de Valparaíso, Universidad Adolfo Ibáñez, as a basis for class discussion rather than to illustrate either effective or ineffective handling of a business situation.

Early in 1992, Anthony Wylie, General Director of Fundación Chile, received two specific requests from the governments of Bolivia and Uruguay: both countries wanted to create "replicas" of his unique institution. Fundación Chile, born as a joint venture between the Chilean government and ITT Corporation (the giant US multinational) for the transfer of technologies that would improve the use of the country's natural resources and productive potential, now had to face one of the most important decisions in its history.

Fundación Chile already had had some experience providing technological assistance services overseas. Since 1985, it had been developing individual projects in several Latin American countries, and had given assistance even to New Guinea and Egypt. However, the response to the requests from countries as close as Bolivia and Uruguay – more than just being two interesting opportunities abroad – could represent the formal, systematic and more intensive starting point of the Foundation's internationalization process. Aware of this potential, the institution's management and the Board of Directors had to take two important decisions. First, they had to determine whether or not international expansion was desirable for Fundación Chile. And then, if this first proposition were approved, they had to decide on a course of action and the way that this process would be implemented.

Historical Background

The history of Fundación Chile could be clearly divided into three principal stages: development, growth and consolidation.

Creation of Fundación Chile

In October 1974, Mr. Raul Saez, Minister of Economic Coordination in President Augusto Pinochet's Cabinet, was commissioned by the Chilean government to solve the difficult situation created by the nationalization – decreed by the former government of President Salvador Allende – of the Compania Chilena de Telefonos, a subsidiary of ITT Corporation.

Part of the solution proposed by Minister Saez was to have an agreement between ITT and the Chilean state whereby they would create Fundación Chile, a non-profit institution, whose objective would be to transfer new technologies, methods and systems that would contribute to the development of the country's productive activities. The idea was accepted by both parties and, on August 3, 1976, Fundación Chile was made a legal entity by decree (law no. 1,528). Each party was to contribute $25 million over a 10-year period, from 1976 to 1985, with almost half of this amount being handed over during the first three years.

The Growth Stage

Throughout the first stage of its existence, between 1976 and 1985, the management of Fundación Chile was entrusted to ITT, which appointed Mr. Wayne Sandvig as Director General.

During those first 10 years, the institution gathered strength in the performance of its mission. It developed a network to carry out an international search for technological and market information. Each year, the organization received a certain amount of assistance from a number of foreign experts, while, at the same time, Fundación Chile officials traveled abroad. It soon became apparent that the areas for action should be the natural resource sectors where Chile had comparative advantages. In these sectors, the government was fostering many attractive advancement opportunities within the market economy, many of which offered wide international possibilities. The agricultural, forestry and seafood sectors were found to be especially favorable and, therefore, the Foundation decided to focus on these areas.

In 1982, a new action channel was developed for handling technological transference: companies using a new technology – either self-
owned or in conjunction with the private sector – were created and
operated. Fundación Chile, realized that the main restraint to introducing and developing new technologies was the scarcity of innovative businessmen who were ready to take this kind of risk. Therefore, the institution decided to explore business opportunities that would provide
private investors with good examples of the advantages that could be
gained when technological development was carefully assessed and
properly managed. During this first period, six "demonstration" companies were to be designed and created in each one of the three specializing sectors. Once they matured, these companies would be sold in
order to finance the creation of new demonstration firms.

The Consolidation Stage

By 1986, the contribution from the parties that had created Fundación
Chile was finally completed, and a change took place in the institution's
management. The contract made with ITT expired at the end of 1985
and, on January 1, 1986, Mr. Anthony Wylie, the former Assistant Director General and Food Technology Director, was appointed by the
Board of Directors to replace Mr. Wayne Sandvig as General Director.

Starting then, Fundación Chile's continuity had to generate the
necessary financial resources on its own. The self-financing level of the
institution's activities began growing steadily, reaching 35% by 1985. By
that point, Fundación Chile had achieved a strong reputation that extended beyond Chile's borders.

During this second stage of the institution's history, 24 new demonstration firms were created, and it was at this time that the first transfers
took place. In late 1988, the Foundation sold Salmones Antártica to a
Japanese company, under very favorable conditions, after bidding on an
international scale produced offers from nine interested parties. Salmones Antártica, a pioneer in the development of a booming growth
sector, had become the largest salmon company in the country. Between 1989 and 1991, Fundación Chile also transferred four other
companies. *(The firms created by Fundación Chile are listed in Exhibit 1,*
along with those already transferred by 1992.)

The pioneering activity performed by the institution in the creation
and development of new industrial sectors, based on the technological
innovations transferred into the country, was also significant. Salmon,

vacuum-packed meat, berries, and other industries were clear examples of sectors where the Foundation had fostered the entrepreneurial activity of many small and medium-sized businesses, helping them to generate dynamic activity in their sectors and others related to them. The boom of the salmon industry in Chile was triggered by the Foundation, from 1982 onwards, through its first demonstration company. Numerous businessmen copied the initiative some years later, thereby achieving sales of $153 million in exports for the sector in 1991. *(In Exhibit 2, a comparison is made – on a more aggregated level – between the growth of Chilean copper exports, total exports, and those exports in the three large sectors where Fundación Chile was working during the years 1976-1991.)*

The Institution in 1992

In 1992, Fundación Chile's specialization in the agribusiness, marine resources and forestry sectors was consolidated. The institution directly employed 244 people, while another 1,352 people worked at the demonstration firms.

The mission of transferring tested technologies to the national productive sector continued to be, in 1992, the great institutional goal of Fundación Chile. That mission materialized by developing routine technological services and technological dissemination, technological assistance services and demonstration firms.

Routine Technological Services and Technological Dissemination

The institution provided laboratory, monitoring and quality control services, the publication of specialized magazines and the organization of seminars. The services given in the agribusiness area, for instance, were basically directed towards the food industry, achieving quality control of raw materials, intermediate goods, processes and finished goods, according to national and international regulations. Fundación Chile had laboratories in Santiago and in its Puerto Montt branch, in the southern part of the country. The latter was devoted to the marine resources area, performing functions similar to those in the agribusiness sector.

It was especially important to determine what the quality control levels for export goods should be – and then fulfill them, since the amount of exporting that the government was promoting meant that maintaining quality was going to be a critical factor. The Foundation's Director General, Anthony Wylie, pointed out:

"Fundación Chile's internal activity is guided by the concept of having business excellence. The Foundation constantly strives to optimize the quality and efficiency of all its products and services."

Joaquin Cordua, Associated Director General and Manager of the Development and Marketing Department, added:

"Since its first years of operation, the Foundation has developed a large program of quality control and certification, including the training of hundreds of monitors. It introduced quality seals for the country's export goods, created chemical and biological analysis laboratories, as well as several laboratories to detect pesticide residues."

In 1991, the Quality Program of Fundación Chile took part in the control of a high percentage of the country's fresh fruit and vegetable exports. In addition, it inspected and certified a great variety of other products: 65% of frozen products, 30% of fruit pulps and juice concentrates, 18% of dehydrated foods, and more than 80% of fresh and frozen salmon. Finally, it granted a quality seal to a significant portion of the country's production of impregnated lumber, among other important activities in this sector.

Technological Assistance Services

At the request of national and international firms and institutions, the Foundation used its inter-disciplinary know-how to give assistance in the fields of technology selection and transferring, technical assistance in technological issues, markets and in assessing investment projects. *(A more detailed view of the type of technological services offered is shown in Exhibit 3, using the Agrobusiness Department as an example.)*

Both for routine service and assistance service offers, the Foundation had competition in Chile from a number of important sources: universities, general and specialized technological institutes, private laboratories, consultants, etc. However, Fundación Chile was favored by its unique image, achievements, capabilities and know-how. None of its competitors had the same overall potential as Fundación Chile in its three areas of specialization.

Fundación Chile's customers were firms in need of technological know-how and technological management. The institutional track was reflected in the sales figures in these areas – called routine technological services and assistance technological services. The total income from these service sales had shown a significant growth, tripling between 1985 and 1991.

The relative size of Fundación Chile's departments was reflected in the amount of their incomes and operational costs. *(Sales of routine and assistance technological services, as well as their operational costs, are shown in Exhibit 4.)* The pricing of these services was market based, seeking to be price competitive and to attract the customer on the basis of quality. On the other hand, the nature of the services and Fundación Chile's own mission explained its policy of not transferring to the customer all the costs associated with this area of activity. It was felt that this kind of economic aid to the private sector allowed better use of the country's resources and that it encouraged business agents to invest in technological innovation matters.

Creating Demonstration Firms

This was the activity that most clearly differentiated Fundación Chile from other technological institutions around the world. It was born in 1982 because the Fundación needed to perform a more active role in the national technological innovation process. Until 1982, many projects had been postponed or rejected because of the risk and slow maturing features perceived by the private sector. The Foundation decided, then, to take up an entrepreneurial role and invest in the creation of demonstration firms.

The Foundation set about this adventure all alone, creating "subsidiaries", or associating with national or foreign businessmen in "affiliate" firms. It sought these liaisons whenever the project's success strongly depended on market knowledge and lengthy experience in a sector, and when projects were bigger than the available resources. But, when these conditions were not a factor, the Foundation preferred to invest in the creation of a new company on its own. Then, project management was easier. there was less potential for a conflict of interest between partners who sought only to maximize profits with short-term investments and the Fundación, whose central goal was to achieve technical and economic success by setting up a firm for the purpose of transferring and disseminating a new technology.

When the objective of demonstrating a new technology's advantages was achieved, the Foundation sold the company. Control of the firm generally was determined – after bidding for shares on a national or international level – by the size of the investment. When the Foundation owned only a minority share, it usually established an agreement of preferred sale to the other shareholders.

The development process of a subsidiary, once it had formally acquired that condition, consisted of two stages. In the starting phase, the company was managed by the Foundation, since the technological element of the project was dominant. Management was generally entrusted to staff people that came from the Foundation itself. This stage was followed by the so-called "weaning" period, after the company had gained a position, had both a clear strategy and structure, and had demonstrated its feasibility.

The first of these demonstration firms was Salmones Antártica Ltda., created in 1982. This subsidiary, devoted to salmon breeding, located its facilities in Chiloé and Aysen, in the extreme southern part of the country. The next one was Cultivos Marinos Tongoy, which devoted years of work to introducing and developing Pacific oysters. They were followed by Procarne and Caprilac, specializing in vacuum-packed meats and products derived from goat's milk, respectively.

Of the 30 firms created since 1982, five had been sold. Of the 25 still existing in 1992, 19 were subsidiaries, i.e., Fundación Chile owned more than 50% of their stock. The rest were affiliates (*refer again to Exhibit 1*). In order to have optimum use of Chile's natural advantages, 27% of the firms were located in the northern part of the country, 19% near the capital, and the remaining 54% in the south.

Patricio Barros, Manager of the Investments Department, who handled the Foundation's investments in all the subsidiary and affiliate firms, proudly explained the novel technology transferring system using demonstration firms:

> "The institution enjoys high credibility in business circles, because it has shown that it takes risks and is able to overcome them. Businessmen have seen that the Foundation has shown its disposition to put its economic resources where its ideas are and to take risks, even before those same businessmen were ready to take them."

Corporate Organization

Fundación Chile had a Board of Directors as its chief collegiate body. In 1992, it consisted of 27 persons, of whom six regular members and six substitute members were nominated by the government, and an equal number were nominated by ITT. As of early 1990, in accordance with the Board's ordinances, there was also one representative from the Instituto de Ingenieros, one representative from the Sociedad Nacional de Agricultura and former US Ambassador Walter Landau participating as ex officio members, able to voice an opinion, but with no voting privilege. The Board's President had to be a Director nominated by the government, and the Vice-President was an ITT Director elected by the Board.

Patricio Barros, Manager of the Investments Department, described the decision-making process that Fundación Chile used to address, for instance, the various and profuse initiatives derived from its staff activity.

> "One of the technical-professional groups works out a program. This program is first submitted to their own department, with questions for directors and businessmen in the area. Department management then presents it to the Managers' Committee. Once the Committee has examined it – including all essential outside consultations, the Director General either approves or rejects it. When the Director General has given his approval, it goes on to be examined by the Sectorial Board. For example, if the project relates to a fishing firm, the Fishing Board sees it. In addition, every initiative has to be given a medium and long-term perspective, so it must be examined by the Strategic Planning Committee as well. Then, after everything else, because it will require funds and will affect the Foundation's equity, it must also go to the Finance committee. With the "blessings" of all these groups, it finally goes to the Board of Directors of Fundación Chile, which will decide to take it or leave it."

The Finance and Strategic Planning Committees were composed of directors, with the President of the institution presiding over them. The meetings were also attended by the Director General and the Investments Manager in the first case, and by the Director General and the Development and Marketing Manager in the second case.

The President of the Board valued the kind of administration that ruled the institution, as well as the multi-dimensional pluralist constitution of the Board in professional and political aspects, and the experience of its members. He commented:

"Finally, everything – and I will maintain that disposition – is agreed upon by common consent. Voting has never been necessary. We know that some initiatives have already been aborted because of disagreements during the previous filtering process. By the time things get to the Board of Directors, they have been sufficiently analyzed."

Financing

Fundación Chile was a private non-profit corporation, but was forced to finance itself. It had, in 1992, three financing sources for its operational activities. One was by selling technological services (laboratories, quality control, technical assistance, etc.). This was, therefore, an operational source; the other two sources were non-operational: income from investing its equity funds in the stock market; income and capital gains from its subsidiaries and affiliate firms.

In 1991, the operational income was 1,815 million pesos, compared to 3,503 million pesos in operational costs, with the self-financing coefficient at 51.8% (slightly lower than the coefficient in 1990, which reached 52.3%), but considerably higher than the 38% of 1985. The interests earned in the stock market were not able to reverse the operational deficit, which was made worse by a negative result in the subsidiary and affiliate firms, the fiscal year thereby showing a net capital loss of 1,113 million pesos, lower than that of the previous year, which had reached 1,529 million pesos.

(*Exhibit 6 presents a summary of the institution's results, as well as its equity situation.*)

The capital loss was a situation that could be accepted for a year or two, but it was undesirable in the medium or long term. Eventually, the Foundation was expected to maintain, at least, the initial $50 million contributed by the founding parties.

The financing contribution that Fundación Chile obtained from the firms it created came, rather than from dividends generated by their operations, from the sale of those firms, which generally occurred when they had reached the point of being able to generate such dividends, after a period of reinvesting profits in them.

However, the firms did make a contribution towards raising the self-financing coefficient. This derived from the internal policy of establishing technological assistance contracts between Fundación Chile and its firms, guarding against subsidizing them or being subsidized by them, i.e., trying to establish a market price for such services. The maximum percentage of self-financing (59%) was achieved in 1988, the year when the Foundation sold its first firm.

International Activities

The international dimension of Fundación Chile was implicit in its mission of looking for and selecting external technologies. From its beginnings in 1976, the institution had invested a great deal of effort in establishing contacts with the main international sources of technology, and later in disseminating the latter inside the country. However, it was only at the end of its first ten years that Fundación Chile's activities – specifically, rendering technological assistance – extended beyond Chile's borders.

Overseas Projects

In 1985, Fundación Chile made an agreement with Fundación Salvadorena para el Desarrollo Economico y Social (FUSADES) to furnish technological assistance in El Salvador's agribusiness sector. This agreement was directed at identifying horticultural farming with export potential and finding cultures that could replace those which Salvador had to import from other Central American countries. In this first international agreement, technicians from Fundación Chile worked for four years in El Salvador.

From then on, Fundación Chile extended its technological assistance and agribusiness project assessment activities to other countries – Colombia, Peru, Bolivia, Argentina, Uruguay, Ecuador, Guatemala, New Guinea and Egypt among them. All those projects consisted of specific services, except the ones in Bolivia and El Salvador, where more extensive programs were carried out. Patricio Galeb, Manager of the Agribusiness Department, outlined the external interests in this way:

> "In most countries we have found the same problems: how to find
> a way to diversify agriculture, to increase exports or to enhance
> product quality, a way to open marketing channels, etc. When we
> were hired in Central America, for instance, the intention was to
> switch from sugar cane, cotton and coffee to other products.
> Today, El Salvador is exporting 10 million boxes of fresh melons to
> the United States, thus reaching one of the goals we had set for

that project. Countries resembling ours are seeking to do things the way we have done them in Chile."

Developing these projects provided Fundación Chile with a valuable source of experience, international projection and income. Likewise, there was also an increase in foreign attendance at the courses and seminars conducted by the institution in Chile. The First International Fruit Congress, sponsored by Fundación Chile in 1989 and repeated in the following years, had special significance. It brought about an awareness of Chile's leadership position as the first horticultural and fruit exporting country in the Southern Hemisphere.

International Marketing

Fundación Chile used, basically, two channels for the international marketing of its technological services. One of its three departments was primarily a technical public relations function – carried out personally by the institution's chief executives, who were frequently asked to speak and participate in congresses and seminars in different countries. These conferences presented a very important opportunity to display the kinds of services the institution could offer to customers abroad. Each department had, moreover, an international prospectus, and a similar one for the institution as a whole was also being worked out.

The second channel was to systematically make a formal approach to financing sources, such as the World Bank, the Inter-American Development Agency (AID), the EEC, etc. Fundación Chile's President himself and the Development Manager conducted the institutional relations with these international organizations.

Though rendering technological services abroad was considered a profitable activity – internally very highly regarded, its executives recognized that the institutional attitude towards them was reactive rather than based on an active search. A very high percentage of the projects in which they had participated had not been "sought out", although each opportunity had succeeded in being swiftly capitalized. On the other hand, Luis Hernan Bustos, Marketing Projects Manager for Fundación Chile, thought that these services had to be better adapted to each market's actual needs. He pointed out.

"The organization is not, so to say, properly adapted to render these international services; basically, it only repeats outside what it is doing in Chile. I think these markets should be addressed in a different way, according to their particular requirements."

In relation to demonstration firms, the international marketing activities were very restricted. The small size of most of them, derived from their initial state – since they were sold in the public market when they developed and consolidated – prevented them from penetrating the international market by themselves. All of them used distributors and agents in destination markets. The international marketing was restricted to export marketing that focused on supplying importers and dealers abroad.

These firms had access to research studies about the prospective foreign markets, but the data was gathered at the beginning of the project, to analyze the firm's feasibility. Once past that step, these firms had to finance themselves and, given their small size, it was difficult to afford new market research. Therefore, they got information through visits to customers, daily contact in the market and participation in international expositions.

International Competition

Fundación Chile faced competition from many foreign consulting firms and institutions. In the United States, for instance, there were a great number of small and medium-sized firms devoted to providing technological and project assistance services, primarily to Third World countries. These firms were closely related to the financing sources, as many of them included former executives from the World Bank or from AID. As well, when any of these institutions – such as AID or the EEC – financed a project abroad, they demanded that the contractors be American or European. In fact, Fundación Chile sometimes was the subcontractor hired by these firms to carry out jobs in Third World countries.

Other very important international competitors were the original purveyors of technology. Fundación Chile, being an institution created to transfer technology into Chile, sometimes had to apply to these original sources of technology. These technology and equipment purveying firms also supplied technical assistance, which made them strong competitors against whom it was very difficult to compete. Many of these original purveyors built facilities and delivered all finished projects to their customers. Fundación Chile, on the other hand, offered assistance in project structuring and development, assessment of the requirements to carry them out and other opportunities, but it did not build facilities and equipment.

Nevertheless, Fundación Chile had certain specific advantages which helped the organization to obtain projects in such a competitive international market. As one high executive said:

"I think that our main advantage is having greater involvement in the projects we carry out. Usually, the individual that we send abroad has successfully developed the same project in Chile. That means actually transferring technology. Most American consulting firms only send an expert who looks at the work to be done, makes a set of recommendations, hands over a bundle of papers and goes away. That is, he doesn't actually involve himself in the project."

Fundación Chile had other distinct advantages as well. A very important one was that its prices were somewhat lower, because its engineers and qualified technicians were paid less than those from the developed countries' institutions. As well, in many Third World – especially Latin American countries, Fundación Chile benefited from knowledge of the language, a cultural affinity, and the experience of having successfully used the particular technology in a developing country.

Requests from Bolivia and Uruguay

Just as groups of private businessmen and institutions from different countries hired Fundación Chile's technical assistance services, some international organizations – such as the World Bank or AID – had shown great interest in having an institution like Fundación Chile in other countries. The knowledge that such an institution could have about technology, businessmen, markets, and the business activity itself permitted it to be more flexible and confident, thus in a better position to benefit from international funds allotted to economic cooperation.

Believing in this idea, during 1991 the governments of Bolivia and Uruguay made specific requests to Fundación Chile asking it to participate in the creation of similar institutions in their countries. Their requests were typical of the interest shown in Fundación Chile by other Latin American countries as well. In April 1991, conversations with a Bolivian governmental organization called Proyecto de Asociaciones Campesinas (Peasant Associations Project), financed by AID, had been initiated. Since this project was almost finished, they wished to perpetuate it by establishing an institution like Fundación Chile and needed the latter's assistance to achieve this end. Later on, some high executives in the Executive Secretariat of PL480 – a Bolivian organization that managed a yearly budget of $20-30 million provided by the US government – intended to allocate part of those resources, some $10 million, to creating a technological transfer institution according to the pattern set by Fundación Chile.

The situation in Uruguay was similar to the one in Bolivia. In October 1991, five executives from Fundación Chile were invited by PENTA, a Non-Traditional Exports Promotion Program, to examine the feasibility of creating a replica of Fundación Chile in their country. They also asked for the latter's assistance in organizing such an institution. At the same time, the possibility of the Chilean institution's assistance in developing the aqua culture, forestry and agriculture sectors of its neighbor was explored. However, unlike the Bolivian project, PENTA did not have a clear and reliable financing alternative. The Uruguayans proposed to pay Fundación Chile for its assistance by evaluating its contribution and applying it towards a percentage of ownership in the new institution.

Internal Debate

At a Strategic Planning Meeting attended by Fundación Chile's management and board members, these requests from abroad and the issue of international opportunities offered to the Fundación were jointly discussed. For a long time, many had felt that Fundación Chile's institutional position regarding international requests needed to be defined.

There were several options for the course of action that Fundación Chile should follow to achieve international status. Some people thought that the institution should benefit from the original and successful model that it had developed by transferring that model to Bolivia, Uruguay and other countries. They claimed that this transference should be paid for just like any other technical assistance; it should not be remunerated by having a part ownership in the new institution, as the Uruguayans proposed. The people at Fundación Chile who felt that the institution should pursue the option of contributing to the creation of replicas in other countries saw it both as a profitable activity and as a way to project Chile's image as an efficient up-to-date country.

However, there were others at Fundación Chile who thought that creating replicas of the institution in Bolivia and Uruguay was an option that would benefit those countries more than it would benefit Chile. They agreed that the institution had to go from a situation of reacting to external requirements to one of designing an international action strategy, but they maintained that it should combine national interests with institutional interests. They pointed out that their own internal customers and the Chilean business sector could raise severe objections about transferring technology and Fundación Chile's model, as then international competition would undoubtedly develop, especially in those neighboring countries with similar competitive advantages in natural resources. Such competition would, in their opinion, strongly affect Chilean exporters in those industries in general and demonstration firms created by the Foundation itself in particular.

There was one Foundation representative who went even beyond the idea of creating replicas of the institution in other countries. He maintained that the Foundation could take an active role in these replicas and Chile did not necessarily have to be involved. This executive explained his proposal:

"The Foundation has developed an expertise that allows it to know how to detect an opportunity somewhere. to know its limitations given the existing technology, how to deal with the technology suppliers and how to adapt a technology to real needs. And, there is no reason why it must be done in a specific place. You can carry out that job in other countries. The internationalization of an institution like this one implies also an 'offshore' technological transfer. In other words, if we develop a project in Bolivia, we do not have to limit ourselves to bringing technology from Chile; we can as well, for instance, import it from France. And why not? If we are in the business of technological transferring, that is our business."

Asked about the incompatibility of that position with Fundación Chile's mission of contributing to Chilean development, the executive added:

"In effect, the best way to benefit Chile is to help its businesses and institutions to be internationally strong. That, naturally, implies changing or enlarging the mission. Chile would go on being the Foundation's operating center, but there would be operations in other countries as well. This external presence would give access to many more technology sources, to more ideas, to more market knowledge. The idea, anyway, would not be to create these replicas all alone, but together with people from abroad, setting up a network that would allow us to do a much better job in Chile."

One director set forth the idea that Fundación Chile's internationalization should follow a different course, closely linked to the creation of "antenna" firms. Their purpose would be to maintain a permanent bond with innovation sources and to have entry windows to technological development ("technological antennas"). These firms could also be on the lookout for opportunities to place products by opening up markets and distribution channels, and by gaining access to a direct knowledge of Chilean export receiving markets ("commercial antennas"). In other words, these antennas would consist of direct investments made by Fundación Chile in developed countries. There were alternatives, like associating with leading foreign firms in the three areas where the Foundation specialized. The same thing could be done with technological institutes, and it was also possible to associate with Chilean firms in order to have access to people who could act on the international scene.

Taking the previous idea in another direction, it was proposed to encourage Fundación Chile's specialists by hiring them out, on a commission basis, for projects of international agencies, such as the BID or the World Bank.

However, some directors and executives did not clearly see the value of establishing "commercial antennas". One of them pointed out:

"To me, the only way of creating market-placed antennas is to work in the markets. An individual sitting in an office and trying to look at what is happening in the markets is of no use. The only way to know about the markets is to participate in them."

He proposed the creation of a subsidiary of Fundación Chile that would buy the products of demonstration firms and other businesses to systematically commercialize them in foreign markets, acting as a trading company. The idea was that this subsidiary, by being deeply involved in the market, would detect new and interesting opportunities. In addition, this trading company would facilitate selling the demonstration firm's products abroad, as several of these demonstration firms – due to their small size or early developmental stage – could not afford an export department. This trading company would also be able to penetrate important markets more effectively, by establishing its own offices and representatives in those countries. This would add value to the demonstration firms, as they would have a better commercial backing.

The proposition that demonstration firms establish their own subsidiaries and commercial organizations abroad, instead of exporting through agents and dealers or through the Foundation in a centralized way, was another idea supported by several people. In fact, by the end of 1991, CENTEC – one of Fundación Chile's wood furniture demonstration firms – was seriously considering creating a subsidiary in the United States associated with an important American customer who owned a wooden furniture store network. This joint venture, with an investment of nearly one million dollars, would provide benefits to both partners. For the Chilean firm, it would mean securing access to the distribution channel, while the American firm would acquire the providing source – by demanding exclusivity from the Chilean supplier.

This option, however, was more complex for small-sized or incipient demonstration firms, as they did not have enough operational volume or margins to finance that kind of arrangement.

Finally, some directors and executives were against all these ideas, maintaining that Fundación Chile did not have enough of its own resources to develop these kinds of activities. They proposed that the Foundation continue only with particular assistance jobs to other countries and that the type of services which could be offered internationally should be defined. One of them stated:

"We should offer those services as long as they are profitable. We can subsidize firms in Chile, but not abroad. Besides, we should do interesting things only, things which will not interfere with our national activity. The Foundation is a small institution, where each individual is very important. So, we should not do anything that might decrease the quality of the job done in Chile in order to undertake international activities. My opinion is that we must not accept more than three or four international assistance jobs per year."

Final Considerations

Through 1991, government, university and business sector representatives had begun to be aware that Chilean firms needed to accelerate the creation process of competitive advantages in the international environment. Marked trends towards a world market approach, building trade blocs, swift innovation of products and processes, increasing technological and environmental pressures, etc., forced everyone to reflect on the future competitiveness of local firms. The country had increased its exports from $3,800 million in 1985 to $9,000 million in 1991. Non-copper exports went from 27% in 1974 to 54% in 1991. That same year, Chilean exports per capita had doubled those of Mexico and tripled Brazil's. Notwithstanding these significant achievements, experts considered that the country had only just reached the threshold of the international markets. Therefore, it was necessary to enter "a second stage" – one of greater presence and participation in the different links of the value chain all the way to the final consumer abroad. At the same time, the value added process of the export product needed to become more dynamic. Anthony Wylie commented:

> "The Foundation's ongoing endeavor is to transform the country's comparative advantages into competitive advantages. To accomplish this goal, there must be an added value in primary products advantageously offered by the country."

Fundación Chile, in the opinion of most experts, could not be left out of this "second stage", since it was the pioneering institution in the technological development of three of the four main exporting sectors of the country. The management and the Board of Directors had started to seriously consider the role that the institution should perform in this new environment. One individual expressed the need of addressing Fundación Chile's international projection, following the new trends observed in the analysis of world scope competition. He concluded that Fundación Chile had to internationalize in order to contribute to the internationalization of Chilean firms.

Submerged in such a complex picture, Anthony Wylie felt entirely clear about only one thing: the answers that he had to give Bolivia and Uruguay involved strategic decisions about internationalization for his institution. The executives and directors should address this decision promptly, but with maximum care. There appeared to be numerous opportunities and options, and the task of reaching an agreement on these various decision levels was not going to be easy.

Exhibit 1: Demonstration Firms of Fundación Chile

Area	Firm	Goods	Year it was created	Year it was transferred	% owned by Fundación Dec. 31, 1991	Equity Fundación Chile (million $1992)[1]
Agri-business	Agricola Esmeralda S.A	Exotic fruits and tropical seeds	1989		100	246.7
	Granjanova S.A.	Packed vegetables free from contamination	1989		100	646.9
	Punto Verdo S.A.[2]	Vegetables marketing			100	–
	Granja Sur S.A.	Fresh apples for export and juice	1989		100	568.9
	Agronova S.A.	Export citrus fruits	1989		100	795.5
	Agroinversiones Huacán S.A.	Paprika experimenting	1990		100	214.8
	Agricola y Vitivinicola Itata S.A.	Export fine wines	1989		100	308.7
	Tecnagro Cautin S.A	Berries and asparagus	1987		55	46.1
	Tecnofrio S.A.	Berries and asparagus processing	1988		55	144.9
	Berries La Unión S.A.-C.P.A	Berries	1985	1990	–	–
	Berries La Unión S.A.	Berries processing	1985	1990	–	–
	Procarne	Vacuum-packed meat	1983	1989	–	–
	Caprilac[3]	Goat milk Cheese	1983		–	–
Marine Resources	Cultivos Marinos Tongoy	Pacific oyster seeds	1983		100	396.4
	Cultivos Achao S.A.	Pacific oysters	1989		100	107.2
	Finamar S.A.	Smoked salmon	1988	1991	–	–
	Salmotec S.A.	Pacific and Atlantic salmon	1988		100	541.8
	Tecnofish S.A.	Turbot juveniles	1991		66	–
	Granjamar S.A.	Turbot juveniles	1990		100	194.1
	Cultivos Mares de Chile S.A.	Turbot fattening	1991		100	316.8
	Semilas Marinas S.A.	Avalon juveniles	1990		100	64.6
	Campos Marinos S.A.	Avalon fattening	1990		100	34.8
	Salmones Huillinco S.A.	Atlantic salmon juveniles	1987		25	121
	Salmonas Antártica	Salmon and Trout	1982	1988	–	–
Forestry	Constructora e Inmobiliaria 2000 S.A.	Energy-thermic housing	1989		100	19.6
	CENTEC S.A.	Furniture parts and components	1989		100	1,218.9
	Ignis Terra S.A.	Lenga sawing and marketing	1991		10	53.6
	Tecnoplant S.A.	Tree nursery	1990		50	91.9
	Lumber Ram S.A.	Structure lumber	1989		33.33	75.5
Information Technologies and others	Auprin S.A.	Industrial automation	1987		76	55.9
	Capitales e Inversiones S.A.	Venture capital	1988		12.5	47.0

[1] For its US$ equivalent, see average exchange rate in Exhibit 7

[2] It belongs to Granjanova S.A.

[3] In 1989 it was transformed into Salmotec, S.A.

Exhibit 2: Chilean Export Growth by Selected Sectors, 1976-1990

Export Value (in US$ millions)			Growth
Sector	1976	1990	Factor
Forestry[1]	166	839	5.05
Agriculture and Cattle[2]	134	1,111	8.29
Fishing[3]	91	881	9.68
Copper[4]	2,083	3,907	1.87

Source: Indicadores de Comercio Exterior, Banco Central de Chile.

[1] It includes uncut timber, manufactured lumber, furniture, paper, cellulose and derived goods.

[2] It includes agro-industrial goods such as: canned fruit, desiccated fruit, fruit juices, milk, meat, etc.

[3] It includes fish meal, fresh and frozen fish, mollusks, canned fish.

[4] It does not include scrap copper or manufactured copper.

Exhibit 3: Services Offered by the Agribusiness Department

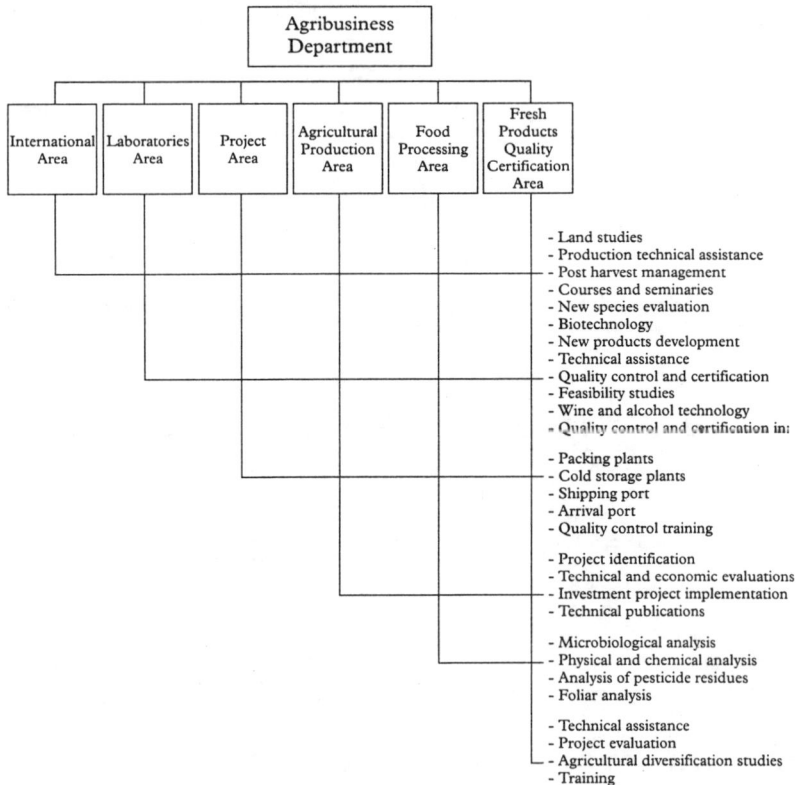

Exhibit 4: Technological Services Income and Costs by Departments, 1991

Department	Revenues from service sales	Operational Costs	Self-financing coefficient
Laboratories	229.9	233.5	98%
Agribusiness	531.9	761.1	70%
Marine Resources	560.4	793.5	71%
Forestry	386.7	597.2	65%
Others[2]	106.7	1,117.6	

(in $ millions by December 31)[1]

Source: Fundación Chile Internal Records

[1]For its US$ equivalent, see corresponding exchange rate in Exhibit 7.

[2]It includes General Management, and the Departments of Development and Marketing, Investments, and Finances and Administration

Exhibit 5: Organization Chart of Fundación Chile

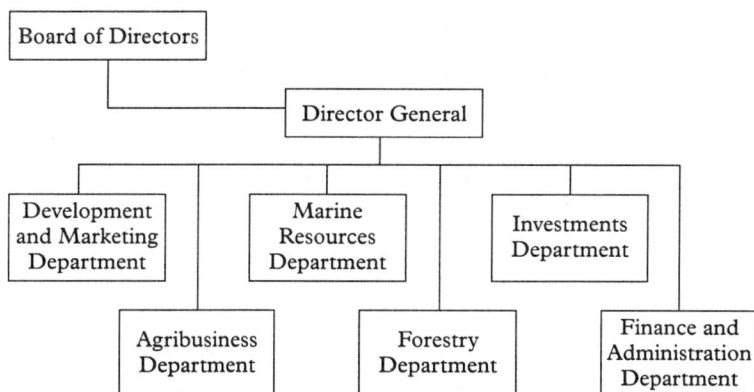

Exhibit 6a: Summary of Results 1991

(in millions of pesos, at December 31)[1]	1991	1992
Operational Revenue[2]	1,815.4	1,631.3
- Operational Cost[3]	3,503.0	3,122.1
= Operational Result	(1,687.6)	(1,490.8)
+ Actual Interests	1,188.7	394.8
+ Firms Result[4]	(428.3)	(256.0)
- Monetary Adjustment		
Due to Inflation	118.4	152.2
- Others	67.8	24.8
= Surplus	(1,113.4)	(1,529.0)
Self-Financing Coef. (%)	51.8	52.3

[1]For its equivalent in US$, see corresponding exchange rate in Exhibit 7
[2]Services Sales + Sale Cost of Goods.
[3]Operating Expenses - Sale Cost of Goods.
[4]Related Firms Income + Capital Gains on Sale of Firms.

Exhibit 6b: Equity State 1991

(in millions of pesos, at December 31)[1]	1991	1990
Financial Investments	10,605.7	13,432.9
+ Firms Investments	6,312.6	5,725.8
+ Net Capital Assets	3,007.8	2,841.6
+ Work Capital	952.6	(8.2)
= Equity	20,878.7	21.992.1

[1]For its equivalent in US$, see corresponding exchange rate in Exhibit 7

Exhibit 7: Some Chilean Macroeconomic Indicators

	1985	1986	1987	1988	1989	1990	1991
GDP (%)	2.4	5.7	5.7	7.4	10.0	2.1	6.0
Inflation (%)	26.3	17.4	21.5	12.7	21.5	27.3	18.7
Unemployment(%)	13.2	8.8	7.9	6.3	5.3	5.7	5.3
Trade Balance (US$ millions)	849	1100	1229	2219	1578	1273	1576
External Debt (US$ millions)	19.44	19.50	19.21	17.64	16.25	17.45	16.41
Average Exchange Rate ($/US$, Dec. 31)	183.66	205.0	238.11	247.49	296.58	336.86	374.51
Real Wages Variation	1.9	2.1	0.5	4.3	3.1	5.0	4.9

Source: Economic and Social Indicators 1960-1988. Banco Central de Chile. Monthly
Bulletin. Banco Central de Chile.

11. Mentec Ltd.

This case was prepared by Professor Per V. Jenster and Sean O. Reagain of the IDA as a basis for class discussion rather than to illustrate either effective or ineffective handling of a business situation.

"We are about to enter the fourth stage of our life as a company with a new revolutionary product aimed at the video conferencing market," said Michael Peirce, founder and Chief Executive of Mentec Computer Systems Ltd., a Dublin-based firm with £17 million in sales and an impressive growth record. "Next week, on June 2, 1992," he continued explaining to his visitor, "my technology manager, Christopher Fairclough, and my trading manager, Frank Waters, are accompanying me on a 4-day tour of the US where we are visiting seven firms interested in doing business with us – all excellent companies with a fine reputation."

"And what's your strategy going to be?" the visitor asked.

"We'll have to figure that out on the plane," Peirce answered. "I know how important it is to think strategically, but right now we have an opportunity crisis and only a small window for exploiting it."

Background

Mentec was founded in 1979 by Michael Peirce, a professional engineer who had quit a career with ICI in England at the end of the 1960s because of national merger restraint policies and conditions, and had returned to lecture in manufacturing subjects at the Engineering School at Trinity College in Dublin. He recalled:

> "I think my salary was only just over £1,000. I received the 4% maximum increase allowed under the Government's income policy but, as a professional engineer with four years of experience, it made me wonder what the world was all about."

Peirce therefore opted to return to Dublin to do research and get a doctorate in the area of manufacturing, focusing specifically on the area of computer implementation of on-line and real-time computing, which was just emerging at the time.

Having completed his research in 1976, Peirce looked around for opportunities to build up project work in industry. To this end, he established a small team within the university engineering department, which soon became involved with some industrial companies. Two projects were conducted for these companies: one providing automatic testing in telecommunications and the other gathering data from machines on the factory floor of a large tire factory. After developing these projects and demonstrating that a commercial opportunity existed, Peirce felt that it was logical to continue by formally establishing a business. Understanding this decision was difficult for his family and friends, many of whom believed that he was crazy to give up a good salary and a secure job. But, Pierce himself had no doubts. "I never really found it difficult, because I was so excited about what I was going to do."

A significant factor in Peirce's decision to set up on his own at that time was that it coincided with the launch of the Enterprise Development Programme by the Industrial Development Authority of Ireland (IDA). This was a support scheme designed exclusively for people with previous management experience who wanted to start their own ventures but who lacked the capital to do so. Under this Programme, a loan guarantee was offered as part of a generous incentive package to these high-potential entrepreneurs. For Peirce, this support was crucial in making the venture happen.

> "With the IDA endorsement – a very important thing to have – it was possible to go to a bank and borrow what, at the time, seemed like a horrendously large amount of money. We had absolutely no equity of our own. The partner's equity from day one was entirely borrowed money."

Peirce himself worked out the details of financing the venture, including the negotiation with the IDA, and he identified suitable people to join him in forming the management team. This team consisted of a close colleague from the university, a former student and two other business people, with Peirce having a 74% interest. The company, which Peirce called "Mentec Ltd.", had a total equity of £40,000 at the outset, of which the IDA subscribed £20,000 in redeemable preference shares. The two owners of the company, Peirce and his university colleague, held 100% of the ordinary equity of the company. Bank facilities of £150,000 were also put in place.

Neither Peirce nor his co-directors had had any previous experience running a business. Although Peirce had held cost center responsibilities at ICI, he had not had much exposure to balance sheet management. However, the IDA – in return for its substantial injection of equity into the company and the provision of a loan guarantee with the banks – proposed a nominee director to the company, Kieran Flynn, who Peirce appointed as chairman. Flynn was a senior industrial figure who had been managing director of a public company and had had more than 20 years of financial experience. Looking back on this period, Peirce explained the significance of Flynn's role:

> "Flynn insisted on the rigor of having board meetings – which we might not have had – as well as monthly accounts, which we certainly would not have done. In this start-up phase of the business, his input was strategically immense: he made us face up to the fact that we were in the investment phase – the loss-making phase – of the business. Flynn was never involved in the company in an operational sense; his contribution was on specific issues. He was physically present in the company two or three times a week, which worked out well because it meant that he was accessible to me and my management team on an almost executive chairman basis. It gave a group of technologists like us, from day one, a very experienced financial man. It was this fact which distinguished Mentec from the many companies that fell by the wayside. He made a big, big difference."

In its initial phase, Mentec was essentially a project organization. Its target market was exclusively in manufacturing systems. It focused on real-time systems, mainly targeting multinationals. In this phase, the company was a project-driven, project-seeking organization whose specific skill was linking computers to manufacturing equipment. The company did not focus on any specific sector, but it operated only in Ireland, and with the distinct and growing multinational manufacturing sector. This meant that, from the outset, Mentec had good references, and that list continued to grow. Moreover, by definition, these client companies could afford to pay: other businesses were pulled down by clients that simply could not pay for the services they had received.

Key Decisions

Mentec's original business focus was clearly on systems design and installation of systems tailored to individual company requirements.

These solutions fulfilled the client's needs from system content to hardware and software design, installation and implementation through to aftercare and maintenance.

One critical start-up decision made by Mentec was to target the process control and support systems market rather than the fast-growing personal computer (PC) market. This market would grow more slowly, but it represented a higher value-added opportunity. This decision meant making a massive commitment of financial resources, a difficult undertaking for a small company at such an early stage. However, the investment did yield a return: when the PC market became more and more price competitive, the process control and real time systems market, though it had been more costly to enter, was offering a larger customer base.

As Mentec's relationship with its clients developed, the market drew the company into additional computing-related areas – e.g., production, inventory and distribution control. Many companies wanted Mentec to set up complete systems, including financial, commercial and manufacturing systems. To capitalize on this opportunity, Mentec established an informal alliance with a company that specialized in financial systems development. Every time an application needed both manufacturing and financial skills, Mentec and its partner made a joint quotation. One of the companies always took the lead role: if Mentec saw an opportunity to win new business, but needed a financial systems supplement, the partner company would provide it, and vice versa. While this arrangement never constituted a legal agreement, it seemed to work exceptionally well for Mentec for eight years.

By 1987, however, Mentec had outgrown its ally. Although the partner company was highly professional, exceptionally well managed and rich in cash, it had made strategic errors where retrenchment was the only way out. While Mentec had focused on real-time systems, its ally had opted for quicker returns by pursuing the multiple system PC market. As that market became more competitive and the products were seen as commodities, the company was left stranded with a lot of smaller customers and inadequate purchasing power in the market. When the principal of the partner company decided to leave, it made sound commercial sense for Mentec to buy the company. It had complementary skills, was cash rich and had a clean balance sheet. The merger proved to be very successful: Mentec's traditional profile of being engineering-focused and workshop-oriented combined well with the partner's more clear-cut, MIS staff profile.

The merger integrated every member of the partner company's staff into Mentec. They physically moved into Mentec's premises, their senior directors were given senior appointments – in the commercial systems area – and they became, as Peirce said, "the leaders of part of our tribe". The blend of the two mind-sets enhanced Mentec's capability so well that, by end of 1989, the two companies were totally integrated.

In addition to the informal partnership that Mentec had developed in 1983 with the other small Irish firm, the company also formed a strategic alliance with Digital Equipment Corporation (DEC), which had two plants in Ireland – in Galway and Tipperary. The relationship consolidated after DEC announced that it had a processing chip for open sale which enabled products to be designed around DEC's PDP technology. Following a visit by DEC engineers, Mentec began purchasing the chip and using it in an R&D program to design a bottom-end data acquisition product based on very advanced technology.

The relationship with DEC allowed Mentec to have a commonly accepted architecture throughout its implementation projects. The downside was that DEC was a relatively expensive equipment supplier and a large proportion of Mentec's revenue tended to revert back to DEC. Mentec remained closely allied to DEC until 1991, although projections showed that the amount of Mentec business accounted for by DEC was changing: having fallen from 95% to 60% in the three years between 1988 and 1991. As DEC's technology matured, management at Mentec concluded at that time that DEC had less to offer in terms of advanced chip technology development. To build on its core skill in single board computer design, Mentec therefore began seeking a second generation supplier. Having surveyed the market alternatives, it formed a technical relationship with Intel to design a range of single board computers based on the Intel 860 processor. By 1991, Mentec had completely minored its achievements with DEC's PDP technology, using the Intel technology instead.

As Mentec's technology developed, its management always put a high priority on ensuring that the organizational structure also evolved effectively. In 1985, the company radically changed its structure, following the recommendation of an international consulting firm. The consultants pointed out that, as Mentec grew, it would be very important to differentiate between its major sources of profits. At that time under Irish tax law, profits from exports were exempt from taxation; as well, dividends paid by exporting companies – whether to Irish citizens or foreigners – were tax free. In effect, companies enjoyed a double tax break. Under the guidance of the consultants, Mentec learned that it was very important to set up its export operation as a separate business, to insulate the profits from this activity.

To avoid having its operations resemble "a piece of spaghetti", Peirce reorganized Mentec into three companies to reflect the three different tax structures it faced: the export company, which had historically enjoyed zero taxation; the system's integration company, which faced 10% taxation in Ireland and 46% taxation in the UK, and the sales company in Ireland, whose profits were all taxed at 46%. The group board consisted of the managing directors of the three companies and reported to Peirce as chief executive. This organization structure worked well, allowing Mentec to clearly establish what its margins were in each area of operation.

The Three Stages

Looking back at Mentec's first decade of operation, Peirce identified three distinct stages in the company's development.

1. *Lift-off:* In this phase, Mentec's focus was exclusively on the home market, it had zero sales abroad. In the company's first year, it earned IR£ 60,000 in sales within six months. In the next year, its first full year of business, sales were around IR£ 260,000. In the third year, sales climbed to IR£ 750,000.

2. *Conscious consolidation, followed by entry into a new growth path:* In the fourth year, turnover growth slowed – with sales of IR£ 875,000. In subsequent years, sales turnover increased to IR£ 1.2 million and then IR£ 1.7 million.

Peirce cited three key factors which helped the company move from stage one to stage two successfully. First, having a chairman with a strong financial background and experience was critical; he was able to win and hold the confidence of the banks during the initial investment phase of company life.

The second important decision was appointing a full-time executive accountant early in the company's life. According to Peirce:

"There is a tendency among technology-driven start-up companies to hide R&D costs in the hope that they will be forgotten once they are profitable. However, in many cases, because these costs are ignored, profitability never is reached and the company collapses. By having an accountant in place, Mentec never allowed itself to hide poor financial performance; it was always forced to face up to and address the facts."

The third and most critical factor was, in Peirce's opinion, the adoption of spreadsheet technology for cash flow management as soon as the company had large sales revenues. While this decision might seem trivial, Pierce viewed it as crucial.

"I think that if we hadn't taken that step, we would have "gone broke" by year three, notwithstanding the Chairman's financial expertise, the bank support, the lot. 1 don't think anything would have substituted for the fact that we did – week by week, 12 weeks forward – cash flow management based on spreadsheet projections. The absolutely critical period was from year three to five. Good banking won't get you through this period when the numbers are going up rapidly. Not even good trading will get you through. You have got to have a financial controller who can look 12 weeks ahead and say that we are going to need IR£ 300,000 more or we will be overtrading."

3. *Divisionalization* (started in 1987): Sales growth was continuing rapidly; annual sales reached £2.7 million, and they continued to grow to IR£ 3.7 million in 1988.

In the company's formative years, overemphasis on cost center definition and performance was not desirable because people tended to be defensive if put under too much scrutiny. However, as strong sustained profit growth was achieved, performance measurement based on cost centers became very important in determining the actual strategic directions to be taken.

The establishment of three separate companies within Mentec represented the first layer of divisionalization. Then, setting up cost centers inside the individual companies created the second layer. The fact that each particular area of company activity could act independently was at the core of Mentec's successful advance into stage three. It was believed that the root of the company's growth could be attributed to having 24 profit centers across these three companies, many of which effectively stood alone. To illustrate the impact and growth resulting from division-alization, one profit center had become as large on its own as Mentec had been three years earlier.

A key issue for Peirce remained how to further develop the divisional structure. He saw his options very clearly.

> "Are we going to grow by developing the existing three com-panies? Or, do we decentralize and put in, say, five divisional direc-tors? Or, do we allow one of the companies to be stripped off and capitalize on its potential to become a new substantial business area? I have got to try to determine the best and most feasible structure, one that will maximize the opportunities which we un-doubtedly have in some of these areas."

The structural dilemma was heightened by Mentec's difficulties in de-ciding how it should reorganize in order to capitalize on the latest op-portunity – the new, and very different, video conferencing market. Ac-cording to Peirce:

> "This opportunity needs each company's strongest capabilities: it needs the trading strength of our direct sales company and the technical strength of our technical company. we are struggling to find the most effective way to put everything together so we can get the best out of both, and we are coming to the conclusion that it may require a fourth company."

Board and Management Structure

In 1992, the Mentec board had seven members. The non-executive Chairman was Kieran Flynn. The executive members were Group Chief Executive, Michael Peirce, the three operating divisional direc-tors: Christopher Fairclough, Managing Director of Mentec Computer Systems Limited, Wyn Gill, Managing Director of Mentec Sales Limited and Frank Waters, Managing Director of Mentec International Limited. Group Financial Director, Christopher Meehan, also acted as financial director to the three operating companies. The role of the other non-executive Board member, IDA nominee director, Pat O'Brien, was to serve as the expert on business practices in the Far East, as well as representing the IDA interest on the board.

The company employed a matrix management structure. In addition to their responsibilities as managing director of one of the Mentec companies, each operating director also had a group role: Chris Fairclough served as Group Technical Director, and Wyn Gill acted as Group Purchasing Director.

(Refer to Exhibit I for the Mentec organization chart and Exhibits 2-5 for Mentec's financial statements.)

Business Strategy

Mentec's current business strategy plan called for clear profit (ROI) targets of 35%, emphasizing low costs, using standard CPU engines available from the major industry players. The company sold into the replacement market for a product with a wide range of applications. In the area of DEC-based products, Mentec entered an established market with a product that was more price-performance competitive than the existing products. Regarding its Intel relationship, Mentec also identified an established arena of activity for marketing a product endorsed by Intel as an extension of its own existing product.

The key element of Mentec's strategy was that it did not address the mainstream markets of DEC or Intel. Rather, it focused on their secondary business areas. Mentec's Technical Director, Chris Fairclough, explained the strategy in straightforward terms.

> "A company like Intel would have current products, other products and new products. You don't hit their current product range because they'll stamp on you. What you do is hit a product range which they are starting to neglect. The market may be a smaller niche for them, not one of their main markets, but still a very large market overall. For example, the Multibus 2 market is a niche market for Intel and other big players. But, the total market goes as high as $500 million, and parts of it would be very attractive for a company like Mentec."

The secret of Mentec's successful pursuit of this strategy was its understanding of the industry and the relationships it had developed with the major players. At the express invitation of DEC and Intel, senior Mentec management had gone to the US to find out more about the strategies of these two companies. A good example of Mentec's strong relationships was seen when DEC announced that it was going to open up the macrochip worldwide. Michael Peirce recalled the event:

"DEC's top quality people in the area invited us to meet them. We told them that we had been working with DEC for ten years, so they knew all about our PDP activity and our INTEL activity. Then, we asked them to give us access to this microchip so that we could identify the areas that DEC was not going to address."

Products

Mentec's operations were divided into three distinct business areas. Its hardware business was based on single board computers (SBCs). Its Irish and UK software business was concerned with the development and sale of software in Ireland and Britain, targeted at DEC users in the manufacturing and distribution sectors. The company's third area of business involved distribution of DEC hardware and requisites in Ireland and the UK.

In the hardware areas, the first generation of SBCs produced by Mentec was based on the DEC J-II chip. Mentec's key customers for this product included Siemens and Italtel in the telecommunications area, and Agfa in the photographic processing equipment area. As such, Mentec acted as a sub-supplier of DEC products, as well as marketer of its own equipment. Its main competitors were Obler, a German manufacturer, and DEC itself – a fact which was starting to strain the relationship.

While this first generation SBC market had ceased growing – because DEC was no longer promoting PDP, technology companies such as Siemens and Italtel had made massive investments in PDP technology, for which they needed continued support. Thus, this market, although not actually growing, remained a worthwhile one for Mentec.

Recognizing the mature stage of its DEC-based hardware business opportunity, Mentec had introduced a second generation of SBCs. It was based on Intel 860 technology, and was aimed at a broader market, though with the same core group of customers. Mentec was focusing the application of this technology on Multibus 2, used in factory automation, which was seen as a growth niche.

In tandem, Mentec was developing a boxed product which was able to run open systems software like Unix, aimed at highly technical value-added resellers who bought all the components except the central processing unit.

The main hardware products which Mentec sold directly were DEC processing units, computer disk drives and memories. These sales covered Ireland and the UK only. While Mentec had a benign relationship with DEC's Irish operation, DEC UK and DEC wholesalers and value-added resellers represented major competitors to its direct sales. Its customers were varied, with no central customer group.

In the software area, Mentec sold its own products and some products of other companies. Its focus was on products that required technical implementation and follow-up training. Its customers included large multinationals such as ICI and firms in discrete manufacturing operations.

A significant addition to Mentec's software product range was the "Network Professor", a network management tool manufactured under license from a US company, T.E. Concepts. When it was launched, this product offered a critical advantage over competitive products, which could not match its facility to manage networks. Mentec's adoption of this product reflected the company's view that future opportunities would lie in the communications aspect of the computing business. Its main customers for this product were multinational companies and other existing customers for solution software products sold through distributors and value-added resellers.

In the sales distribution area, Mentec's products covered planning systems determining manufacturing requirements, financial cost information systems, and sales and distribution systems.

Markets and Distribution

Mentec had notable success in establishing its products in its major hardware markets – the UK, Germany, Italy and Japan – and in the rest of Europe to a lesser extent.

Its software business focused on Ireland and the UK, with its operations based in the North and Midlands of England. Much of Mentec's software business represented capital investment through purchasing companies, because it was linked to equipment purchases and implementation programs. Thus, Mentec's business was vulnerable to recession, when capital programs were pushed back.

When it began to consider operations on an international scale, Mentec recognized that – as a small company – it would be critical to establish an effective international distribution network. The company believed that it had two options: to sell directly in international markets or to appoint distributors or some other form of third-party sales agent in each target country. It initially opted for single outlet supply and negotiated an arrangement with a major US corporation. This turned out to be very unsatisfactory from Mentec's point of view and, after one year, Mentec ended the relationship. Michael Peirce recalled the situation:

> "They took advantage of our naiveté to lock us out of negotiations with other outlets. In the process, though, we learned an important lesson. We resolved, from then on, to spread our risks with our distributors: no more single distributors or exclusive worldwide distributorship. we now have two distributors in every European country for our SBC business."

By 1992, Mentec used 40 distributors in all, with the most successful ones found in Germany, Italy, the UK and Japan. In most countries, one distributor became more dominant. For example, in both Germany and Italy, one distributor handled 80% of the business. There were three distributors in the UK, but one of them did 90% of the business.

Mentec gave priority to building up a two-way trust with its distributors. For example, if the company received an inquiry from an Italian telecommunications company and then visited that company, the distributor was always involved in the meeting. While Mentec did work to capture new business, it always then passed the client over to the local distributor.

An important part of Mentec's competitive strategy was in the way it handled the business system. Not only did the company outsource its raw materials and components, it also subcontracted production. With downstream functions delegated to distributors, this unbundling of the business system allowed the company to concentrate on the key value-adding activities – design, assembly and testing, and marketing.

Michael Peirce leaned back in his chair and smiled at his visitor. Glancing at his watch, he said:

> "Our new product idea can be attributed to our understanding of computer and telecommunications technology. Our experience gives us the ability to launch into new markets with fantastic growth potential. To exploit this window of opportunity, we must act quickly. Our task next week is to determine how and with whom we can pursue this new market. And, our strategy is to take advantage of this opportunity!"

Exhibit 1: Mentec Organization Chart

**Mentec Ltd.
Holding Company**

Chairman: Kieran Flynn
CEO: Michael Peirce
Directors: Christopher Meenan (Financial)
  Christopher Fairclough
  Frank Waters
  Wyn Gill

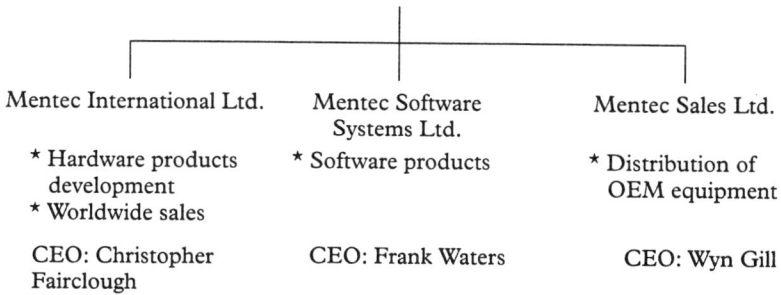

Mentec International Ltd.	Mentec Software Systems Ltd.	Mentec Sales Ltd.
* Hardware products development * Worldwide sales	* Software products	* Distribution of OEM equipment
CEO: Christopher Fairclough	CEO: Frank Waters	CEO: Wyn Gill

Exhibit 2: Mentec Limited and Subsidiaries Consolidated Balance Sheet as at 30 June 1992

	1992		1991	
	Ir£		Ir£	
Fixed Assets				
Intangible Assets	1,789,334		1,307,980	
Tangible Assets	2,182,445		1,920,282	
Financial Assets	6,202	3,977,981	2	3,228,364
Current Assets				
Stocks	1,614,861		1,549,988	
Debtors	7,320,562		6,296,181	
Cash at Bank and in Hand	1,058,464		160,907	
	9,983,887		8,007,076	
Creditors:				
Due within One Year	(5,346,613)		(4,258,883)	
Net Current Assets		4,647,274		3,748,193
Total Assets Less Current Liabilities		8,625,255		6,976,457
Creditors:				
Due after One Year		(1,757,082)		(1,979,086)
Provision for Liabilities and Charges		(36,437)		(97,412)
Net Assets Capital and Reserves		**6,831,796**		**4,899,959**
Called up share capital		1,050,782		1,048,259
Share premium account		1,745,612		1,748,135
Revaluation reserve		519,783		519,783
Other reserves		(518,457)		(496,708)
Profit and loss account		4,022,016		2,053,490
		6,819,736		4,872,959
Minority interest		12,000		27,000
		6,831,736		**4,899,959**

Exhibit 3: Mentec Limited Balance Sheet as at 30 June 1992

		1992		1991
		Ir£		Ir£
Fixed Assets				
Financial Assets		2,233,201		2,227,001
Current Assets				
Debitors	2,078,360		2,392,237	
Creditors: Due Within One Year	(486,067)		(307,677)	
Net Current Assets		1,592,293		2,084,560
Total Assets Less Current Liabilities		3,825,494		4,311,561
Creditors: Due after One Year		(729,100)		(1,215,167)
Net Assets		**3,096,394**		**3,096,394**
Capital and Reserves				
Called up Share Capital		1,050,782		1,048,259
Share Premium Account		2,045,612		2,048,135
Profit and Loss Account		-		-
		3,096,394		**3,096,394**

Exhibit 4: Mentec Limited and Subsidiaries Profit and Loss Account for Year Ended 30 June 1992

	1992	1991
	Ir£	Ir£
Turnover	23,681,365	15,661,266
Cost Of Sales	807,033	11,561,758
Gross Profit	4,874,332	4,099,508
Distribution Expenses	(114,560)	(75,903)
Administrative Expenses	(2,380,375)	(2,094,260)
Other operating Income	4,562	49,898
Interest Payable and Similar Charges	(145,127)	(186,990)
Profit on Ordinary Activities before Taxation	2,318,832	1,792,253
Taxation on Profit on Ordinary Activities	(286,133)	(163,447)
Profit on Ordinary Activities after Taxation	2,032,699	1,628,806
Minority Interest	(25,000)	(25,000)
Profit on Ordinary Activities Attributable to the Company	2,007,699	1,603,806
Dividends	(39,173)	(668,126)
	1,968,526	935,68
Profit and Loss Account at Beginning of Year	2,053,490	1,117,810
Profit and Loss Account at End of Year	4,022,016	2,053,490

Exhibit 5: Mentec Limited and Subsidiaries Consolidated Statement of Cash Flows for the Year Ended 30 June 1992

	1992	1992	1991	1991
	Ir£	Ir£	Ir£	Ir£
Net Cash Inflow from Operating Activities		3,058,344		2,081,632
Returns on Investment and Servicing of Finance				
Interest Paid	(140,101)		(177,066)	
Interest Element of Finance Lease Payments	(5,026)		(9,924)	
Dividends Paid	(127,423)		(693,126)	
Net Cash Outflow from Returns on Investment and Servicing of Finance		(272,550)		(880,116)
Taxation				
Corporation Tax		(316,946)		(24,003)
Investing Activities				
Purchase of Investments	(6,200)			
Purchase of Tangible Assets	(480,500)		(344,191)	
Investment in Intangible Assets	(705,383)		(709,901)	
Sale of Fixed Assets	1,797		3,029	
Net Cash Outflow from Investing Activities		(1,184,286)		(1,051,063)
Net Cash Inflow before Financing		1,284,562		126,450

Exhibit 5: Continued

	1992	1992	1991	1991
	Ir£	Ir£	Ir£	Ir£
Financing				
Repayment of Bank Loans		115,530		632,935
Repayment (drawdown) of Shareholder Loans		243,033		(500,670)
Capital Element of Finance Lease Payments		28,442		23,926
Proceeds from Issue of Share Capital		-		**(64,675)**
Net Cash Outflow from Financing		387,005		91,516
Increase in Cash and Cash Equivalents		897,557		34,934
		1,284,562		**26,450**

12. Benetton S.p.A.

*This case was prepared by Senior Research Associate J. Carlos Jarillo and Jon
I. Martínez, as the basis for class discussion rather than to illustrate either effective or ineffective handling of an administrative situation. The case authors
gratefully acknowledge the assistance of Mr. Franco Furnó, manager of Organizational Development at Benetton S.p.A., in the preparation of this case.*

"I should say the new strategy relates to our intention of structuring Benetton as a proper multinational company. That means we
plan to create a complex global manufacturing systems to advance
our mission to reach the two-thirds of the world where we do not
have a presence. It is in this light that our recent choice to diversify
into the field of financial services must be interpreted. The financial services companies that we operate - generally in partnership
with important banks and financial institutions - have to be con-
siderate and provide the necessary support for Benetton's new development policy. In addition, the new and more sophisticated system that we are going to build in the field of services (not only financial services but the service industry overall) may help us in our
attempts to implement the entrepreneurial formula that I have
tried to explain to you."

With these words, Mr. Aldo Palmeri, General Manager of Benetton
S.p.A., outlined the strategy for the future development of Benetton, a
strategy designed to keep the outstanding rate of growth the company
had enjoyed since its inception.

I. History of the Company

The Benetton story was a tale of huge success built from humble
origins. Started some 25 years ago, the company had reached $1 billion
in worldwide sales, building from its strengths in one of the most mature, labor-intensive industries in labor-expensive Western Europe.

The firm was a typically Italian family concern, with four siblings -
Giuliana, Luciano, Gilberto, and Carlo - involved from the beginning in
the company operations. The eldest brother, Luciano, was born in 1935,

and spent his childhood through the harsh time that Second World War brought to northeastern Italy. Upon his father's death, he had to leave school at the age of fifteen to take at job in a men's clothing store. In 1955, Luciano, who had just turned twenty, told Giuliana he was convinced that he could market the bright-colored, original sweaters she used to make as a hobby, so why shouldn't they leave their jobs and start a business?

With thirty thousand lire, obtained from the sale of Luciano's accordion and Carlo's bicycle, Luciano and Giuliana bought a knitting machine, and soon afterward Giuliana put together a collection of eighteen pieces. Luciano was immediately able to sell them to local stores. Sales increased steadily over the next few years, until Giuliana had a group of young woman working for her and Luciano had bought a minibus to carry these employees to and from a small workshop the Benettons had set up near their home.

In the early nineteen-sixties, Luciano Benetton put into practice several innovative ideas that helped turn the company from a small enterprise into a giant. The first idea was to sell only through specialized knitwear stores (as opposed to department stores and boutiques selling a wide range of clothes), whose owners would presumably be more interested in pushing sales of his particular product. Luciano made use of another idea unusual at that time: to offer retailers a 10% discount if they paid in cash on delivery of his product. At that point, Benetton sweaters did not bear the family name (they used foreign names, like "Lady Godiva" or "Trés Jolie"), but they already had the Benetton characteristics of medium-high quality and stylish design at a very reasonable price.

Two more new ideas emerged, this time for lowering production costs. The first was a novel technique for making wool soft, like cashmere; it was based on a method Luciano had observed while visiting factories in Scotland, where rudimentary machines with wooden paddles beat raw wool in water. The other idea was to buy and adapt obsolete hosiery-knitting machines, at a price of $5,000 apiece, a fraction of the cost of a new machine. The refurbished machines did their job perfectly.[3]

Benetton was formally incorporated in 1965 as "Maglificio di Ponzano Veneto dei Fratelli Benetton". The small enterprise consisted Lu-

---

[3] The biographical notes in the preceding paragraphs are adapted from "Profiles - Being Everywhere," *The New Yorker*, Nov. 10, 1986, pp. 53-74.

ciano, Giuliana, and their younger brothers, Gilberto and Carlo. Gilberto was placed in charge of financial issues, while Carlo headed the production system. In the same year, the first Benetton factory went up in the village of Ponzano, a few kilometers outside Treviso, in Northeastern Italy.

In 1968, the company opened the first independent outlet in the mountain village of Belluno, not far from Venice. With its appealing merchandise and its spare, intimate interior, the shop was an immediate success. The store occupied only about 400 square feet, in part because of limited Benetton product line at the time, but it set the pattern for the stores to follow. "It was conceived on the idea of the specialized store, the desire for an alternative to the department store," said Luciano Benetton to an American journalist. He added: "From the beginning, we wanted to create an image – the right people to open our stores, the décor, the colors."[4]

Through the late sixties and early seventies the Benettons concentrated their efforts on capturing the domestic market. By 1975, the distinctive white and green Benetton knitting-stitch logo had become the symbol of a phenomenon in the Italian commercial scene. Approximately 200 Benetton shops had opened in Italy; many of them, but not all, bore the Benetton name. The idea of having other names – Sisley, Tomato, Merceria, 012 – with a different decoration and selection of Benetton clothes, grew out of the intention of appealing to different segments of the market and of avoiding mass flops: if one Benetton store was a failure, others in the same area wouldn't bear the stigma. Over the years, however, none of these names had achieved much importance, and many of them were being folded back into the Benetton brand.

In spite of the early opening of their first foreign outlet in Paris, in 1969, international sales had remained negligible for the company for most of the seventies. In 1978, 98% of the company's sales of $80 million were in Italy, where opportunities for continued high growth were diminishing. Consequently, the firm launched a major expansion campaign into the rest of Europe, always following their systems of only selling through specialized, Benetton-named outlets. Sales boomed as the network of shops spread North into France, West Germany, Britain, Switzerland, and the Scandinavian countries. In the early 80's, most young women in Europe seemed to be buying Benetton sportswear, in-

---

4 *The New Yorker, op.cit.,* p. 58.

cluding Princess Caroline of Monaco and Diana, Princess of Wales, which gave Benetton worldwide publicity. By 1982, sales had grown to roughly $311 million. In 1983, Benetton had sales of $351 million, from 2,600 stores in Europe.

Though the Benettons still expected some growth in Europe, they saw greater opportunity farther afield. By the end of 1983, the company had already placed 31 shops in department stores throughout Japan, and 27 shops in major cities of the United States. Interviewed by an American magazine, Luciano Benetton confessed: "Being in America is like a dream – it is so big, so prestigious. If we do well, it will help us in Japan because they like whatever is big in U.S."[5] Progress in both countries had been difficult at the beginning, however. Instead of opening European-style shops, 18 of the 27 U.S. shops were in department stores, like Macy's where Benetton had small boutiques from which it obtained a percentage of the profits. The "joint-venture" was short-lived, perhaps due to the Macy's practice of quickly marking down prices on slow-moving items, which went completely against Benetton's philosophy.

The company set up some manufacturing units outside of Italy. The existing factories in France, Scotland and Spain were joined by an American facility in North Carolina in 1985. However, production outside Italy was not started for economic or technical reasons, but to by-pass protectionism in those countries.

The complexity of handling an ever-expanding network of shops, production volumes, materials flows and employees kept increasing. By the late seventies, everybody in the company felt that something had to be done. The decision was made in 1981 to recruit professional managers. Aldo Palmeri, 36, a highly executive at the Bank of Italy (Italy's central bank) in Rome, was hired as a consultant and after a year became the new managing director. Although he had several ideas for reorganizing Benetton, his limited experience in industrial companies obliged him to recruit an experienced manager to put them in practice. This man, in charge of personnel and organization, was Mr. Cantagalli, who joined Benetton in 1983 from a similar position with 3M, a large American multinational, in Italy.

They proceeded to recruit experienced managers from other large companies to form a "professional team." The newly created organiza-

---

5 "Benetton: Bringing European Chic to Middle America," *Business Week*, June 11, 1984, p. 60.

tion department had to implement an organization development program to bridge the old "handshake management" culture with the new and more formal one. This process of creating new functions and written procedures lasted three years and finished in October 1986.

The Board of Directors was composed of four members of the Benetton family and Mr. Palmeri. However, the Benettons didn't play the conventional, distant role of members of the board and took part in many day-to-day decisions. Although it didn't appear in the organizations chart, most of the senior functional managers had two reporting relationships: a formal one to Aldo Palmeri, and an informal one to a member of the Benetton family. Hence there were two different groups of young adults that had to coexist at the top: the self-made Benetton siblings, and the well educated ex-multinational executives. The main task of the organization development department was to join both cultures. According to Mr. Franco Furnó, manager of this department, "there has been a lot of improvement in this mutual understanding process in the last three years, but the job is not finished yet."

Until July 1986, the four Benetton siblings shared 100% of the company's equity. After reporting strong 1985 results (see Exhibit 1), the company offered a total of 16.5 million common shares to the public. Eleven million were listed in the Milan and Venice stock exchanges, 4.48 million in the Euromarkets, and the rest was offered to Benetton's employees, agents and clients. The total stock issue represented about 10% of the company. In addition, the company sold lira- (70 billion) and Deutsche Mark-denominated bonds (200 million) with warrants. It was estimated that the whole financial operation represented about 20% of the company's equity, bringing in around $200 million.

Exhibit 1: Financial Highlights

Consolidated balance sheet as of December 31*

Assets	1986	1985
Current assets	833,192	494,891
Investments and other		
non-current assets	5,431	6,372
Fixed assets (net)	134,636	80,335
Intangible assets	15,548	10,215
Total assets	*988,807*	*591,813*
Liabilities and stockholders' equity		
Current liabilities	373,663	317,203
Long-term liabilities	251,148	76,730
Capital gains roll-over reserve	–	130
Minority interest in consolidated subsidiaries	2,437	4,742
Stockholders' equity	361,559	193,008
Total	*988,807*	*591,813*

* *Millions of Italian lire $1 approx. 1,400 Italian lire*

Consolidated statements of income*

	1986	1985
Revenue	1,079,060	879,535
Cost of sales	701,818	558,501
Gross profit	377,242	321,034
Selling, general and administrative expenses	169,303	150,653
Income from operations	207,939	170,381
Other (income) expenses	1,878	6,368
Gain from disposal of treasury stock	–	3,198
Income taxes	(87,008)	(69,788)
Deferred income taxes	(5,468)	–
Income before minority interest	113,585	97,423
Income to minority interest	(556)	(1,226)
Net income for the year	*113,029*	*96,197*

* *Millions of Italian lire*

II. The Company in 1987: An Overall Description

Benetton was a vertically de-integrated company, not only in manufacturing, but also in the three other main activities that constituted its value chain: styling and design, logistics and distribution, and sales. The company relied on external people and companies for the major part of these crucial activities. It employed some 1,500 people at the end of 1987.

The styling or design of the garments was done outside the company by number of international free-lance stylists. Giuliana Benetton, with a staff of about 20 people in the Product Development Department, interpreted the "look" created by the stylists and performed the modelling phase.

More than 80% of manufacturing was done outside the company, by 350 subcontractors that employed about 10,000 people. In-house production accounted for the remaining less than 20% (mainly dyeing) and was performed by 700-800 people.

Logistics and distribution activities were also performed mainly by outsiders. The company did the storage phase by using a single, huge warehouse for finished products. In addition, the Logistics Department at Benetton was in charge of delivering the finished garments to the stores all over the world.

Finally, the company utilized an external sales organization of almost 80 agents that took care of a retailing systems of nearly 4,000 shops spread all over the world. The internal part of this activity was performed by 7 area managers that coordinated the selling system as a whole divided by territories.

The Operation Cycle

There were basically two fashion seasons: spring/summer, beginning in February and ending in July, and fall/winter, beginning in September and ending in December. The large volume of business done by the company required that production planning for woolen and cotton articles began far in advance of shipment to the stores. Roughly, twenty-one months elapsed from the preparation of clothing designs for a particular selling season to the final payment of commissions to Benetton agents.

Basic steps in the operating cycle were: preparation of final designs; assembly of a few samples of each of the 600 items in the total collection; a "pre-presentation" meeting was then held between Giuliana Benetton, manufacturing managers, and some of the company's 80 agents, which eliminated about a fourth of the models; the remaining were then produced in small quantities for presentation by area managers to agents and by agents to store owners; upon receipt of the first orders, the planning department "exploded" a rough production plan for the season, by fabrics and styles; purchases were made according to this plan, and capacity with the subcontractors negotiated; finally, production was started and deliveries begun just in time for the selling season. They were scheduled so that each store could present 80% to 90% of all items (fabrics, styles, and colors) in its basic collection to its customers at the outset of the selling season.

Although shops committed orders seven months before the selling season, giving Benetton time to Schedule, produce and deliver, the production plan did allow some flexibility for the retailer in three ways. First, from August through early December, as they gathered more information about color preferences, shop-owners were allowed to specify colors for woven items that had been held in "gray" up to that point, with a limit of 30% of the total orders for woolen items on such orders. Given the popularity of colorful weaves and jacquards in the last three to four years, "gray" stock had only represented about 15%-20% of all orders. This trend was expected to change in the coming years, which would mean a return to more "gray" orders.

The basic production plan was also adjusted through the presentation of a "flash collection" just before the season. The flash collection corrected styling mistakes in the basic product line and usually included about 50 new designs based on "hit styles" presented by fashion houses (competitors) during the two main seasonal shows.

Finally, orders could be adjusted through "reassortment," which was the most critical phase in the production plan, requiring great coordination and follow-through by retailers, agents and producers. Reassortment occurred during the last third of each selling season, when retailers were allowed to add orders to their original ones based on sell-through of popular items. Juggling retail orders to match manufacturing capacity for thousands of shops in a five week period was not an easy task. There was a minimum economical production batch, so sometimes when the reassortment order was not enough to fill the minimum batch, the marketing people would get in touch with shop managers to propose some alternatives. As Benetton moved into new geographic area the complexity of reassortment grew incessantly, because the best sellers for different areas tended to vary widely.

Payments to subcontractors, representing a major cash outflow, were made 70 days after the end of the month in which production occurred or, in the case of the spring-summer collection, in October. Collections from retail stores were based on a season beginning date of March 30 for the spring/summer season, with one third of payment due 30, 60, and 90 days after that date or the date of actual receipt of merchandise. This was designed to minimize retailer's investment in inventories.

Manufacturing Activities

The company was divided into three divisions: wool, cotton, and jeans. In 1983, Benetton had seven plants in Italy. In 1985, the number of plants decreased to five, and in 1987 the company owned just three production units, one for each division. The reason for this reduction in the number of plants was simply a matter of the company's philosophy of vertical de-integration and external production as a mode of organization. All those divested plants acted in 1987 as Benetton subcontractors.

As shown in Exhibit 2, Benetton utilized three different kinds of raw materials. In the wool division the raw material was basically thread, no matter whether it was acrylic, cotton, or actual wool. In the other two plants, the raw materials were basically fabrics. The wool division's technology was mainly knitting, while the other two divisions' technology was essentially cutting.

Benetton was the biggest purchaser of wool thread in the world. It purchased about 9 million kilos of thread per year. The other two divisions bought raw materials (fabrics) from 80 to 90 different suppliers. The company centralized all the purchasing activities as this was perhaps the main source of economies of scale in the industry. In 1987, 37 tons of yarn and 40 tons of fabrics entered the production system daily, to be transformed into 180,000 garments, adding up to 40-45 million garments per year.

The wool division worked with 200 external production units. Benetton owned a percentage of the equity of the largest of them. The cotton and jeans divisions worked with other 150 external production units.

Benetton gave the external contractors the exact amount of raw materials (calculated by computer), technical documents, an idea of the time needed to perform each single production activity, etc. Therefore, although these production units were external, Benetton provided much of the technical ability needed to run them, as most of them worked exclusively for the company. In addition, Benetton advised subcontractors about the required machinery to buy, and offered them financial aid through its own leasing and factoring companies. The contact with the subcontractors was also facilitated by the fact that, according to an Italian journalist, it could be said that there was no manager at Benetton who was not at the same time owner, president, or director of a leading subcontracting company in the Lombardia-Veneto area.

Exhibit 2: Flow of Materials

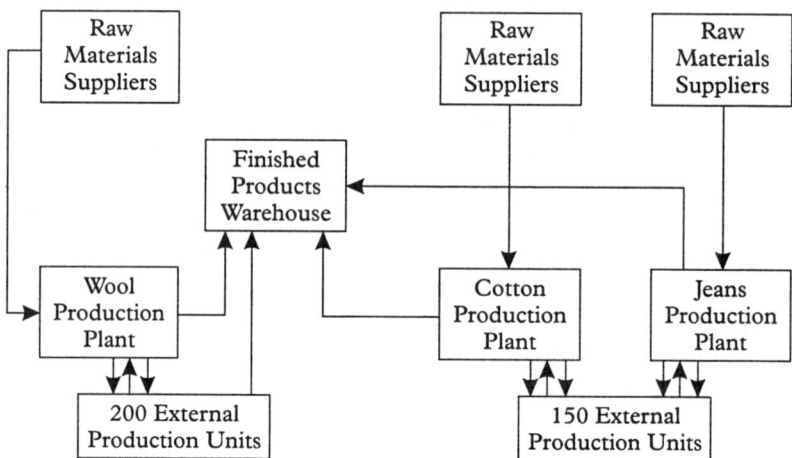

Although most of the manufacturing activities were externally performed, some were centralized at headquarters in Ponzano Veneto. Among these were all purchasing, production planning, technical research, product development, acquisition and exploitation of patents and rights, cutting by computer and dyeing.

Even allowing for the added costs of shuttling raw materials and semifinished products among subcontractors and Benetton's factories, the savings brought by decentralization resulted in total production costs for woolen items almost 20% below those of garments of comparable quality made in Europe and on a par with those made in the Far East. The following pages explain in detail how the wool division worked to achieve those results.

The Wool Division

The wool division consumed 55% of all raw materials used by the company, and woolen garments represent about 47% of total sales in units. Three out of four woolen garments (that is, 15 million garments) were sold in the fall/winter season. The remaining 25% were sold during the spring/summer season. They were manufactured following a process made up of four sequential phases: knitting, assembling, dyeing, and finishing.

Knitting

Once the agents had collected the orders from the stores and sent them to headquarters, the technical department prepared the portfolio order for each of the three divisions. Thus the manager of the wool plant received an order portfolio that only included the articles to be manufactured in that plant.

The proportion of internal work in the knitting phase had decreased in the last five years. In 1982, only 40% of the knitting of wool had been performed externally. As shown in Table 1, just 1% of the knitting phase was done internally in 1987, and 90% of that 1% was concentrated in a very specific type of knitting machine. Benetton had decided to keep in-house that kind of machine because it had a lot of problems finding those machines in external companies. That machine was very expensive and, therefore, risky for external contractors. The company also used its internal production to have first-hand information on the productivity and coating of the knitting phase.

Table 1: Summary Chart of the Manufacturing Process in the Wool Division

Production Phase	% Performed Internally	% Performed Externally	Number of Contractors	Degree of Exclusiveness
Knitting	1%	99%	70-80	90%
Assembling	0%	100%	100	100%
Chemical Treatment	25-30%	70-75%	3	100%
Dyeing	100%	0%	-	-
Finishing	5%	95%	20	100%

Benetton worked with 70-80 subcontractors in the knitting phase, and nearly 90% of them worked exclusively for Benetton. Mr. Morelli, plant manager for the wool division, argued that there were pros and cons to that exclusivity: "the main advantage is that the company can count on them to plan its production, as it knows their production capacity, kind of machines, number of shifts, etc. But the main disadvantage is that the company has to assure the saturation of their machines, which is risky for both Benetton and the external contractors."

Assembly

This phase of the manufacturing process was completely performed outside the company by more than 100 external contractors, who worked exclusively for Benetton. In 1982, only 60% of this activity had been done externally. Most contractors had less than 15 employees for Italian law imposed many regulations on larger companies. 14-15 was also a good number to set up an assembly chain.

According to Mr. Morelli, Benetton didn't perform the assembling phase internally because "first of all, it goes against the philosophy of the company, that looks for de-integration and flexibility. Secondly, there are some economies in doing this job externally because these small subcontractors have to pay less in terms of social costs according to Italian law, although the salary level is almost the same."

Dyeing

The early seventies saw the development of Benetton's perhaps most widely publicized production technique: the dyeing of assembled garments rather than yarn, for single-color garments. Until then, it was the yarn that was dyed, and then the parts knit and the sweater assembled. The Benettons discovered that, to some extent, the critical fashion factor was color, not shape. They decided, therefore, to knit and assemble a large part of their production undyed ("gray") and wait until fashion trends for colors became clearer to make the final color decision. They thus avoided overproduction of sweaters in non-appealing colors and ensured they could meet demand for the "best hits" of the season. The process was slightly more expensive but had the advantage of allowing production to respond quickly to public demand. It also allowed the company to maintain almost no inventory, and to produce mainly to order.

The company kept 100% of the dyeing phase internally. In 1982, half this phase had been performed outside the company. The whole process was concentrated at home because of the great importance of the dyeing phase for a company whose main distinctive product characteristic was its colorful style, and the ability of its garments to produce color-coordinated sets of clothing. In addition, dyeing was both the most complex and the most capital-intensive process, which made it risky for external subcontractors.

Before the dyeing phase, every article had to pass though a chemical treatment to soften and de-wax the wool. The pieces that used already-colored threads had to pass through this chemical treatment, too. This phase was also a capital intensive one but, technically speaking, was not as sophisticated ad dyeing. The main part of this chemical process (70-75%) was performed outside the company by three external companies. Two of these plants had belonged to Benetton until 1985, when it sold them to their plant managers. These plants became joint ventures between these new entrepreneurs and Benetton. These plants employed about 100 people each.

Finishing

Only 5% of this phase was performed in-house, in contrast to the 80% done internally in 1982. The 20 subcontractors that performed the other 95% worked exclusively for Benetton. This Phase was labor-intensive and didn't require particular machinery. It was split in two parts: quality control of each single garment, and packaging.

Some Problems in the Benetton-Subcontractors Relationship

Mr. Luigi Muzio, managing director of one of the largest external firms in which Benetton had an important equity position, commented: "the main problem in working for Benetton is the great number of changes in articles, colors, etc., they do in a very short time. We have to adjust the machines weekly or even nightly to follow all these changes. This means a large number of different articles produced in small batches each, which, from a manufacturing point of view, is very inefficient." This subcontractor also complained about the machinery that was suggested by Benetton. In his opinion, they had a "final product orientation" instead of a "process orientation," not taking into account the productivity or the suitability of the machinery to the subcontractor's characteristics. Thus, he maintained that the machinery suggested by the company was often more suitable to a craftsman than to an industrial concern.

Subcontractors ran a big risk when they decided on the purchase of a certain type of machine. The key factor that decided the usefulness of the knitting machines was the thickness of the thread. Fortunately, it didn't vary so rapidly as the styles, colors or fashion in general. However, the company had experienced some problems of this type in the past, for some subcontractors had been stuck with machines that were useless for the current fashion trends. The firm had facilitated the change of the machines both by buying them or by allowing the contractors wide margins on some orders so they could re-invest this money in new machinery. For this reason, Benetton tried to concentrate in-house the most expensive and fashion-dependent activities.

Mr. Muzio realized that working exclusive for Benetton involved a risk, but on the other hand it had the advantage of allowing them to dispense with a sales and marketing department: "the constant work provided by Benetton enables this company to concentrate in manufacturing, with just a few people in change of administrative and financial tasks. Working only for Benetton means one invoice per month, fixed payment conditions, etc. We often receive requests from potential clients, but I'd rather work this way." Mr. Morelli, head of the wool division, pointed out that "one of the main problems in working with external firms is to achieve the required flexibility in them. They have to completely adapt to Benetton demands in terms of working periods, vacation, etc." Another Benetton executive voiced this concern: "this is neither a 'just in time' systen nor a very scheduled one."

Subcontractors worked normally 8 hours a day, but when the company was in a hurry they had to work over the weekend, and twelve or more hours a day. Nearly 10% of all subcontractors were released every year because they didn't meet quality standards.

One of the highlights of the company's network of subcontractors was described by Mr. Morelli: "Benetton maintains a sort of 'umbilical cord' with external contractors. They are considered part of our family, and feel confident in telling us their problems." Plant managers knew personally each subcontractor and some of them became friends, to the point that they talked about their personal problems and asked for advice. Manufacturing people visited subcontractors very often. In addition, they were permanently in touch by phone. This daily communication allowed them to work in real-time, solving little problems and making production adjustments.

According to the firm, the less experienced the subcontractor in the apparel industry, the better it would adjust to Benetton's philosophy. It was more difficult to create this "umbilical cord" with people that had previously worked for other clients. The experienced contractor tried to impose its conditions before starting the relationship.

Finally, there was a strong identification with Benetton, not only within the company, but also among subcontractors' employees. Luigi Muzio said: "workers in my company are fully identified with Benetton. They feel very proud of belonging to a worldwide-known group born in an ignored province of Italy. It is the first time that an apparel producer of this region develops into a world-class company, and this means a lot for this people."

High-tech Production Processes

Many experts in the apparel industry agreed that the Benetton success formula was based on the company's ability to combine fashion with industry, using advanced technology. Luciano Benetton confirmed this to an American business magazine: "there are many elements to our success, but the real point is that we have kept the same strategy all along - to put fashion on an industrial level. Most of the rest of Italian fashion is still on an artisan level."[6]

For production, Benetton used numeric control knitting machines linked to Apricot (a British firm) computer-aided design personal computer terminals. Designers using the 10 CAD terminals could play around with knitwear colors and patterns on a video screen. Once a designer decided on a particular pattern, the computer prepared a tape that would direct the knitting machine to automatically produce the fabric, in an easy-to-assemble form of pieces. Since 1980, they had also used a Gerber Camsco CAD system that they had connected to a Spanish-made Investronica automatic cutter, turning the system into a CAD-CAM unit. The CAD-CAM system's automatic cutter followed pattern pieces stored in the computer's memory, which turned out 15,000 full garments every eight hours, wasting less than 15% of the cloth.

Logistics

Logistics played an important role in the Benetton strategy. Stores carrying Benetton products were designed with limited storage space for back-up stocks. Upon arrival at the store direct from the company, merchandise often was checked and placed directly on the display shelves. This required both a carefully prepared schedule of shipments

---

[6] "Benetton Takes on the World," *Fortune,* June 13, 1983, p. 116.

to stores, and a large and efficient warehouse to store finished products at headquarters.

The new robotized warehouse in Castrette, the main symbol of Benetton's high technology, became fully operational in February 1986. With a cost of over 42 billion lire (about $32 million) to built and outfit, the warehouse was a huge automatic box run by a Digital Equipment Corp. minicomputer that directed several robots via remote control. The robots could read bar codes on boxes, and then sort and store them. The operation of the warehouse was totally automatic and there was no human handling in the whole process. A staff of five specialists just monitored the movements via computer.

Selling Activities

There were three groups of actors involved in selling activities: the company, the agents, and the shop owners and managers.

Although his only formal position was as a member of the board, the real marketing manager was Luciano Benetton, who in the past had formally occupied this position many times. Under him, the commercial director and the area managers composed the marketing department. Nearly all the members of the commercial organization had been hired by him, and were used to working directly with him. Area managers were company employees in charge of territories run by a number of agents. There were 7 area managers for the nearly 80 agents. All the area managers were Italians.

Riccardo Weiss, the area manager in charge of the U.S., Canada, Japan, and countries of the Eastern block, described one of the tasks of an area manager: "he does every month what agents do every day: have a look at each shop and its problems. We are always watching the movement store by store. Sometimes we talk directly with shop-owners, although agents don't like that. But they need to hear the voice of the company from time to time." Mr. Weiss went once a month to the U.S. and talked almost daily with every agent by phone.

Another important task an area manager performed, was the collection of the money from the shops. On average, an area manager devoted 30-35% of his time to follow payment problems. His rush periods were May-June for the spring/summer collection, and October-November for the fall/winter one.

Agents

As shown in Exhibit 3, the agents constituted the interface between Benetton and the shops. They were not Benetton employees, and had exclusive rights over a sales territory. Luciano Benetton had personally hand-picked most of the 80 agents. Right from the start, Luciano looked for a new kind of agent, who could fit with the particular philosophy of the emerging company. He wanted "personal attitudes, rather than business experience." As an executive put it, "the thing that really strikes Luciano is the entrepreneurial spirit in an agent, rather than anything else." The company's relationship with its agents was managed largely on a verbal basis of trust: only in 1984 had formal contracts begun to be written between Benetton and the agents. Agents rarely had had to be replaced for failure to meet expectations.

Exhibit 3: Distribution network

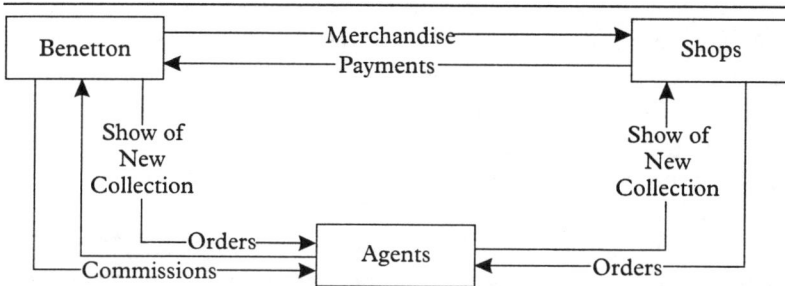

Twice a year, all agents had to spend one week at headquarters getting to know the new collection for the season and selecting a sample of 30-40% of the 600 items of the total collection. After this, every agent went back to his territory and took about 30 to 40 days to present the sample collection to each shop owner. Then the agent helped the shop owner in selecting the most suitable articles for each particular shop, and asked for orders. At the end of each day, the agent sent the orders collected in that day to headquarters. Articles were shipped directly to the shops from the central warehouse, without passing through the agent. During the season, the shop owner sent the money directly to Benetton, dividing the total payment in three quotas, which were paid 30, 60 and 90 days from the date of actual receipt of the merchandise. After this, the company paid the agent a 4% commission on the value of goods shipped from the factories.

Mr. Manlio Tonolo was the agent for the Northeast region of Italy. He had joined the company in 1969 as the manager of the second shop opened by the company in Padova. He had worked with Luciano Benetton in a men's clothing store when they were teenagers. Mr. Tonolo explained the criteria for selecting an agent at that time: "the candidate had to have an enthusiastic predisposition towards the work itself. Luciano was looking for people who could be potential consumers rather than agents, who could understand the product - the multicolored sweater, which back then was completely unconventional - and believe in it."

The main responsibilities of the agents were: a) To select the location of new shops. b) To find and select potential investors for new shops. c) To help new clients in starting shops and train them, usually in the agent's stores. d) To look after the shops and help owners to manage and control their shops. e) To present the collection to shop managers and help them in choosing goods. f) To collect orders and transmit them to headquarters. g) To encourage image competition among shops.

Agents were also encouraged to re-invest part of their commissions in opening new shops, thus becoming clients themselves. This mechanism produced a "self-multiplying effect" in the retailing network. This policy of encouraging agents to have and run their own shops helped them to get first hand knowledge of the retail business and its problems in practice. For instance, Mr. Tonolo owned 35-40 shops out of the 200 he supervised in northeastern Italy. More than competitors, the shops owned by him served as examples to the shops recently opened in terms of such factors as window dressing, products display, overall image, etc. Besides this according to Mr. Tonolo, the concentration of shops in an area of a town, instead of reducing the sales of each one, tended to increase them.

Agents had normally a small organization to perform their multiple activities. Although agents visited the shops regularly, they usually hired young assistants who controlled the shops' overall image and problems on a weekly basis. In addition, the assistants helped the agent in the task of monitoring the new trends in young's people culture. They had to visit the places where they met (discotheques, bars, etc.) and see how they behaved, not only what they wore.

The majority of European agents were Italians, and so were almost 50% of the U.S. agents. Some of these had started in Europe and then moved to America. Benetton had found it difficult to find agents with the "right mentality" in America, so they had to replace them with Ita-

lians, already familiar with the firm. These had had their share of difficulties to penetrate the American market, because of their ignorance of
laws and regulations. "They had too much of the Italian mentality," as
one executive pointed out.

Shops

Fewer than 10 of the Benetton stores worldwide were owned and operated by the company. These were located in key cities such as Milan,
New York, Rome, and Düsseldorf. The rest were set up by independent
entrepreneurs, who often owned several shops in the same area. Benetton approved location of the shops and Luciano personally oversaw the
more strategic sites.

Shop owners were not retail experts. As Luciano Benetton put it: "We
have caused a new type of retailer to become important who until the
day before was perhaps a florist or a hairdresser. His prior career was of
no importance, but he had to have the right spirit to work in a Benetton
shop." Mr. Weiss, area manager for North America, Japan and Eastern
Europe, commented: "experts in retailing are not good shop owners
(and managers) because they don't understand very well the particular
Benetton system." When asked about this "shop philosophy", he mentioned the following characteristics:

- New window display every week.

- Good sales people in stores, good service.

- Competition among Benetton shops in the same area based on
  image (window decoration, garments diversity and display).

- No price competition: prices were set directly at the factory or at
  least "strongly suggested," as in the U.S. In addition, markdowns
  could not be taken before discussing them with the agent.

Turnover among shop owners was low. For example, of the 200 shops
controlled by Mr. Tonolo in the northeast of Italy, which were owned by
50-60 people, only 5 or 6 shop owners had been replaced in a period of
10 years.

The growth of the network of shops had been enormous, as can be
seen in Table 2.

Table 2: Stores in Operation at Year-end

Year-end	1982	1983	1984	1985	1986	1987*	1988*	1989*	1990*
Stores	1,917	2,296	2,644	3,200	3,893	4,650	5,300	6,200	7,000
Change	n/a	379	348	556	693	757	650	900	800

* Morgan Stanley Research Estimates

Retailers didn't sign franchise agreements (Luciano Benetton hated bureaucracy and found that the current arrangement "stimulates the full capacity of the owners"). Also they were neither required to pay Benetton a fee for use of its name nor a royalty based on a percentage of sales or profits. Therefore, the term "franchising" in describing the Benetton retailing network was a misnomer.

All Benetton outlets were required to follow basic merchandising concepts, the most important among them being that all merchandise must be displayed on open shelves accessible to customers, who could touch it and try it on. The open displays in an otherwise undecorated space create an impression of great color and fashion to the window-shopping customer. Important also was the selection of the adequate salespeople: they must be young and very customer-oriented. They had to be able to advise the customer on which garments coordinated well, and what were the best colors to wear for a particular person. Benetton used five mechanisms to control its "identity" in spite of the dramatic increase in the number of shops:

• Standardization of the shop image. Retailers had to choose among 12 basic layouts and fixture selections. This furniture must be provided by only three Italian suppliers, located near headquarters.

• Central supply of advertising material, which was produced at headquarters and shipped to the shops all over the world. Shops were allowed to do some advertising in local media (mainly newspapers) after the company had checked the advertisement.

• A strict pricing policy. The computer back at Benetton printed the price in local currencies in each tag attached to every article. For the U.S. market it was a "suggested" price.

• Benetton shops could only sell Benetton products.

• Strong initial training of shop owners by the agent.

Many people called Benetton "the fast food of the fashion industry", a comparison Luciano Benetton didn't disagree with: "I like the idea that we are similar to fast food in the sense of organization, the efficiency, the cleanliness of image, the publicity."!7•

Promotion Strategy

Employing one agency in Paris for France (Eldorado) and another in New York (J. Walter Thompson) for the rest of the world, the company had coordinated its advertising worldwide. Since the product was the same all over the world, the company had been able to maintain the consistency and international character of its ads. The themes, "Benetton - All the Colors in the World," in 1983-1984; and "United Colors of Benetton," from 1985 on, had appeared on outdoor billboards and in numerous magazine all over the world, always in English. These campaigns were the results of brainstorming sessions held by Luciano Toscani.

About 4% of Benetton's sales was spent on direct advertising. Additionally, the company sponsored sports events, including rugby and basketball teams, and a Formula 1 auto racing team.

Global Outlook

When Luciano Benetton was asked if he wanted Benetton to become another McDonald's, he commented: "Not McDonald's for the same level of goods, the same consumer, but, yes, for the distribution all over the world. I would like us to be everywhere. Another company we might compare ourselves to might be Coca-Cola or Pepsi-Cola since we aim our product at young people. The idea behind Benetton - which was basically that of mass-produced, medium priced fashion that moves with the trends yet maintains something classic - had not changed since our clothing started to become not just a strictly European product but a product for the whole world. In America, in Australia, in Japan - where we envision having two hundred shops - it has been consistently accepted. In all these countries, the prototype client remains the same - young and female. Naturally, there are regional differences. In America, for example, we reach a public a little different from that in Europe - a

---

7   *Wall Street Journal Europe,* June 24, 1986.

more sophisticated public, which travels, and might have seen the product first in Europe."[8]

In spite of their general success entering new markets, there were certain countries where the company had found serious difficulties due to tariffs, import quotas and other protectionist barriers. Benetton decided to invest in local facilities in order to avoid current or potential protectionism. Benetton Sarl., in France; Benetton S.A., in Spain; Tabando Ltd., in Scotland; and Benetton USA, Inc., were the four foreign manufacturing subsidiaries set up by Benetton International N.V., based in Holland. There was no international manufacturing network at Benetton: these manufacturing units outside Italy produced only to satisfy local needs, and they didn't supply all the goods needed in those countries. For example, the plant located in North Carolina produced only about 5% of what was sold in the U.S. market.

In other countries - where Benetton couldn't enter through exports and wasn't interested in building manufacturing facilities or in developing joint ventures with local partners - licensing agreements to use the Benetton trademarks were signed. Thus, local companies in Brazil, Mexico, Japan, Portugal, India, and Argentina paid royalties to Benetton for each item they produced and sold. There were a total of 183 licensed operations in these six countries. Although these operations generated only a 5% license profit for the firm, they must adhere to Benetton standards. The range of products and the manufacturing technology were exactly those of Benetton's, because all these licensees visited Ponzano Veneto's factories, bought the machinery under the firm's supervision, etc.

Information Systems

The company had committed itself to using the best information systems available and to improving them when they could. Benetton spent about 1.2% of its annual turnover on this, including hardware, software, and personnel. As the company was growing at a rapid rate each year the information system was always being restructured to cope with the new demands.

The most important of these systems was the connection between the agents and the firm. They had started with a dedicated network of mini-

[8] *The New Yorker, op.cit.,* p. 63

computers located in seven European cities, that acted as nodes, connected to the company's miniframes in Italy. As retail operations had grown, this dedicated network became increasingly expensive. Then, after a successful test in North America, agents were connected to the Mark III General Electric Information System's value-added network service available round the clock in 250 cities in 25 countries. The service provided network access and data filing software. All application software was Benetton's own. Mark III replaced the need to operate the Information System Center at headquarters 24 hours a day and relieved the burden of long distance, often transcontinental, telephone charges for data transmissions. Use of Mark III was indispensable during reassortment.

"Keeping track of the financial information of each one of the 4,000 shops in the world is completely mad and useless", argued Bruno Zuccaro, the manager of information systems at Benetton, and former executive of Zanussi and Honeywell. This had been an information systems project in the past, but had failed due to administrative and technical problems. The project consisted of having a cash register in each single shop to keep track of the shop's sales and financial situation. This would have allowed the company to know the cash-flow of each shop and the money it had. However, it was neither accepted by shop owners nor by the Italian law that specified a certain type register for tax purposes.

The Information Systems Department was working on a project to connect a sample of a few representative shops all over the world. The sample contained shops that started selling early in each season due their condition of international centers where trendy people went, such as upscale ski resorts. By installing a computerized point of sale (P.O.S.) system in each of these shops, the company could gather information about fashion trends in design, colors, etc., well in advance of the season, which was critical for planning and producing the reassortment articles. This project was being tested in five Italian shops to see how it worked and how well it was accepted by shop owners and agents.

Each shop owner was free to manage his or her shops as he or she pleased, but the Information Systems' staff had developed a software package for retail shop management that it planned to encourage retail shops to buy. The software ran on an IBM personal computer equipped with a bar code reader, for all garment tags came from the factory with critical information printed in bar code. The system processed sales, inventory, orders and receipt of goods.

The Information System Department had not done much to connect the subcontractors network. The firm felt that they were too many and most of them too small for attempting this task. The company knew the production capacity of every subcontractor, but the production scheduling and the allocation process of the production plan to each contractor was not done by computer. Therefore, Benetton didn't know the exact amount of work that each subcontractor had in a given moment.

III. Ideas for the Future

Changes in the Subcontractors' Network

Benetton was working with a constellation of 350 subcontracted production units. The idea was to simplify the complex problem of being in touch with so many external firms, and deal only with the 9 or 10 largest subcontractors. These, in turn, would be in touch with all the medium-sized and small contractors, the Benetton family - not the company itself - would own shares in all of them. It was also planned to integrate those larger subcontractors into the company's own information systems.

The U.S. Subsidiary

Benetton was planning to increase the production volume and the range of products in the U.S. subsidiary located in North Carolina. It was currently making t-shirts and classic trousers there, which only accounted for 5% of the total U.S. consumption of Benetton products.

There were two main reasons to manufacture in this overseas facility: to avoid protectionism problems, and the fact that some Americans preferred garments "made in U.S.A.". Other reasons for producing locally rather than importing from Italy were the wild gyrations of exchange rates, and the tariffs and transportation costs the company had to bear. As a result of this last factor, final prices to consumers were 35-40% higher in the U.S. than in Europe. Benetton had to pay 24-25% in tariffs, and 7-8% in transportation.

Financial Matters

The company was planning to go public on the New York Stock Exchange, because it wanted to reinforce its international image and to secure funds for a planned diversification process, although the company had already accumulated a substantial amount of financial resources in the last years.

Diversification of the Benetton Group

In December 1985 the holding company changed its name from INVEP S.p.A. to Benetton Group S.p.A. and increased its capital stock from 8 billion lire to 70 billion lire by capitalizing reserves.

The INVEP holding, created in 1981, encompassed all the business activities controlled equally by the four Benettons. The main business of the group had traditionally been Benetton S.p.A., counting for about two thirds of the group sales. In December 1985, the three different companies named Benetton Lana S.p.A., Benetton Cotone S.p.A., and Benetton Jeans S.p.A., were merged into Benetton S.p.A., becoming its three manufacturing divisions.

The group from the beginning in related business activities, such as the 50% share in Fiorucci S.p.A., the Milan-based design firm, acquired in 1981, and the 70% of Calzaturificio de Varese, an Italian shoe manufacturer, bought in 1982. The first investment allowed the company to enter into the more rarefied realms of European fashion, and the second provided them with shoes for sale along with sweaters and shirts in Benetton shops around the world.

However, both investments were only marginally profitable. At the end of 1983, Luciano Benetton commented about Calzaturificio de Varese: "As an experiment it has been quite interesting, but the factory is old and there have been many problems."[9] However, after two or three years of operations, this company began to show positive results and it was considered a success. On the other hand, the investment in Fiorucci S.p.A. was sold in 1985. At the time of that sale, Benetton purchased 5% of Nolan Norton Italia S.r.l., a company in the computer industry.

Benetton had taken advantage of its well known trademark in licensing agreements covering a wide rage of consumer products, like cosmetics, perfumes, socks, toys, household linen, etc. It had also arranged successful alliances with Bulova to sell watches with the Benetton name, and with Polaroid for the manufacture of Benetton sunglasses.

---

[9] *Fortune, op.cit.,* p. 119.

The diversification process of the company had gone beyond related business activities and entered into the financial services sector. Some of these investments were: 70% of In Factor S.p.A., a factoring subsidiary with a capital stock of 5 billion lire; a 50% stake in two leasing companies: Leasing S.p.A. and Finleasing Italia S.p.A.; a 20% of the private Banco de Trento e Bolzano in northern Italy; and a 10% stake in leasing companies in France and West Germany, which were run by Banca Nazionale del Lavoro, Italy's biggest bank.

Luciano Benetton had announced new projects for the coming years: "The future will include diversification in retailing, financial services in banking and elsewhere, in Italy and abroad."[10] According to Aldo Palmeri: "Benetton's plan to develop financial services will call for the company to achieve, within two years, a 50-50% mix in group turnover between industrial and financial revenues."[11] *Benetton was planning to:*

• Expand its factoring and leasing subsidiaries both in Italy and abroad. It had received authorization from the Ministry of Foreign Trade in Rome to operate in the factoring business outside of Italy.

• Form a financial services and venture capital company in Milan that would engage in currency swaps, syndicated loans, corporate finance, underwriting, and other investment banking activities for the clothing and textile sector, in partnership with another big Italian clothing manufacturer.

Carlo Gilardi, Benetton's finance director admitted that "although we have a handful of Citicorp specialists in currency swaps, factoring and leasing, it will be necessary to enlarge our human and managerial resources substantially to reach our goal."[12]

---

[10] *Financial Times,* May 23, 1986.
[11] *Ibid.*
[12] *Ibid.*

5. Case Research Acknowledgments

Case research has become an integral part of modern management development in both universities, business schools, regional development and in-company training. Cases on issues of management are invaluable in exposing the inherent kinds of issues which organizations face, forming an understanding of market behavior and strategic choices, and drawing experienced-based generalizations about sound management practice. Good cases should thus enable the students the essential practice in analyzing and evaluating options and choices, as well as the trade-offs in the implementation.

As industry after industry undergoes radical change, however, timely cases are becoming more important (not to say that one cannot learn from classical examples). As with all research, the skills, time and dedication to develop outstanding case material are a scarce resource. We are therefore indebted to our IMD colleagues and their research associates whose efforts appear in this book, as well as to the executives in the companies who cooperated in making the material possible. We are particularly grateful for the financial support provided by the Industrial Development Authorities of Ireland for development of 7 of the cases appearing in this book.

Our colleagues at IMD would welcome any comments you might have about this book or the cases in it, or any specific errors or developments. The address is IMD, P.O. Box 915, CH-1001 Lausanne, Switzerland.

5.1 Description of Case Authors

William A. Fischer
American. Manufacturing Management. D.B.A. George Washington University. M.S. Industrial Management and B.S. Civil Engineering, Clarkson College of Technology. Dalton L. McMichael Sr. Professor of Business Administration, University of North Carolina. Work experience in technology management in both industry and government in the U.S., the People's Republic of China, the Far East and developing world. Research interests: International manufacturing and technology transfer.

Kamran Kashani

Iranian. Marketing. D.B.A. Harvard University. M.B.A., B.A. University of California, UCLA. Teaching experience includes marketing strategy, sales force management, industrial marketing, international marketing and general management topics. Formerly on the faculties of INSEAD, Babson College (Visiting) and the Iran Center for Management Studies. Consultant to U.S. and European companies. Research interests: Global marketing strategies.

J. Peter Killing

Canadian. General Management. B.A., Ph.D. University of Western Ontario. Associate Professor, School of Business Administration, University of Western Ontario. Visiting Professor at IMD 1985-1986. Consultant to local and multinational firms in North America, Europe, Australia and Brazil. Research interests: Management of alliances.

Jon I. Martinez

Born in Chile, Prof. Jon I. Martinez holds a doctoral degree in business from IESE in Barcelona and carried out post-doctoral studies at MIT. He is a professor of international business and marketing at the University Adolfo Ibanez in Santiago and a Visiting Professor at UCLA. Prof. Martinez has published widely in the field of international business and is a consultant to many corporations in Latin America.

Dominique V. Turpin

French. International Marketing Strategy. Egon Zehnder Fellow of International Management. Ph.D. from Sophia University, Japan, Dipl. ESSCA, France. Extensive experience in teaching and research both in Europe and Japan. Consultant to several consumer goods and industrial service companies. Research interests: Strategies of Japanese firms in and outside Japan.

Sandra Varldermerwe

Irish. International Marketing and Services. D.B.A. Stellenbosch University. M.B.A., B.A. in Sociology, University of Cape Town. Formerly Professor of Marketing, Witwatersrand University, and Visiting Professor in Europe, U.S. and Canada. Working experience in sales and marketing management. Consultant to consumer, industrial and service companies. Research interests: Market-driven change, marketing strategies, transformation in services management.

5.2 Biographical Statement

Dr. Per V. Jenster

Professor Jenster is a faculty member of the Center for International Management and Industrial Development, and formerly of IMD, Lausanne, Switzerland, with responsibilities for teaching and research in the areas of strategic management and marketing. Prior to joining IMD in January of 1989, he spent nine years in USA as a strategy consultant and a faculty member at the University of Virginia. At IMD, the Professor is director for the Institute's programs, Managing Industrial Market Strategy and The Owner-Executive Program. In addition, he has been responsible for a number of programs tailored to specific companies. With the Institute's Business Associates and Sponsored, Dr. Jenster has be program chair for the Workshops on Corporate & Strategic Planning. He is also director of the Center for OwnerManaged Business Research at IMD.

Born in Denmark, Per V. Jenster received a cand. oecon. from the University of Arhus. He was awarded a Fulbright Scholarship for advanced studies in USA and earned a doctoral degree in strategic management and information systems from the University of Pittsburgh in 1985. His award winning research is widely published in more than 35 articles, books and case studies. The co-authored book, *European Cases in Strategic Management* has just been released, and two new books are forthcoming.

Dr. Jenster's industry experience includes extensive senior management consulting in the areas of strategic management, marketing planning, competitive analysis, and cost evaluation studies. As principal of an international consulting firm, Senior Management Co. Ltd., his past clients include diverse organizations such as Alcoa, Westinghouse, IBM, Philips, Unilever, Nestle, Business Week International and the Danish Ministry of Finance, as well as a number of other organizations. Prior to his academic studies, he worked in product management of industrial goods bound for Africa and the Far East for the East Asiatic Company.

In 1988, Professor Jenster was appointed by U.S. Secretary Varrity as advisor and member of the Virginia Export Council, U.S. Department of Commerce. He is also board member of several entrepreneurial organizations, and serves on the Executive Board of the Journal of Strategic Change (Wiley). In addition, Dr. Jenster holds the royal appointment as Honorary Danish Consul to Switzerland (Cantons Vaud, Valais, Neuchatel, Fribourg).

Dr. J. Carlos Jarillo

Professor Jarillo is a faculty member at University of Geneva, and formerly of IMD in Lausanne. His areas of teaching include strategy and international business. Prior to joining IMD he taught at Instituto de Empresa in Madrid and IESE in Barcelona, and served as a Senior Research Associate at the Harvard Business School.

Prof. Jarillo holds a Doctorate in Business Administration from the Harvard Business School, a Doctorate in Economics from the Autonomous University of Barcelona, and an MBA from ESE. He has published widely in the fields of strategy and international business: to date, three books and dozens of articles, some in journals such as Strategic Management Journal, Journal of International Business Studies, Long Range Planning, etc. Some cases he has authored have been repeatedly included in casebooks.

His direct professional experience includes work as consultant to many companies and governments, and has served recently on the evaluation panel of the Brite/Euram program of the Commission of the European Communities.

Terry Hadlock - home ec
725-2121

Easy to take, easy to tolerate.

PCE®

erythromycin particles in tablets